"AN EXTRAORDINARILY MOVING ACCOUNT"

Saul Bellow

"Dorothy Rabinowitz is keenly alive to her subjects' scars—to the nightmares that will not stop; the tranquilizers; the special sorrows of weddings and barmitzvahs; the dark-toned and tattered photographs of the dead, as precious as any relics ever were; the instability of the marriages rashly entered into after the liberation by frayed people bereft of bread or companionship; the accidental livelihoods that stifle talents; the craving for security and the certainty that there is no such thing."

The New York Review of Books

"Masterfully orchestrated. . . . A work of poetic reportage"

Kirkus Reviews

"OUTSTANDING"

The Miami Herald

NEW LIVES

SURVIVORS OF THE HOLOCAUST
LIVING IN AMERICA
BY DOROTHY RABINOWITZ

AVON
PUBLISHERS OF BARD, CAMELOT AND DISCUS BOOKS

AVON BOOKS
A division of
The Hearst Corporation
959 Eighth Avenue
New York, New York 10019

Copyright © 1976 by Dorothy Rabinowitz
Published by arrangement with Alfred A. Knopf, Inc.
Library of Congress Catalog Card Number: 76-13709
ISBN: 0-380-01790-3

First Avon Printing, November, 1977

AVON TRADEMARK REG. U.S. PAT. OFF. AND IN
OTHER COUNTRIES, MARCA REGISTRADA,
HECHO EN U.S.A.

Printed in the U.S.A.

Contents

Acknowledgments

I am grateful to the National Endowment for the Humanities whose grant of a senior fellowship enabled me to carry on the writing and research for this book. The idea of a work on the holocaust survivors in America originated with Morton Yarmon, who first posed the subject to me.

For indispensable source material on Bergen Belsen, as well as conversations from which I profited, I am obliged to Sam E. Bloch, Secretary-General of the World Federation of Bergen-Belsen Associations. The American Jewish Committee's valuable study, *The Eichmann Case in the American Press*, provided source material on which I drew heavily in the chapter dealing with the Eichmann trial.

Harry J. Alderman, head of the Blaustein Library of the American Jewish Committee provided advice and generous use of the library facilities.

Of the numerous people who aided me in locating survivors, the following were particularly helpful: Sonia Krevitt, Betty Lande, Morton Silverman, Leonard Goldhammer, Ernest Weiner, Lillian Hoffman, Albert Sheldon, Morton Gaber, Sheryl Leonard, and Dora Zaidenweber.

For willingly providing answers to innumerable questions and facilitating my efforts to obtain material on the Braunsteiner case I am indebted to William Gurock, Chief Counsel for the United States Immigration and Naturalization Service in New York, and also to William H. Oltarsh.

For discussions relating to this book's subject, from which I benefitted, I thank Dr. Mortimer T. Ostow. Thanks are due as well to Professor Frances K. Barasch for reading a portion of the manuscript. Stephen Koch read the text in its entirety and provided criticism of a high order. I am indebted to former Knopf editor Regina Ryan for her interest in this project and to my current editor, Ann Close, for concerned and expert attentions to the manuscript. Yvonne Lancaster typed and retyped the manuscript and in the process provided valuable editorial comments as, also, did Barbara Hawkins.

For words spoken at crucial periods during the writing of this book I am forever thankful to Midge Decter. To Lucy S. Dawidowicz, who offered help unstintingly and provided information and support at every turn, I owe more than it is possible to express here. My largest debt, finally, is to the survivors, each one of whom expanded my knowledge and enabled the work of this book to go forward.

Introduction

No one can speak with certainty of the figures, but it is most likely that four to five hundred thousand European Jews survived the German Occupation in the years 1939–1945. These fell, generally, into three categories: the some seventy-five thousand who survived the camps; those who had lived in hiding or on false identity papers; those who survived in the woods fighting with partisan and guerrilla groups. By far the largest part of the Jewish remnant emigrated to Israel, while the United States took in the second largest in the ninety-two thousand or so European Jews admitted during the postwar period, 1945–1951.

It is with the latter group, the holocaust Jews who came to America, that this work is concerned. It is, in addition, concerned with the mainstream of Jewish survivors, which is to say that it is not about intellectuals, holocaust spokesmen, or writers. One heard, in the course of interviews conducted with some hundred and eight survivors in New York, Philadelphia, Chicago, Kansas City, St. Paul, Minneapolis, Denver, Los Angeles, San Francisco, Houston, and New Orleans—in narratives from sensibilities of every sort—certain insistently recurrent themes. These played no small role in determining the choice of material to be presented here: which stories to tell, whom to portray. It was my intention to represent as wide a range as I could of the survivors I encountered, but the portraits here, it should be stressed, are entirely of individuals, not composites. In many instances, whether at the request of some of those I interviewed or because it seemed to me to be appropriate, I have not used real names. Where this is so, I have indicated the use of a pseudonym with an asterisk.

D.R.

1 | The Witnesses

Spectators file into the small courtroom of the United States Immigration and Naturalization Services building in New York, for on this late-September day of 1972 there is to be another session in the deportation hearings of Mrs. Hermine Braunsteiner Ryan, a German-born Queens, New York, housewife. The spectators are press and television reporters, present in numbers far larger than those usually seen on these premises: the case is a unique one, representing as it does the first attempt on the part of the U.S. Justice Department to deport an American resident on grounds pertaining to war crimes. According to the charges drawn up by the Immigration Services prosecutor, Mrs. Ryan is the former Hermine Braunsteiner, a Vice-Kommandant of the Maidanek and Ravensbrück concentration camps between the years 1939 and 1944. In that capacity, the government avers, Hermine Braunsteiner beat inmates to death and contributed to the murder of untold numbers of others.

The hearings began in the winter of 1972. Since then, former Maidanek inmates have been brought in a steady stream from all over the United States, Canada, and Poland to the upper-floor courtroom at 20 West Broadway, in keeping with the prosecutor's intention to reconstruct Hermine Braunsteiner's career as Vice-Kommandant of the women's camp at Maidanek, and thus to pave the way for her deportation.

There is no statute of limitations in immigration law.

However, the chances are not good, in the opinion of the prosecutor's colleagues in the Immigration Service, of obtaining a deportation, on charges having their origin in events that took place thirty years earlier, against an American resident and the wife of an American citizen. The chances are better that the case will stretch on for years, with the possibility of many appeals following a deportation ruling. Nevertheless, prosecutor Vincent Schiano, a fiftyish man of white-faced intensity, determinedly searches out witnesses and prepares the case he has sought for years to bring to trial.

This day's witness has the wasted look that sudden illness visits on the faces of the formerly robust. A man in his early seventies on whom a high thatch of wiry gray hair confers the one and only suggestion of sumptuousness, Jacob Korman* leans forward agitatedly in an effort to grasp the questions being put to him by Mrs. Ryan's attorney. Korman has testified that he saw Hermine Braunsteiner beat two women with a horsewhip until they were dead. The women were two of five who had been picking grass in the space between the barbed-wire fences at Maidanek. Had he seen the whip? Mrs. Ryan's attorney, Mr. Barry, now asks.

"She wasn't without a whip."

For watching the beating, Korman states, he himself was given twenty-five lashes on his return to the men's camp. Mrs. Ryan's attorney, a large and ruddy man, inclines his head. With what was the witness beaten? The SS used a rubber-tipped whip, Korman answers.

"That beating never disturbed the ten gold pieces you had in your rectum?"

"No."

"They were secure in there?"

"They didn't—"

"Objection," snaps prosecuting attorney Schiano.

The ten gold pieces refer to the witness's previous testimony: he had hidden the gold in his rectum just before his arrival in Maidanek, so as to have money to barter for his life. Mrs. Ryan's attorney has several times directed the witness to tell how he hid gold pieces in his body. On their arrival at Maidanek, Korman replies, the prisoners were ordered to surrender all their valuables, and put them in appropriately marked receptacles outside the bathhouse; there were separate receptacles for American money, Polish money, and for jewelry. Some people kept money back and hid it in their clothes, thinking that they would get them back when they came out of the bathhouse. But it wasn't so; they never saw those clothes again.

"What about that money you had, the paper money?" Barry asks.

"I'm telling you—you put it there, and you never got it back."

"You never got it back?"

"No."

"And the only thing you had was the twelve gold pieces in your rectum?"

"Yes."

"And each time you had a bowel movement, I would assume . . ."

"Very bad . . . it was very bad."

"The gold pieces dropped down out of your rectum and you put them back in again?"

"Yes."

"And this continued for a period of eight or nine weeks?"

The prosecutor objects and is sustained. The witness reiterates under more questioning how he hid twelve gold coins in his body, after the fall of the Warsaw ghetto. Explaining how the prisoners were stripped and shaved on their arrival at Maidanek, the witness speaks in broken English, some of it difficult to understand. Time and again, the Special Inquiry Officer (the presiding judge at Immigration Service hearings) has to direct Korman to speak up or sit closer to the microphone.

"They took away from you every hair that you had on your body," he tells the court in a low voice in which now there is so fresh a note of stupefaction as to make the event, lost so long ago in time, seem suddenly near.

Mrs. Ryan's attorney interrupts here, saying he does not want to hear any speeches.

"Let's get back to the gold pieces. How many of the gold pieces did the witness use in Maidanek?"

"Two," he is told.

"Then you put the other ten back in the rectum?"

"Yes."

"And you kept them?"

"Yes."

"And do you have any of them today?"

"No."

"Never saved any of them? Used them all up? What did you do with the others, then?"

"I bought—"

"You bought your way out again?"

Mrs. Ryan's attorney asks the questions in rapid succession. Well before he finishes, a foot-shifting, thickening silence takes hold in the courtroom, one of those spells of hot discomfort that can course through an audience in an instant, banishing noise, jolting the indifferent. In a betrayal of feeling unusual among members of his profession, a television reporter winces and closes his eyes. Next to him, a young reporter for a metropolitan daily stares down at her lap.

The cross-examination moves on to the witness's testimony on Maidanek. The first two days there, he and the other prisoners had been made to do exercises continually, from early morning until nighttime. Marching. How many hours? There were no watches, the witness tells Mrs. Ryan's attorney.

"They hold us from morning to night. You ask me to tell you hours."

Even while they ate at night, the prisoners were not permitted to sit down, he tells the court. And to keep clean was impossible; you could not wash yourself. On the third day in Maidanek, he asked other prisoners in his block what he could do to survive. People told him that if you had money to pay somebody, you could work in the kitchen. A day or so later, having bribed the *Blockälteste** with twenty rubles, he obtained a job in the kitchen where

* Inmate block leader.

at least there was a chance to keep clean and get something to eat. The kitchen workers hauled enormous food wagons from the camp kitchen, which was in the third field of Maidanek, to the women's compound, in the fifth field. Having this job was how he came to see the events in the women's camp to which he now bears witness.

This part of the testimony produces a flurry of questions, both from Mrs. Ryan's attorney and from the judge, as to how the food was put on the wagons, the number of men working on each, and the distances they traveled between camps. Forty prisoners were required for the job of loading the thirty or forty large vats of food and hauling them by wagon to the fifth field.

"How far was the third field from the fifth field?" Mr. Barry asks.

"For us, pulling, it was very far."

The judge intercedes, patiently but with a look of strain; the cross-examination has generated a tension in everyone. "Can you tell us how far it was?" he asks the witness.

"I can't tell you. I didn't look up. You have to understand what the concentration camp at Maidanek was like." There is a sharp display of temper now from two sides: Mrs. Ryan's attorney charges that the witness is making speeches; the witness retorts, in a voice no longer difficult to hear, that he has not come there to make speeches.

"Mr. Barry, you can restrain yourself," the judge warns severely. "The witness understandably may not, but I expect you to."

"Mr. Korman is a sharp man, don't worry," Mrs. Ryan's attorney murmurs, sitting down.

Under further questioning at the end of this exchange, the witness tells how the prisoners who hauled food had to wait a half-hour or more outside the women's compound for the empty cans to be brought back: how, at other times, they might wait an hour for the SS guards who accompanied them to be done with their visits to the women's barracks. Earlier, on direct examination by the prosecutor, he has given testimony on events that took place in or near the women's camp, which he saw while working as a horse.

"You were what?"

"A horse," the witness reiterates in answer to the prosecutor's query, in the patient, faintly surprised tone of one on whom it has fallen to explain the self-explanatory. They were horses, the prisoners who hauled the food wagon: a team of twenty people pulling in the front, twenty others pushing from the back. On the sides are the SS men, who hit the horses, he starts to add, but here the prosecutor cuts him short so as to draw him back to the subject of Hermine Braunsteiner. How many times had he seen people killed in Maidanek? Schiano asks the witness. Every day is the answer. Maidanek was a death camp. But this particular time is one he cannot get out of his head. One day he and the other prisoners hauled the food rations to the women's camp, as usual, but were not permitted to enter because three or four hundred women were assembled in front of the entrance. The women, most of them with children, had just arrived in Maidanek where Hermine Braunsteiner was now talking to them.

"And she said to them they have to give the children to the people on the wagon; they are going to a summer camp and they will get milk in the morning and at night."

But the mothers held on and would not give the children up—little ones, two, three, four years old. A second time Braunsteiner told the mothers they must give up the children, and when they would not let the children go this time, Braunsteiner began to beat an old woman holding a child of about two or three in her arms. The old woman was not the mother of this child she held in her arms, but its protector. Braunsteiner hit the old woman again and again, and then both woman and child were on the ground. Afterward he and the other horses had to carry away their corpses, and then there continued this scene he could not forget: himself and the other horses hauling the food wagon in; the screams and cries as the SS fell upon both the women and the children; the sight of the children being carried to the two trucks, and of the truckloads of terrified children driving away, finally. Everyone knew where they were going.

Hauling the food wagons was not the only means by

which he learned what went on in the women's camp. The coal pile that provided fuel for the kitchen was located next to the fifth field women's barracks. Here, while shoveling coal along with some forty other male prisoners, he saw Hermine Braunsteiner whip to death the two women who had been picking grass between fences. This testimony generates a long and bitter exchange between Mrs. Ryan's attorney and the witness. One of those killed was a twenty-six-year-old woman, Sara Forminska, whom he knew from Warsaw, the witness says; the other was a thirty-year-old woman, whose last name was Sakalavich. Both of these are important pieces of testimony, because the witness is naming names, which factor gives a crucial specificity to his evidence against Mrs. Ryan. The witness had a coal shovel in his hand at the time? Mrs. Ryan's attorney asks. The witness had. And the forty or so other men with him, Mrs. Ryan's attorney asks, they had shovels? Some just had brooms. Could the witness tell how long Hermine Braunsteiner beat the two women, and how many blows of the bullwhip she gave them? Maybe twenty minutes, maybe less; he had not counted the number of blows. The camp inmates did not need too many blows to be killed.

"Did the other women between the wires come to help the two women?" Mr. Barry asks.

"How will they come to help?"

Several times more Mr. Barry asks the question: "And the others, they never came over to help the other two?"

"What are you talking about, help? She would kill all of them. I don't understand you."

"They never came over to help?"

"How could they help?"

"But they didn't?"

Twice more Mr. Barry asks whether the other prisoners had come forward to aid the women who were being beaten.

The witness peers into the very mouth of his examiner during the course of these inquiries, as if seeking, by intense concentration on their source, to fathom them. Not that he does not recognize the intent of the questions, which suggests that Maidanek was a place like any other in the world: that it housed a society like any other, composed of people who might choose between one form of behavior and another, and who could, if they but would, intervene when they saw their fellows victimized.

"You just watched also? And the others never came over to help?"

For a long moment he says nothing, until, in the struggle between fury and propriety that the questions have produced in him, propriety wins; the place to which he has come to be a witness this day is a court, after all, with a judge and lawyers, where questions put to witnesses must be answered. Subdued by the consciousness of this fact, the witness sits back in his chair and answers the questions, the last of them in a monotone that bespeaks resignation, if of a very temporary sort.

"You just watched also?"

"Yes."

"And the other forty or so men, they just watched?"

"Yes . . ."

Survivors often have this look of restraint he wears now, a thin veneer beneath which the massed energies of the unspoken perpetually stir. The courtroom imposes severe limits on testimony, and he is not unaccustomed to such limits, the witness's cloudy, resigned look says— these proprieties which dictate that only so much and no more may be told. Nevertheless, prepared as he had been to obey the requirements of the courtroom, including the submission to a harsh cross-examination, the questioning has clearly taken its toll of him. The call for a recess is a relief; at once, the witness is out of his chair, the prosecuting attorney's arm under his as the strangely formal-looking processional of two makes its way to a corner of the courtroom opposite the one where Mrs. Ryan sits with her attorney.

Where Korman lives, in Yonkers, the houses are old two-family structures, eccentrically shaped and set on graded streets, which design spares the neighborhood the monotony of certain of the more modern suburbs. Still, it is not an area that people of means would choose to live in. The neighborhood is essentially working-class, for there is industry in this city, in addition to the sporting life of the Yonkers Raceway. The largest part of its population is of Italian Catholic origin, with the second largest part divided between the Irish and those listed in the census as being of Polish and Russian extraction. Among the latter two nationalities are a good number of Jews, some thirty-five to forty thousand altogether in this community which borders New York City on the north.

The houses are neat enough, though the small signs of disrepair in most of them have a suggestion of permanence, proof of the owners' acquiescence to the fact that the neighborhood is old and not likely to attract buyers with money enough to be particular. Korman's house sags with the rest of them on the block, though he is not actually the owner but the upstairs tenant of the two-story brick-and-wood structure. A small hall and sharp turning staircase, whose highly polished banisters gleam in the dimness, lead to the apartment where he has lived for more than fifteen years.

His history, after his arrival in the United States in 1951, is similar to that of many a holocaust survivor. In his fifties in 1951, with a wife and infant to support, he began piecing together several tentative livelihoods, trying this and that and settling finally on real estate, a field whose potential for entrepreneurship was to attract many. There were, perhaps, additional reasons why holocaust survivors, the remnant of a universe laid waste, should have immersed themselves in careers having to do with houses—with building. Whatever the reasons or combinations thereof, whether "building" represented a symbolic assertion of renewal, a strategy against the encroachment of nihilism, or simply practical opportunity, the fact is that survivors in considerable numbers involved themselves in building and construction careers—immensely successful ones, as it turned out, for some of them.*

* The Shapell brothers of Los Angeles, survivors of Auschwitz, are counted the leading manufacturers of prefabricated houses in America.

Jacob Korman's own career was a módest one. At fifty, a fair number of years older than the average survivor arriving in the United States with a wife and young family to support, he was not destined for the all-consuming undertakings and enterprises that some of the younger men in their twenties and thirties, also recently emerged from the displaced persons' camps, were to engage in. Before the war he had been a businessman. He had been born and brought up in Germany, of orthodox parents, one of eight children of a manufacturer of small arms and military supplies who moved the family to Poland in the late 1920s. Jacob Korman, the youngest son, had by then completed his Jewish seminary studies. In Warsaw he became proprietor of a textiles store and married a woman of orthodox Jewish background. In September of 1939, when German armies invaded Poland, Korman fought with the Polish Army until its capitulation, in less than a month, to overwhelmingly superior forces.

Korman returned to Warsaw, whose dense Jewish population was, like the rest of Polish Jewry, already submerged in the unparalleled reign of terror begun immediately upon the arrival of the Germans. In November of 1939, he was caught in one of the roundups that became a regular occurrence in the Jewish quarters, during which German soldiers descended upon a crowded street without warning and encircled the passers-by. The men and boys trapped in the dragnet were then marched to waiting trucks, which would take them to other parts of Poland or, like Korman, to Germany, where they performed slave labor in a variety of capacities.

At Dachau he worked building barracks. Transferred in a few months' time to Buchenwald, he escaped shortly thereafter—thanks to the comparative laxness of the non-SS guards in that early period of the war—by walking away from a work detail, and made his way back to Warsaw. By 1940, the Jews of Warsaw were sealed into the ghetto, their famished, disease-ridden population swollen by hundreds of thousands of Jews deported from other parts of Europe. It was strictly forbidden to bring food into the sealed-off ghetto, although smugglers, many of them chil-

dren, regularly risked the extreme punishments meted out
by the Germans to anyone caught bringing food in from
the outside. The rations "legally" allotted to the ghetto and
distributed under the auspices of the Judenrat, the Jewish
Council, were just sufficient to maintain half of its inhabitants on starvation fare. In this hunger-haunted world,
where death by starvation was a daily occurrence, Korman
held a not insignificant job: inspector in the Judenrat
kitchens, with the work of supervising his sector's ration
distributions. The pay was food, a wage beyond price.
Until the Warsaw ghetto was destroyed, he survived in it,
together with one sister—his wife and the rest of his family having by then been deported or killed. In this period,
Jewish police had twice arrested him and twice he had
managed, though brought to the *Umschlagplatz*,* to escape
being put on the train to Treblinka.

Finally, early in May, 1943, when the revolt of the
Warsaw ghetto was in its last hours, he was captured by
the Germans, along with thousands of Jews flushed from
underground bunkers, and marched out of the flaming
Jewish sector.

The circuit of concentration-annihilation camps through
which he was to pass after this was a long one. He was
first brought to Maidanek. How, Mrs. Ryan's attorney had
asked during the cross-examination, had he left that camp?
On a certain day, the court had heard, the SS came into
the barracks and ordered the inmates to get out into the
field stripped naked and do gymnastics.

"They have taken only the people who were completely
fit and sane," the witness explained. The few hundred
people who passed the gymnastics test, himself among
them, were then all put into one barracks. After the SS
came in and made a list of their names and numbers, they
were taken to another barracks where they were confined
for a day or perhaps two—he could not remember which.
When they were let out of the barracks, they were made
to stand in a line, like soldiers; but "soldiers" was not quite
the right word, not precise. What was the correct word?

* The staging area where Jews were assembled for deportation.

the witness asked suddenly of the court-assigned German interpreter, a personage whose existence he had theretofore ignored, for the most part, on the ground that an American citizen was entitled to testify in English.

"A military division," the interpreter provided. Korman nodded, satisfied. The inmates had to stand in lines like a military division, and then they were put on trucks and taken to Treblinka where, on their arrival, the SS picked out the healthiest-looking of the transferred prisoners and put them back on the trucks. Korman stayed in Treblinka with the rest; he was now forty-three—an advanced age in the concentration camps—but in sufficiently fit condition to pass the physical tests designed to separate the inmates still capable of producing labor for the Reich from those who could not. Lack of labor capacity generally marked inmates for annihilation sooner rather than later.

From Treblinka he was transferred after some months to Auschwitz—from there to Mauthausen, Nordhausen, and finally the Bergen Belsen camp, where he was liberated in April, 1945. Korman was, in 1945, one of the relatively small number of surviving Jews past their middle forties, the average age of most of the survivors at the liberation having been somewhere between eighteen and thirty-nine. He was by then entirely without family; his wife, parents, three brothers, and four sisters had all been killed in Treblinka and the Warsaw ghetto.

A photograph of him in 1946 shows a husky man with large features wreathed in a formal, faintly contentious smile. It must be hard to believe, Korman suggested to a visitor to his house, that he and the man in the photograph were the same person; and there were grounds for this suggestion. He was now a greatly shrunken version of the man in the photograph; the well-fleshed face and throat had disappeared and left in their place bones and hollows, thin reminders of the materiality that had vanished.

"I was strong, like if you take a piece of iron," he observed, putting the photograph away.

The picture had been taken when he was about to marry his second wife, a German-born Jew more than twenty years his junior, whom he had met in the Belsen concentration camp. In 1947 she bore him a daughter—he had had no children by his first wife—and for the next three and a half years the family lived in Germany and France where Korman began again to earn a living selling textiles. In 1951 they obtained visas to America, for they were, like the majority of survivors, determined to leave Europe and its memories behind them.

He sat in his sunlit, chilly living room on a winter's day, his wife listening with great care as he described the ghetto. She was more than content that her husband should do the talking, and she had indicated from the outset in a manner at once polite and impervious to argument that that was how matters would remain. Occasionally, she supplied her husband with a word or detail, after which contribution, usually, she withdrew into her characteristic busy silence. There were several reasons for this silence, the first and most important having to do with her belief that in the presence of strangers one was better off weighing words and being watchful, particularly now that her husband had become involved in the business of the trial. Now, in her estimate, he—their entire family—was confronted with a variety of potential dangers, some of which, such as the possibility of crank phone calls and threats in the night, were clearly defined in her mind, while others, more subtle, had yet to be named, given shape and form. But experience had clearly told her one did not have to be able to name dangers to know their presence. One could wait and watch: the threat, be it to body, spirit, or good name, would announce itself. Clearly, too, she felt that watchfulness was best performed in the guise of something else, and so she dusted or set the table while listening, her down-turned eyes and busy hands denying all interest in what else might be going on in the room.

It was she who had urged her husband to speak in Yiddish: inasmuch as he was talking, she would have him precise, the way he himself wished to be, as he showed in the courtroom when searching out the proper word for military division, as survivors often wished to be when recalling the past. Particularly did images that seemed to stand clear in the mind's eye warrant exact description.

However minor they might appear to others, the small, so clearly recalled details of the holocaust past—such as the way inmates had to stand in formation on leaving Maidanek—were bound up with the central life experience of the survivors and therefore had the weight of biographical fact. To permit a false or imprecise description of a detail, or to allow the wrong word to be assigned, was, then, the equivalent of letting a loose description or a misstatement of one's personal history stand.

Yiddish provided Korman all the exactness he required for a description of the ghetto. Under its liberating influence, he parodied the trembling and amazement that had been in his voice when he saw that the Jewish policeman taking him away for deportation was one of his oldest friends. "Yankel, you take me?" he had asked. "Whom shall I take, then, myself?" the policeman asked in turn. "Tell me, shall I take me or you?"

For his own role—a naïve questioner invoking claims of friendship—he displayed a certain mockery: the Jewish police had to deliver a certain number of Jews up for deportation or be taken themselves, with their children and families. Korman rendered the policeman's answer to him with unmistakable conviction, for it was the answer the policeman had given, not the question he had been asked, that better expressed the realities of existence under the Germans.

The dead in their thousands lay everywhere in the streets of the Warsaw ghetto. Their families and Jewish communal leaders tried to keep secret the identities of those who died, so that the ration cards of the dead could still be used to obtain food for the living. As kitchen inspector in the ghetto, Korman's job had been to observe closely the way in which the soup ration was doled out, to guard against the possibility of favoritism; it sometimes happened that the person distributing the meager ration would give one person a thick, more nutritious portion scooped from the bottom of the soup vat, while other people got only the watery rations from the top. One saw pinched, starved faces everywhere, and among them, on the streets of the ghetto, one could also see fat, well-fed faces—Jews who had found a way to keep themselves provided with plenty.

"That's not necessary," Mrs. Korman murmured. She had been moving, busy and noiseless, never out of range of her husband's voice. She kept her own demurely low; still she could clothe the words "That's not necessary" with irresistible authority whenever her husband and his visitor spoke of things she considered best not discussed—"unnecessary details," as she called them. It was not necessary, in a hostile world, that controversial comments about fellow Jews should come from her husband's mouth; everyone knew how comments could be twisted around and made to mean something other than the speaker intended. Really, she urged one, in a firm but silken voice such as you might use to inform a visiting relative's child that the glassware was not a good plaything, it was not necessary to deal with irrelevant details. It was not necessary either, in his wife's view, to be sharply critical, as Korman sometimes was, about his government's political errors, particularly what he considered to be its leniency toward political extremists. Not, as she affirmed, that she believed criticism of the United States government would call down any sort of punishment on them—but simply that such comments were unnecessary.

"I think this is really beside the point," she would say thoughtfully whenever the conversation took a dubious turn of this kind.

Her husband made no objection to these interruptions; clearly, he considered them to be his wife's right to make. She knew what she was about, his whole behavior to her said; it would not have occurred to him to interfere in the performance of her clear and proper role as the family pragmatist and mediator between himself and the world.

With uncustomary sharpness, she once observed that her husband, whom she referred to with grave and pointed formality as *Mr.* Korman in the presence of strangers, had encountered not the smallest concern for his dignity when on the witness stand. Present to hear her was prosecutor Schiano's assistant, DeVito, in the Braunsteiner case.

"Wasn't there someone to stand up and protect him from all this?" she demanded. Her reference was to Mr. Barry's constant questions about the hidden coins and the general harsh treatment to which her husband had been submitted.

The prosecutor's assistant, a kindly-looking man in his fifties, shook his head sadly.

"Somebody to stand up for him and say, 'So far, and no more'—somebody should have seen to it that he was not talked to in this way," she added, looking into assistant DeVito's face.

Her husband made a small, halfhearted wave of the hand to show that the matter was of no importance to him. Mrs. Korman paid it no attention, but left the dining-room table, where lunch was in progress, throwing over her shoulder one final observation about how surprising it was that a witness should be afforded no protection whatever. She walked with a determined air, her brow furrowed in a way which said that while she had no immediate answer about the way the circumstance her husband had faced in the courtroom could have been avoided, one could have been found, beyond doubt. Once or twice only, she volunteered a personal comment: one—a degrading memory summoned to mind, perhaps, by her anger over the rough treatment her husband had received in the courtroom—of being shoved down into a pile of mud and human waste by a guard at Belsen and of being unable afterward to wash the stench out of the single garment she had to wear.

"There was no soap and very little water. I scrubbed it with what water I had, I rubbed it and aired it, but it didn't help. The smell stayed. I carried that around on me till the liberation."

The deportation hearing was not the first case in which her husband had been summoned as a witness. Several years earlier, he had been scheduled to fly to West Germany to testify at the war crimes trial of two SS men, but the night before his flight the phone rang and an anonymous caller told Mrs. Korman that her husband had better not make the trip to Germany the next day. The call was particularly frightening because they had kept the news of the forthcoming journey to themselves, which signified to her that the caller was no harmless crank. The only way the person telephoning could have known of the trip was through the West German consulate office, which had arranged it, and such a person would have to be well placed to have access to information from the embassy—someone with connections and, perhaps, the power to make good on threats. As a result of the call, and largely at his wife's insistence, Korman canceled the trip to Germany.

Matters were at once simpler and more pressing in the Braunsteiner case, so far, at least, as his giving testimony was concerned. This time, there had been no phoned threats in the night, and even if any had come, Korman asserted, they would not have prevented him from testifying. He could forgo a journey to a West German court, which, considering the speed with which convicted war criminals were turned loose, might very well have been a waste anyway, but Braunsteiner's trial was a different matter entirely, involving not only who she was but where she was. When pictures of Mrs. Braunsteiner Ryan appeared in the *New York Times* and the *Jewish Daily Forward*, together with the information that she had for thirteen years been living in America, Korman called the Immigration Service office. He informed the prosecuting attorney that he remembered the woman in the paper very clearly, not because of the picture so much as the name, Hermine Braunsteiner; everyone in Maidanek knew the Vice-Kommandant of the women's camp.

Compared with her complicated postwar history, the route that had brought Hermine Braunsteiner to Maidanek, and to her post as Vice-Kommandant of the women's camp was a straightforward one. Not that the early route was without its ironies, for some time before she took her first job in a concentration camp, she had applied to the Blue Sisters, one of the three nursing organizations in Germany; she had hoped to be a nurse, tending the sick in hospitals. The application to the Blue Sisters had to be sent to Berlin, and took a long time to process. About this abortive attempt to join the nursing organization, she was to tell an American court in 1972, "And then I thought, no letter will ever come back, that nothing will come." The sisters did accept her application, but by then Hermine Braunsteiner had already left her native Vienna and gone to work in a munitions factory in Berlin, where she was to make the connection that led to her first job as a concentration camp guard.

Her origins were humble. Born in Vienna in 1919 to a Roman Catholic couple, Friedrich and Maria Braunsteiner, Hermine Braunsteiner completed one grade beyond elementary school before her education came to an end. For the next several years she worked as a domestic in Vienna and in England, leaving England in 1938, when war between that country and Germany appeared imminent. Once back in Vienna, she found employment in a brewery. From this work, which she found difficult, and having given up expectations of becoming a nurse, she went to the munitions factory in Berlin, to a job that turned out to be harder than the one at the brewery, and also more dangerous, since here she had to work with phosphorus. Because of the dangers of the job and her need for better employment, she told the Immigration Service court in 1972, she had been receptive when the German police chief of Lichtenberg—at whose house she boarded during this period—had introduced her to a Colonel Kröger, SS Sturmbannführer. Sturmbannführer Kröger asked her whether she would be interested in taking a job "watching some women at a camp," she recalled. Having told the Colonel she was interested, Hermine Braunsteiner was directed to report for a personal interview at the Ravensbrück concentration camp, where she was accepted immediately, and where she was to begin the career that was to result in a war crimes conviction, a prison term, and ultimately, twenty-seven years after the defeat of the German National Socialist regime she had served, in the deportation proceedings brought against her by the United States government.

The war crimes conviction was handed down in Vienna in 1949, the formal charge of the Viennese People's Court stating that, as camp guard at Ravensbrück, 1941–1942, Hermine Braunsteiner had "brought into a condition of agony and grievously mistreated camp inmates."

In sum, the woman who had at one time entertained hopes of working in hospitals ministering to the sick stood convicted of the charge, among others, that she kicked and trampled on Ravensbrück prisoners, including old women, until they bled, and of being, in the court's description, one of the most dreaded of guards. Declaring that it had no reason to doubt the essentially unanimous charges of the witnesses, the Viennese People's Court noted that the defendant, Hermine Braunsteiner, had herself admitted committing acts of violence against the prisoners, whom she described in her defense as "asocial persons." In addition, the court took up the charges that at Maidanek, the camp she had transferred to in 1942 after leaving Ravensbrück, Hermine Braunsteiner had set dogs on prisoners, and let the dogs tear the prisoners to shreds, and that she had punished other people with a lead-tipped whip. On the Ravensbrück charges, she was sentenced to three years' imprisonment. The presiding justice dismissed the Maidanek charges for lack of concrete evidence, ruling that the difficulty of obtaining the necessary witnesses was too great, since the place of residence of all those who had given Maidanek depositions was Poland.

Released from prison in May of 1950, after serving nine months of her sentence, Hermine Braunsteiner went to Corinthia, Austria, where she worked principally in shops and resort hotels. There, in 1957, she met a thirty-seven-year-old vacationing American, Russell Ryan, an electronics inspector for a New York firm, whom she married the following year. The wedding took place in Canada, to which Hermine Braunsteiner had obtained a visa with comparative ease, without informing the Canadian immigration authorities of her conviction record. Similarly, she failed to inform the American consul in Canada of her war crimes conviction when, as Mrs. Russell Ryan, she applied for an American visa. She did not remember, Hermine Braunsteiner Ryan told the Immigration Service court in 1972, whether the American consul officials in

Canada had asked any questions about prior arrests; and she herself had volunteered no information on this part of her history. Prosecutor Schiano's response to this declared lapse of memory was to cause Mrs. Ryan to repeat her answer several times. This she did without wavering; when, however, the prosecutor asked what she had answered, when applying for U.S. citizenship papers in 1963, to the question about whether the prospective citizen had been arrested at any time, Mrs. Ryan—aware, perhaps, that a copy of her citizenship application was certainly in the hands of the Immigration Service and was about to be thrust under her nose—recalled that such a question had come up and that she had answered "no" to it. The Austrian government had granted her a legislative amnesty for her crimes in 1957 and therefore she felt she did not have to tell about her conviction, she said in reply to prosecutor Schiano's probings. Both Mrs. Ryan and her husband adhered firmly to the contention—like so many arguments based on intent, an impossible one either to prove or disprove—that they believed the amnesty had expunged Hermine Braunsteiner's record and conviction and that therefore her "no" answer to the question of prior arrests had been given in the belief that it was a truthful one. As he had understood the amnesty, Russell Ryan testified, in the humble but faintly defiant voice of a schoolboy contending that his errors and misinformation merely represent what was taught him by last term's teacher, "it eradicated this record as far as that matter in Austria is concerned."

"And you believed that everything she did in Germany during the war was completely wiped out?" Schiano asked him.

"Yes, sir."

Later, when their troubles began in the United States, he believed that the Austrian government's grant of a complete amnesty would solve the problem. Only then, Russell Ryan said, did he inspect the amnesty document closely and discover that the word "partial" appeared in it.

Hermine Braunsteiner Ryan left Canada in 1959, her

American visa granted, and settled down with her husband in Queens. For the next five years she worked as an operator in a knitting mill, tended to her husband and her house, and made, as defense witnesses were later to testify, a good neighbor; the turmoil of her life seemed permanently to have come to an end. Then, in 1964, Hermine Braunsteiner Ryan's background was brought to the attention of the Justice Department by Simon Wiesenthal, concentration camp survivor and internationally renowned head of the Jewish Documentation Center in Vienna, an organization devoted to information-gathering on the whereabouts and activities of suspected Nazi war criminals. The charges with which Wiesenthal concerned himself in regard to Hermine Braunsteiner had to do with crimes committed in Maidanek, and were of a far greater scope and seriousness than those which had been cited by the Viennese People's Court in 1949. When a *New York Times* article first disclosed the accusations against her in the summer of 1964, Mrs. Ryan terminated her job at the Jamaica, Queens, knitting mill where she worked. She did so in the fear that certain of her fellow employees would kill her, her husband testified in court, leaving unspecified who they were or why they might have wished to kill her. His wife had had to take another position at half the salary and so suffered great economic loss; then, four years later, there were more news stories about her, Russell Ryan declared, with the result this time that his wife was discharged from her job.

But Mrs. Ryan's main troubles were of a legal, not an economic kind, and these began in earnest in 1971 when a United States attorney obtained her consent for the revocation of her citizenship. The revocation was made on the ground that Mrs. Ryan had failed to list her prior war crimes conviction record, on both her visa and her citizenship application, and when she consented to it, thereby saving the government the extremely drawn-out process of denaturalizing a citizen, the way was open to the Justice Department to begin deportation proceedings against her; she was now an alien, one believed, in the language employed in immigration law, guilty of having committed crimes involving moral turpitude.* Both during and after the deportation hearings, the reasons for Mrs. Ryan and her attorney consenting to the revocation of her citizenship remained a mystery to immigration lawyers. It was supposed in some quarters that her attorney had wished to keep his client out of federal court, where her case would necessarily have gone into a legal battle against denaturalization; there was the danger that an adverse federal court decision, stripping Mrs. Ryan of her citizenship, would exert a considerable influence and weigh heavily against her when, as an alien, her case then came to the Immigration Service for a ruling on deportation. Her attorney may have thought it desirable that, by quietly yielding her citizenship, Mrs. Ryan would bring herself directly under the jurisdiction of the Immigration Service, thereby securing a less auspicious, less formal setting for the examination of her case and background than a federal court would provide. Whatever may have been the motives for Mrs. Ryan's decision to relinquish her citizenship, they were to result in deportation hearings the following winter.

In the beginning, the bulk of the defense testimony came from Mrs. Ryan's husband, a man with anxious eyes set in a small V-shaped face that seemed to want to recede into the rest of him. Russell Ryan explained, under direct questioning by the Ryan attorney, the grave difficulties he and his wife would have in the event that she had to leave the United States, the difficulties they had been having all along since the stories about Hermine Braunsteiner Ryan had begun appearing in the newspapers. "For five years, life has been full of hardship," Ryan said. "For five years I lived with a shotgun about three feet away from my bed when I slept."

"What has transpired, with regard to your neighbors and friends where you live, since these matters have appeared in the public press?" Mr. Barry asked.

---

* In immigration law, crimes involving moral turpitude are defined as acts considered abhorrent to the norms of community and society.

"This charge has been following us like a plague, this charge of twenty-five years' standing. They don't want to talk to us, they don't want to come into our house, our home, and they don't want us to call them," Ryan added, referring to his friends and neighbors.

It was here that he told how, in 1968, when the stories about her background were published in the newspapers, his wife had lost her job.

"Do you happen to know, were her employers Christians or Jews?" the Ryan attorney asked.

"They were Jews."

The general thrust of the testimony that the Ryan attorney then began to elicit from Russell Ryan had to do with his entirely American roots: the number of his junior high school in Queens, the name of his Elmhurst high school, the length of his service with the U.S. Air Force in World War II and the Korean War, and the information that his great-great-grandfather had been born in the United States—all were designed to establish clearly the injustice of putting so very American a person in a position of having to leave his country, which would be the case in the event that the Justice Department succeeded in deporting his wife.

His wife had informed him the year he met her, 1957, that she had once been a concentration camp guard and served a prison sentence after the war, but that she had received an amnesty from the Austrian government that same year, Ryan testified. During the cross-examination that followed, Ryan was asked questions concerning his knowledge of the concentration camps, to which he gave answers in the same respectful but faintly defiant tone that he had used when talking about his understanding of the amnesty his wife had received: he knew what he knew, that tone said, what he had been led to believe; he could not help it if people were now telling him that matters were other than what he had been told. Now in the question of the concentration camps, his understanding was made up largely of information given him by his wife, and illuminated by what he had seen himself when he visited such a camp after the war.

"From your understanding of concentration camps now, from what you saw, what do you think they were?" prosecuting attorney Schiano asked Russell Ryan on cross-examination.

"From the ones I saw—well, I had heard they were horror camps, and this was not the truth."

Had he ever visited any of the camps? He had: the camp where his wife had formerly served—Ravensbrück.

"And you were in that camp at Ravensbrück?" Schiano asked.

"Yes."

"Did she tell you that that was a concentration camp?"

"No, sir, it amounts in my mind to a rehabilitation camp."

"To rehabilitate who?"

"The inmates, sir."

"Is that what she told you?" Schiano pursued.

"Yes, sir."

Schiano, interested in establishing Mrs. Ryan's attitudes concerning the concentration camps, asked him again what his wife had told him about Ravensbrück. This time Ryan's answers were more wary, if also more surprising.

"You have indicated," Schiano queried, "that this was a rehabilitation center?"

"Her remarks indicated that."

"But she didn't tell you that?"

"In my mind that was a rehabilitation center."

"Well, did she tell you that there were no rehabilitation programs being carried out?"

"She told me that about two days ago."

On this subject, the supposed function of the concentration camps, there were to be a good many more complicated exchanges when Schiano examined Mrs. Ryan, for Russell Ryan's talk about rehabilitation was a foreshadowing of the general line of defense his wife would maintain throughout the hearings: that she had entered upon her work as a camp guard at Ravensbrück in the understanding that it was a place for people who needed rehabilitation through discipline, and that even at Maidanek, which she described as an extermination camp, her own role had continued to be no more than a supervisory, disciplinary one so far as the inmates were concerned.

The hearings were held in the spare-looking fourteenth-floor courtroom of the Immigration Service building, a setting whose general austerity was considerably relieved by a brace of Manhattan skyscrapers looming up intimately from a wall of windows behind the judge's bench. Directly in front of the judge was the long table equipped with microphones where the witnesses gave testimony: where, in February of 1972, Hermine Braunsteiner sat answering Schiano's questions. Mrs. Ryan took the stand appearing more composed than her husband had and looking physically far more substantial: a rangy blond woman of fifty-three, with youthfully coiffed bangs that did not offset, but seemed rather to highlight, the profound angularity of her face and features.

Schiano, a stonily efficient interrogator during cross-examination, spent a long time examining Mrs. Ryan on the nature of her duties at Ravensbrück, eliciting from her first her understanding of the camp structure. She was not aware, Mrs. Ryan replied in answer to the prosecutor's question, why exactly people had been put in Ravensbrück, only that they were criminals or asocial, and that the badges they wore indicated their problem. Jews wore a special badge? They did. Jehovah's Witnesses wore a badge? They did. Why had she wanted to work in a concentration camp? It was not a concentration camp when she started; the word that they used for Ravensbrück was *Umschulunglager*, reschooling or reeducation camp.

"What was the reeducation all about?" Schiano asked in his characteristic manner, which was without overtones other than the suggestion that there was a gap in his information that, possibly, the witness could fill.

"I think they hoped when they go in the camp they will change their thoughts and many times, I have to say, many of these inmates, they got released."

"How did you know they got released?"

"We saw every morning when somebody gets released, they were taken to the bathroom and put in clean clothes again." Released people were then driven by truck to the railroad station, some distance away, Mrs. Ryan explained.

"Did you see any Jews being released?"

"No."

The first months in Ravensbrück, she had worked eight hours a day guarding prisoners in the punishment block and others assigned to construction work; meanwhile, the camp population was expanding with the influx of new prisoners.

Here the judge intervened with questions. Special Inquiry Officer Lyons inquired whether she had tried to get another job after some months in Ravensbrück. She had not.

"You were satisfied with the position, with the work you were doing?"

"Well, the work was not satisfactory there because it was stand-up the whole day, and it wasn't easy, either."

Judge Lyons, a man of waspish temperament at times, but also often a patient one, persisted in this line of questioning, the more so after Mrs. Ryan said that she had, in fact, tried to quit after the first year in Ravensbrück, but that she had been told this was possible only if she were going to have a child.

"You said you tried to quit after the first year—that would be 1940?"

"Yes."

"Why?"

"Why?"

"Yes, why?"

"I didn't like it. I wanted to get something better."

"What didn't you like about it?"

"Well, standing the whole day. I have very bad veins in my legs and I wanted a more pleasant job."

This answer was not the kind the judge had probed for. A graying man with prominent lips that were pursed habitually in a stubborn line, he hunched forward, a not quite majestic but nonetheless formidable figure in his black robes, and attempted again to satisfy the question that was in his mind.

"Was that the only reason?"

"Yes."

After Schiano resumed the questioning, Mrs. Ryan said she had been transferred from Ravensbrück in 1942 for a combination of reasons, most of which had to do with difficulties in her relationships with another woman guard, as well as with one of her male superiors at the camp. The prosecutor's queries were concentrated now on the physical layout at Maidanek. There were crematoria at Maidanek, and a gas chamber, Mrs. Ryan said, but she could not recall that she had ever seen gallows at the camp or witnessed a hanging, the latter a piece of testimony of some significance in the light of later aspects of the case. As the questions put to her seemed to grow more pointed, Mrs. Ryan's answers, which had been fairly straightforward, became at times hesitant and contradictory. When Schiano asked her whether children had been in Maidanek, she answered "no" flatly, several times; asked yet again, she testified that children had been in Maidanek, "but not in the beginning." Children as young as three, did she remember? Schiano asked.

"I can remember only one little boy, who was nine years old." Query by query now, Schiano elicited a description of camp procedures and her role in them. On the witness stand, even confronting an adversary, it is easier to answer questions truthfully than to evade them when it is not clear how they are dangerous; there is no time to sort out the dangerous from the neutral queries, nor for the witness to reason that all the adversary's inquiries must be presumed dangerous; the impulse, unless the question is an obvious one, is to answer simply because the answer is in one's possession. Mrs. Ryan's behavior on the stand in no way departed from this principle; given a great many questions, she provided a great many answers, not knowing how one would lead to another, nor the design into which they would all ultimately fit.

When new female inmates came to Maidanek, they were first brought to the bathhouse and given clean clothes before being marched off to the field house of the women's camp, Mrs. Ryan testified. Yes, she was one of the people who met new arrivals at the gate and guided them through this process. What was the distance, in Maidanek, between the bathhouse and the gas chamber? Schiano then asked.

"There was no difference, it was the same room." Women picked out for gassing during the selections were put in special barracks and then, at night, the SS would come to take them away, Mrs. Ryan said. No, there were no guards assigned to these barracks; the women were just locked in there. But she had helped bring these women to the special barracks once they were selected for gassing? She had.

According to the rest of her testimony, she had been sick during most of her tenure at Maidanek, and she had seen very little: not more than one or two selections, no massacres of Jews. A query about beatings brought a crisp reply: "Sometimes." When? When she had a hard time lining people up. Had she used a stick to get people out of the barracks? No. Fists? No.

"What did you use?" Schiano asked.

"My open hand."

Mrs. Ryan answered Schiano's questions in clear unemphatic tones. Hands folded neatly on her lap, testifying or listening to others testify, she bore herself with ladylike calm that seemed ruffled only by the approach of reporters: from these, clearly—representatives of newspapers, which had already done so much harm in printing the stories about her—she expected nothing but enmity. Making a stiff, small gesture, she waved away those coming toward her with notebooks and microphones and turned her back, murmuring her replies to the air: "No questions. No questions."

Despite the difficulties with neighbors and acquaintances that her husband had testified were their lot since the news stories had begun to appear, she was nevertheless not friendless. Four witnesses, a man and three women, came to give testimony in Mrs. Ryan's behalf; all had known her for several years, they said, in answer to the questions put to them by Mrs. Ryan's attorney, and had found her to be of good moral character, with an excellent reputation for truthfulness.

"From your observations of her over the years and the contacts you have had with her, would you say that she is a kind, considerate person?"

"Exceptionally kind and considerate."

"Would you wish her to be your neighbor for the rest of your life?"

"I would."

The prosecutor's cross-examination of the first witness consisted of a single question: "Does it make any difference to you whether she is innocent or guilty of mistreating inmates in the concentration camps?"

"No, not necessarily."

To the second witness: "It would make no difference to you?"

"No."

Of the subsequent witnesses, attorney Schiano asked the same question and received the same or similar answers, a result not altogether valueless to a prosecution: displays of uniform and unconditional loyalty that render suspect the judgment and perhaps the integrity of the character witnesses are not among the most desirable contributions those witnesses can make for the defense.

In temper, background, and, above all, in efficacy, the witnesses for the prosecution were a varied lot. One of the defense arguments made regularly, both directly and by implication, was that the deportation proceedings against Mrs. Ryan were largely the result of political—particularly Jewish—pressures. "This may all be good cannon fodder for these ladies and gentlemen of the press, the TV, and so forth, and it may certainly sell newspapers, and the Jewish community may be most happy to see this thing go on forever," Mrs. Ryan's attorney told the court once, by way of arguing that the government should not be retrying the Maidanek charges against his client. In the light of this defense contention, it was not a happenstance entirely that two of the witnesses the prosecution chose to present were non-Jews, and that this fact should emerge prominently in their testimony.

One of them had, however, qualifications of much more

significance to the prosecutor's case than the fact that she had been born a Roman Catholic. Dr. Danuta Czaykowska-Medryk, of Warsaw, and former inmate of Maidanek, had kept a diary of her camp experiences and had written a book on Maidanek, published in Poland, in which Hermine Braunsteiner's name figured several times. A fair woman with aristocratic features, Dr. Czaykowska-Medryk testified, through a Polish interpreter, that Hermine Braunsteiner had pushed and made prisoners run by means of a whip, that she was known as "the mare" because of her habit of kicking inmates, and that she chased the women who were selected for death.

"She beat them, kicked them, and pulled them back into line, pulling them by the hair back into line."

In the course of hearing this testimony, Hermine Braunsteiner sometimes made notes, which she handed to her husband. Each time, Russell Ryan's alarmed eyes moved rapidly from witness to paper to wife, a circuit made again and again before they stopped and fastened on the note. Next to him, her writing done, Mrs. Ryan folded her hands and listened to the witness.

During the selections of Jewish women for the gas chambers, Dr. Czaykowska-Medryk testified, the SS doctor had missed some whose legs were in bad condition: "The ones that he missed, she showed him, and pushed them toward the group of women selected to be sent to the gas chamber."

What, Schiano asked his witness, was the next memory of Hermine Braunsteiner? The day Jewish children were being rounded up, when Braunsteiner had slapped the face of an inmate policewoman who had refused her order to grab the children and bring them to the trucks.

"If you can, tell us how many children were involved in this operation," the judge intervened.

"Two trucks full."

"What was the age group?"

"Those who were able to walk, very young, just beginning to walk, up to twelve years of age—after that, they are considered adults—and these children were sent to the gas chamber. They were gassed."

She herself, the witness said, had been whipped and beaten, her head shoved down into icy water by Braunsteiner, during the time she had been in Maidanek. Did the witness recognize Hermine Braunsteiner today? Schiano asked.

"The moment I walked in I recognized her," Dr. Czaykowska-Medryk replied coldly.

"Do you see her?"

"Yes."

"Where is she?"

"Here." The witness pointed a finger at Hermine Braunsteiner Ryan, sitting in the courtroom.

During her cross-examination, Dr. Czaykowska-Medryk revealed that the book she wrote on Maidanek had been begun in 1946. She did not have a copy of it with her, she told Mrs. Ryan's attorney, who asked her many questions about it: she had not written the book for the purposes of these proceedings.

"What did you write it for?" Mr. Barry asked.

"To state for memory the facts which occurred in Maidanek. To pay tribute to the women who lost their lives, and those who are still alive, and for the purpose that our children should know the truth about the concentration camps."

Did her husband encourage her to come to America to testify at these hearings? Mr. Barry wanted to know. She was surprised, the witness retorted, to have such a question put to her.

"What is the answer?" The judge's question was mild.

"But I am grown up. I know what I went through, and nobody could influence me or my decision." The defense attorney repeated his question. Finally the witness replied: she had not consulted her husband, who had been away on vacation at the time she agreed to testify. Where had her husband gone on vacation? The Baltic. What did he do for a living?

"Objection," from Schiano.

"Overruled."

"A dentist," came the affronted reply.

Was she a member of the Communist Party of Poland? No. Did she have any religion?

"Yes, I am a Roman Catholic."

"Do you practice your religion?"

"I don't understand that question, do I practice."

"Do you go to church?"

"Whenever I feel like it."

"Do you receive the sacraments?"

"Objection."

The prosecutor's objection overruled, the witness glanced up at the judge. "Have I to answer that question?"

The judge listened with a small frown that was an unconscious aping of the one on the witness's face.

"I think," she continued, "it is enough that I took an oath to tell the truth."

"That's all we're asking you to do," interposed Mrs. Ryan's attorney.

"I am afraid you will shortly ask me for my sins."

The question finally was struck.

During the rest of a lengthy cross-examination, a piece of testimony emerged that supported Korman's, given earlier, about the way the kitchen workers from the men's camp at Maidanek had brought the food rations to the women's camp, by which means Korman, a kitchen worker, had come to be on field five and to witness Vice-Kommandant Hermine Braunsteiner's activities.

"They came with a German *capo*.* They looked like skeletons," Dr. Czaykowska-Medryk told the court. "We couldn't believe that they had drawn the wagon or had the strength to even walk. Or do anything. They looked like skeletons with clothes on."

More questions about the book. The witness answered that it had not been possible to include in it everything that had happened in Maidanek.

"Well, you mentioned Braunsteiner in your book five or six times, didn't you?" Mrs. Ryan's attorney asked.

"It was too little. Too few times, too seldom mentioned."

By the time the witnesses for the government appeared

* Camp trusty.

on the stand, they had been tested and questioned at length by the prosecuting attorney, the histories in their immigration files scrutinized, if they were Americans citizens, to establish that they had been in the concentration camps when and where they said they had. They must be precise, the witnesses were told, and they must try to avoid emotional outbursts. But a number of times during the hearings, these warnings proved of no avail. One witness, a fifty-two-year-old Brooklyn woman, entered the courtroom trembling with a visible violence, and several times in the course of giving testimony earned the judge's rebuke for volunteering statements.

On the whole, the witnesses refused talk about revenge, not needing to be told the unwisdom of suggesting that their testimony was motivated by vengeance. Like most survivors, they were long accustomed to the cultural prohibition that made shows of vengeance or any talk of it a form of behavior to be strictly avoided. They wanted only justice, each witness said one way and another, not vengeance.

The solitary exception was the Brooklyn witness, Rachael Berger, a stocky woman whose broad Slavic face exuded defiance of many aspects of the proceedings: its formalities, its restraints, its wealth of questions about times, dates, and distances—all of which, her answers were designed to show, could have issued only from madness or stupidity. The train carrying them to Maidanek had been gassed as they approached the station, and when it stopped, someone dragged her across the bodies and she had jumped down. And she had been taken off the train at Maidanek? Mrs. Ryan's attorney asked. She had jumped down.

"How far was it from the railroad station?"

"You want it in centimeters? Or in millimeters?"

"If you can," Mrs. Ryan's attorney retorted. "You're the mathematician."

She had, she testified, been a student of mathematics at the University in Warsaw before the war. The evidence she had to give the court included testimony that Hermine Braunsteiner had beaten her and—in more detail, delivered in a hard rising tone and spat toward Mrs. Ryan's attorney —a description of the way Hermine Braunsteiner and the other Maidanek women guards had behaved during the death selections: happy and festive. Because of her memory of this behavior, she was going to celebrate this day in court as her holiday, the witness said. Why was today her holiday? Mr. Barry inquired.

"Because it is a Jewish holiday,* I will celebrate and dress like she used to dress herself for the selections."

During a break in the proceedings, journalists crowded around the witness to ask the reason for her emotional behavior and what had prompted her to come and testify— particularly since the experience was such an upsetting one, a reporter suggested in richly neutral tones that owed much to the psychoanalytic mode.

"Why? Why I am here? For our dead," the witness said in a voice that pierced the general clamor in the room. And did she have anything to say about Mrs. Ryan?

"Yes. There she sits before you, blooming." Reporters wrote. Mrs. Ryan, her husband, and her attorney walked out of the courtroom.

"Blooming!" the witness called after her.

Later she divulged that the sight of Mrs. Ryan had enraged her: "Gray suit, immaculate. Hair, immaculate. Over her knees she had these two hands and her hands were so big, her legs were so strong, so young. My whole family came to my mind. I remembered the eyes of my aunt, selected for the gas chamber, standing in line. A young woman—but for the camp middle-aged—and looking at me with such force, such eyes, to say maybe I can do something. My two classmates, taken out during the roll call because they had dysentery and had to relieve themselves. This was enough to send you to death. I had a little cousin, eight years younger than I. I remember once she came to my barracks and I saw her the first time, kneeling down all yellow, destroyed. And my little sister? I loved her so much, gassed. Destroyed. And here I see *her* sitting in this courtroom, with these paws on her lap, folded so. So strong, so fresh, so well-looking!"

Witnesses continued to appear for the government until

* The witness's court appearance fell on the holiday of Shevuoth.

March 21, 1973, when the hearings were terminated. One of them, a Kew Gardens woman, testified to the beatings Hermine Braunsteiner had given to her and to others at the camp, and told how the Vice-Kommandant had put the children on the trucks that took them to the gas chamber. She came, the witness said, with no hate in her heart, but when she had seen Hermine Braunsteiner Ryan's name and picture in the paper, she knew she owed it to come and testify.

"You owe to whom?" the judge asked.

"To those less fortunate than I, who died."

Another government witness, a woman artist and former inmate of Maidanek, submitted four sketches she had made of a Jewish girl who had been hanged on field five in the summer of 1943 for attempting to escape. The sketches were being submitted as corroborative evidence that a hanging had taken place, the government attorney told the court, in reply to the objections of Mrs. Ryan's attorney that the evidence had no bearing on his client's case: Mrs. Ryan had testified that there had been no hangings in the women's camp the summer of 1943, that she had never seen a scaffold at Maidanek. A doctor, a former inmate of the small camp of Genthin, to which Hermine Braunsteiner had been transferred in 1944, appeared in the Immigration Service courtroom subsequently to testify to the beatings she had seen Hermine Braunsteiner administering to inmates there, and to the blows she herself had received from her. She had been inmate doctor at the camp, the witness said, and recalled one instance especially, when she had watched a young Russian girl being punished. The instrument of punishment was a riding crop, struck very hard.

"Who did this?" Schiano asked the witness.

The witness pointed a finger at Hermine Braunsteiner. "The Obersfehrin Braunsteiner."

How many times was the girl hit with the crop? Twenty-five times.

"Did you treat the girl?"

"No, I wasn't allowed to treat this girl. I was the doctor, but she had forbidden me to treat her."

Was it not true, Mr. Barry asked during the cross-examination, that the witness had not been admitted to medical practice until the year 1946? Yes, but she had worked as a doctor in the concentration camps; she had finished her studies and could perform local surgery, but had not done her thesis until 1946. Did the doctor know, Mr. Barry asked, of what the Russian girl had been accused? Sabotage. Also of being a Communist. Did the witness know any of the rules at the camp?

"Yes."

"Doctor, you knew the rules, didn't you?"

"We were supposed to know them."

"And you knew the consequences of the rules?"

"Yes."

"So that, in plain English, if you broke the rules you were punished?"

"Yes."

"And that girl was accused of sabotage, right?"

"Yes."

Had anyone died in the camp to her knowledge? Mrs. Ryan's attorney asked. No. This was not a death camp but a work camp, where people had to be on their feet.

"And you took care of them?"

"I think I did a good job of it. No one died. I hope it was due to my work. I hope so, even without my thesis."

The doctor who had given this testimony was a French Jew. The majority of the witnesses were, however, citizens of the United States. "Why does it take so long with Braunsteiner?" and "Why is she still here?" these witnesses asked many times during the period of the hearings, defying their own understanding of legal complexity and due process to which some of them had so decorously given themselves in the witness stand. They were the inhabitants of two worlds, one past and one present, and at times, such as occurred regularly during the hearings, the logic of one world rendered that of the other absurd: they knew it was perfectly proper to question details in a courtroom, but to the witnesses there was only absurdity in queries about the hour and date events had taken place in the death camp.

What, further, could be meant by questions about why they had come to give evidence?

The question "Why is she still here?" moved toward a solution on March 21, 1973, when the hearings resumed after a hiatus of many weeks. New witnesses prepared to take the stand, but it soon became apparent they would not have to testify at all. For as the morning session was beginning, the news arrived that the West German government had officially requested the extradition of Hermine Braunsteiner Ryan on multiple murder charges. At virtually the same time, the Polish government filed its extradition request for Hermine Braunsteiner Ryan, but the United States, in accordance with its extradition treaty, ruled on the West German request, which had come in first.

The Immigration Service hearings were suspended. The prosecuting attorney thanked his witnesses, who had come that day to no purpose. The same night, March 21st, United States marshals arrested Hermine Ryan, removing her to Riker's Island prison, and the following morning she was arraigned in a Brooklyn federal court as a fugitive from West Germany. During her arraignment, she complained through her attorney that she had been made to share quarters with prostitutes on Riker's Island, with the result that she was brought to Nassau County prison, where she remained until federal court Judge Mishler ruled on the extradition request.

Mrs. Ryan's attorney waged a desperate battle in federal court, arguing that his client was a citizen of the United States, and that the motion stripping her of her citizenship should be vacated: that, additionally, her extradition would subject Mrs. Ryan to double jeopardy, inasmuch as she had already stood trial in Vienna, in 1949, for crimes allegedly committed in Maidanek-Lublin, and been acquitted for lack of evidence. In rejecting both of these arguments, the court called the claim that Mrs. Ryan was a citizen a spurious one. On the claim that she was being tried twice for the same crime, there was, Judge Mishler held in his decision, no constitutional right to be free from double jeopardy resulting from extradition to a demanding country

—that double jeopardy related only to crimes committed in this country; that, furthermore, the charges cited in the bench warrant which the Düsseldorf court had issued for Mrs. Ryan's arrest were not those she had been acquitted of in Austria.

The extradition request issued by the Düsseldorf court included depositions from Polish witnesses, who stated that during the death selections Hermine Braunsteiner supplied candidates for extermination on her own when she felt that they had been overlooked by the selecting officer. The bench warrant charged Hermine Braunsteiner with having killed people in Lublin, Poland, in the period October, 1942, to March, 1944, by several independent actions on her own or jointly with others: "Of having in a cruel manner killed a woman prisoner in the fall of 1942; of having participated in a selection of Jewish women and children in the spring of 1943 on field five of Maidanek, the women and children being selected and sorted out for the purposes of being killed in a gas chamber; of having participated in the selection of 100 women prisoners in April of 1943, the women prisoners being selected and sorted out for the purposes of being killed in a gas chamber; of having cooperated and taken part in the hanging of a Jewish girl on field five."

In the deposition supporting the last charge, the witness, a Polish survivor, stated that Hermine Braunsteiner ordered the young girl to get up on a stool. SS guards then hanged the girl, who had hoped to escape the gas chamber by claiming Polish parentage. The execution had taken place before the eyes of other Maidanek inmates, ordered to watch as an object lesson to them. The signer of the deposition had been one of the onlookers that day.

On August 6, 1973, the petition of the West German government having been granted, Hermine Braunsteiner was brought to the airport in the custody of U.S. marshals. Her husband, Russell Ryan, preparing to forsake their Queens home for the long visits he would be making to Germany, appeared before the television cameras. Full of solidarity and hopelessness, his small jaw thrust forward, he stated that his wife was guiltless of the charges against her and repeated ónce more that Jewish interests in the television and newspaper media and Jewish political pressures were behind the tragedy that had befallen her now. Implicit in this many-faceted and often reiterated charge was a question: who but the Jews would care what happened in Maidanek? Would Americans other than Jews concern themselves with what his wife had done in Maidanek?

This, in one form or another, was also the question in the minds of the former Maidanek inmates, who asked so often why Mrs. Ryan was still in America. On the part of the small band of American witnesses and other survivors, who followed every particle of news about it, the deportation trial of Hermine Braunsteiner was in no small way a struggle for possession. The long and the short of this struggle was the wish—indeed, the demand—that the country which had received and nurtured them after 1945 should not also receive and nurture her, and in so doing confirm a belief that the survivors themselves were given often to pronouncing but did not, like a number of their judgments, wish to see proved, least of all by Americans: that the holocaust was a matter of indifference to everyone but its victims, the Jews; that the world had taken no lessons from it; that it had changed nothing, taught nothing, meant nothing. Vincent Schiano, the prosecutor who had fought to bring the case to trial—having done as he had done, he later said, because he had found intolerable the idea that aliens were deported for having stolen a chicken in the old country, while one with the blood of innocent women and children on her hands was still here—had contributed to their capacity to believe otherwise. For this, the survivors honored him with a formal reception, making no secret of their gratitude.

2 | 1945

In the spring of 1945, elements of the United States First Army and the Soviet Union's First Ukrainian Army met in the center of Germany. There, on the River Elbe, the soldiers of General Courtney H. Hodges and Marshal Ivan S. Konev cut Germany in half, proof that the doom which had been closing in so inexorably on the German armies all spring was now upon them. By April 30th, the American flag flew over Nuremberg. Munich lay a heap of dust and rubble, around the battered Hofbräuhaus, the favored meeting place of Adolf Hitler and his party leaders, and around the Feldherrnhalle, a building consecrated to the memory of Hitler's early speeches. The residents of Munich made their way, that cold and desolate spring, over the piled bricks and glass of their ruined city, scavengers as all the populations of German cities had become after months of bombing. The people of Munich, it was reported, seemed friendlier to the American occupiers than those in a good many other places in Germany, for in the preceding months the SS, of which the city had a particularly rich endowment, had become jumpy; they were quick to be suspicious of gatherings of three persons or more on the streets, and quicker to make arrests, as the end of the Reich grew near. Since the invasion of Normandy in June of 1944, the European war had moved steadily toward its conclusion, to be preceded by a final, furious rush of events in the spring of 1945.

On April 28th, Benito Mussolini was killed by Milanese partisans, his body mutilated by onlookers in an orgy of violence that threatened to turn his remains to dust there on the streets of Milan.

Three days later, Adolf Hitler was reported to be dead in his Chancellery. The German radio proclaimed that Hitler had fallen at his command post, a soldier in the battle of Berlin; Russian sources promptly announced that the news of Hitler's death was a Fascist trick. Hitler's successor, Admiral Dönitz, announced for the benefit of the Americans and the British that, to save Germany from the Soviets, the war would continue against the Russians and also against all armies that fought as allies of the Russians. Two days later, Berlin fell to the Russians; seventy thousand Germans surrendered to the troops commanded by Marshals Zhukov and Konev, after twelve days of bloody street fighting.

The following day, all German forces surrendered in Holland, Denmark, and Northwestern Germany. On May 7th, in a schoolhouse in Rheims, France, military representatives of the Reich signed the document of unconditional surrender: Germany was defeated. It was, Winston Churchill observed, "the signal for the greatest outburst of joy in the history of mankind."

General Alfred Jodl, who signed the surrender for Germany and who would die by hanging in 1946, by order of the International Military Tribunal for war crimes, observed in a brief formal comment after the signing, that "the German people and its armed forces had perhaps achieved and suffered more in the five years of the war than any other people on earth."

In fact, the achievements of the German people and her armed forces, which were known to the world by 1945, were principally of the sort that caused the International Military Tribunals to be planned and the hangman to ready his skills. All that April, the Allied press carried the grim news of Dachau and Buchenwald, and although the Allied governments and their populations had known of the existence of the concentration camps throughout the war years, it was not until the 42nd and the 45th Divisions of the United States Seventh Army overran Dachau and reported what they had found there that the details began to imprint themselves on the imagination of a world already hardened to the knowledge of death and misery by years of war. In America and England, grim outraged dispatches filled the newspapers daily with the stories of the crematoria and the torture rooms, of the skeletons in striped suits—the prisoners, of whom the Americans found 32,000 alive when they took the camp. While the appalled cadres of American and British correspondents were still filing their stories on the crimes uncovered at Dachau, the 80th Infantry Division of the American Third Army entered Buchenwald, near Weimar, Germany, where, it was estimated, 32,700 people had met their end by shooting, hanging, beatings, starvation, or in brutal medical experiments.

By order of the United States Army, German civilians were brought to view Buchenwald. A long and reluctant line of Germans had first to behold the display of human skin, the "parchments" that had been collected from the prisoners by a German doctor with a special interest in tattoos. As they looked, a German-speaking American soldier told them what the parchments display was. The German civilians were then led through the camp barracks where, in three-tiered bunks, seven thousand sick and dying Buchenwald inmates lay. Afterward they viewed the laboratories where the prisoners had been injected with typhus, and also the special room where the children were kept who were inoculated with the disease in order to produce typhus serum for the Germans. The death rate of those inoculated, camp doctors estimated, was ninety-eight percent. The civilian visitors then moved to the crematoria, where they saw the stoves with their human ashes, and nearby some of the little receptacles in which the remains of those the Germans considered to have been privileged prisoners were sent home to their relatives. Afterward the visitors saw the gallows and the torture devices, and everywhere around them the crowds of ambulatory skeletons.

Once uncovered, Buchenwald brought delegations of British M.P.s and American congressmen on firsthand inspection tours. Even as they returned to their home countries, having seen the evidence of Buchenwald and the deeds done there, which they all reported to be the ultimate in Nazi depravity, the British were sending out the first reports on the Belsen concentration camp. In Belsen, which the British Second Army had liberated on April 15th, they found, in the typhus-infected compounds, more than ten thousand unburied dead who had met their end by starvation, shooting, and disease, and lying among them the living —for many thousands of whom, it was clear, the liberation came too late.

Near the town of Gardelegen, where, under the direction of an older SS man, sixteen-year-old German boys in SS uniforms had marched eleven hundred slave laborers into a barn lined with gasoline-soaked straw and set it on fire, scores of American soldiers beheld the mound of charred bodies that remained. The American military commander decreed that the German citizens of Gardelegen would have to bury the remains of the dead men in individual graves, with coffins for each that measured six feet long and three feet wide, and that such burial would take place at the point of bayonet if necessary. In Landsberg, Germany, American troops discovered hundreds of emaciated corpses, which the German guards had not had time to dispose of in the camp's crematoria before making their retreat. An American colonel from Kentucky ordered six hundred citizens of the nearest German town to be marched to the camp where he told them, "This is a prime example of your vaunted German culture. You may say that you are not responsible, but you supported the regime that committed such crimes."

With every day's news of the camps, and of the long chain of similar atrocities the Allied armies found as they made their way across Germany in the final spring of the Reich, there came the warnings of worse news yet to come. The American troops had by then discovered Thekla, near Leipzig, where three hundred people had been locked into a boarded-up barracks in the middle of the afternoon, told to go to bed, and incinerated. As bad as Buchenwald and Dachau were, one American correspondent reported, Thekla was worse than any of these, and Thekla, he pointed out bitterly, was a suburb of Leipzig, a city that prided itself on being the cultural capital of Germany.

Outside Dachau, the Americans found a train halted on a siding and guarded by German soldiers. At first sight of the train, the Americans opened fire on it. At once, people in striped rags tumbled down the embankment from every car and began to run. As soon as the American armored column had identified the train's cargo, the firing stopped, but people continued running across the field toward the American tanks. The German guards made no attempt to stop them, and the headlong flight from the boxcars went on—a swift, striped riot of people running from the trains across the fields straight toward the American armored column. On the road, the driver of an American jeep watched a boy of about sixteen crawl toward his vehicle. When he got to the jeep, the boy pulled himself to a standing position, eyes first on the soldier and then on the dashboard full of chocolate bars. The driver, no older than nineteen himself, said something in English to the boy, who understood none of it, whereupon the soldier scooped up all the candy bars and handed them to him. While the boy ate, the soldier began automatically going through the pockets of his uniform and his knapsack for more candy and food, as though he had done this many times before and was now practiced at it.

The train the Americans had liberated had grown longer in the course of its aimless journey around Dachau; the Germans had coupled boxcars of Hungarian Jewish women to the original train, making altogether twenty thousand people who had been locked up for seven days without food or water. Confronted with so many people perishing of hunger and thirst, the Americans saw the necessity of feeding them as quickly as possible, without requiring them to stand in line and wait for their turn, an effort that would pose clear dangers of riot. They directed the liberated prisoners to arrange themselves along both sides of the road, which resulted, when it was done, in a double-edged file of people that stretched along the sides of the road as far as the eye could see. Immediately after, the first trucks came cruising down the road of survivors, each with four American soldiers in it. From both sides of the truck, the soldiers leaned out and tossed food in packages and kits at the feet of the people on the road. The trucks traveled back and forth along the line, an operation that began in the afternoon and ended at dusk, leaving each person on the road in food up to his knees.

In a town near Theresienstadt, which the Russians had liberated, a Soviet officer offered a newly freed survivor a gun, and invited him along to shoot Nazis. The man, who had just stripped off the garments he had worn for seven months, answered, as he stared down at the lice-covered shirt, that he could not shoot Germans he did not know. He was a Polish Jew; his wife and three children were dead. He picked the lice from his skin and walked to a small river nearby to wash himself.

Fifteen kilometers from Dachau, the American soldiers tried to talk to the women they had liberated from a cattle car. One of the girls from the train made her way through the crowd to an American officer who seemed to know some Polish; she explained to him that they were Jewish prisoners of the Nazis, and that they had been penned up in the train for many days, and driven back and forth in order to evade the oncoming American troops. While they talked, and the soldiers emptied their pockets of candy and cigarettes, the SS who had accompanied the trainload of prisoners as guards were marched under a tree and stripped of their arms. Some of the prisoners crowded around to watch, among them the girl who had found the Polish-speaking American officer, whom she now seized by the arm. The American let himself be pulled forward by the girl and up to a large SS woman. Trembling, as she was to recall years later, and holding on to the American, she slapped the SS woman—a blind, unaimed blow that landed on the bulky shoulder of the guard. It was a guard who had beaten her many times, the girl told the American. And if the guard had not beaten her, she added bitterly, she had beaten others—it made no difference.

Dwight Eisenhower had been among the first visitors to Ohrdruf, near Gotha, not a major institution as German concentration camps went, but one with its full complement, nevertheless, of skeletal survivors sitting among piles of the dead and dying, its torture instruments, its abundant evidence in the form of torn bodies that some of the dying had tried to feed upon the corpses of the dead. While another member of the visiting party, General George Patton, went off to one side to vomit, Eisenhower required of himself that he visit every corner of the camp, which he did, ashen-faced, observers recorded, and in order, as he later said, that he could have firsthand evidence to which he could testify in the event that the world disbelieved the reports of the Nazi crimes.

As it was, the evidence of those crimes was put on film and shown in movie theaters all over England and America. The public saw the stacked bodies and the crematoria, and similar pictorial testimony of Dachau, Buchenwald, Mauthausen, Nordhausen, Belsen, and nameless smaller camps. The London *Daily Mirror* reported that in one instance British moviegoers were so horrified at the atrocities they saw in a newsreel at a Leicester Square theater that they started to leave it, only to be turned back by British servicemen who directed them to go back and see what other people had endured. Such was the temper of the times in Britain, a society that did not lightly brook interference with the private impulses of its citizens so long as those impulses were legal.

The British 11th Armored Division entered Belsen on Sunday, April 15th, the Germans having surrendered the camp in advance of their arrival. The prisoners were to remain under guard because of the outbreak of spotted typhus among them. Upon being asked, the concentration camp Kommandant, Josef Kramer, told the ranking British officer, Derrick Sington, that the prisoners were of several sorts, most of them regular criminals. Sington asked whether there were other people among them. There were, Kramer affirmed, a certain number of political prisoners as well.

Inside the camp the British found men and women packed by the hundreds in barracks that were meant to hold a quarter of their number. Four and five people lay head to foot on each of the bunks that ran in tiers from the bottom of the building to the top. The stench, which could be smelled many miles away from the camp, had become stronger with each step the soldiers took toward the barracks; inside, it was overpowering. Decomposing bodies lay side by side with the living, some of whom were in the last stages of their lives. Outside, the smoke of the entering tanks provided an unnecessary touch of the dreamlike to the place. At the side of a compound, a wall of dead naked women stretched seventy yards long and thirty yards wide. Periodically, shots rang out from the guns of Hungarian SS guards, not yet disarmed, who had discovered hungry prisoners trying to dig up potatoes from the camp garden: in all, in the first hours of liberation, scores of liberated prisoners were shot by the Hungarians before they could be disarmed. The people had been shot, the Hungarians explained to their British captors, because they had been trying to steal food.

"This is a fine hell you have made here," Sington told Kramer,* who observed, in return, that it had become that way in the last few days.

Belsen's inmates were of every nationality, most of them Jews brought from Auschwitz when that camp was liquidated at the end of 1944. Belsen had become the dumping center for the sick, the receiving center for inmates from all the concentration camps in the East, which had been evacuated by the Germans as the Russian armies advanced. There was, in Belsen, no mass destruction machinery as had been set up in the extermination camps in the East, but that which existed operated effectively enough to have brought death to 18,168 people in the final month prior to liberation.

"It is my duty to describe something beyond the imagination of mankind," R. W. Thompson reported in the London *Times*. Describing how the female SS guards had tied a dead body to a living one and burned them together while dancing around the pyre singing, with their hands joined, he ended his dispatch: "These Germans are without hope. They are not as other men. The thing is satanic." Captain

---

* Derek Sington, *Belsen Uncovered* (London: Gerald Duckworth & Co., Ltd., 1946), p. 18.

Sington, whose troops liberated Belsen, recalled that though he had at first been amazed at the sight of the prisoners in the striped suits whom he encountered as the first British tanks rolled in, "the half-credulous cheers of these almost lost men, of these clowns in terrible motley who had once been police officers, landworkers in the Ukraine, Budapest doctors and students in France, impelled a stronger emotion in me and I had to fight back my tears."

In due time, the camp Kommandant's legs were manacled and the Hungarian SS guards disarmed, leaving their captors to wonder why, given the evidence of Belsen, they had waited around to be caught. The British were astounded by Kramer and his guards, none of whom showed any signs that they thought they were guilty of wrongdoing, until they realized that the SS Kommandant and his men—who were not the brightest of their generation—had somehow been led by their superiors to believe that if they handed Belsen over in orderly fashion, the British would welcome them as helpers and administrators of the plague-ridden camp.

When the camp was secure, the healthier survivors squatted around small fires all over the campgrounds, cooking their meal of potatoes; they tended their fires and ate, wholly oblivious to the corpses lying only inches away from them. Behind them, British Army photographs of Belsen show, the shoes of the dead were piled up ready for use as fuel. Here and there, a solitary coat or dress flapped in the wind while airing out atop the wall of shoes, which stood ten feet high. By the side of a hut, a woman poured water over the hands of another, who sat on the ground. A girl of about twenty leaned out of a barracks window nearby, smiling a faint dry smile at odds with her eyes, which mirrored pure excitement. At the entrance to Barracks 22, a small girl sat alone and cried, while the entrance of Barracks 23 bustled with the efforts of some of the stronger women to carry out the corpses of the people who had died the night before. A man in a striped prisoner's suit lay propped up on one elbow and tried in that position to drink from a bowl of soup; another, in a tattered formal-looking

coat, picked his way across the body-strewn grounds, his
soup bowl held firmly in front of him with both hands.

While the survivors who could attempted to clean and
feed themselves, Glyn-Hughes, the Chief Medical Officer
of the British Second Army, set about trying to stop the
spread of spotted typhus. Some ten thousand dead had first
to be buried, in which effort the British drafted the captured
SS men and Germans from towns near the camp. Before
the liberation, the Germans had had the prisoners dig
enormous pits in an attempt to bury some of the bodies that
lay about the camp. The effort was to little effect, since
there were so many corpses, and since the inmates died of
exhaustion and hunger as they worked, thereby adding to
the number of unburied bodies. Now, after Belsen's liberation, SS marched in orderly fashion, four abreast, behind
the wagons carrying the dead to the enormous pits. Their
work was not done at a leisurely pace: while the British
held guns on them, the SS men ran around the perimeter of
the pit at a trot, carrying bodies from the wagon, which
they threw into the pit.

There were half a dozen mass graves in Belsen. Some
were filled by British soldiers who shoveled the bodies in
with bulldozers, but for the most part the three-day task of
gathering the dead and filling the graves was performed by
SS and local civilians. The Germans from nearby towns
who were pressed into the burial detail had first to gather
the bodies, which lay all over the roads leading to the camp,
and carry them in open coffins that had been mounted on
poles. The weight of the bodies they carried was not great.
Under the eyes of the British, the civilians marched
somberly in twos, each carrying one end of a pole: some
of the Germans were young; all of them looked frightened.

When the largest grave was full, Fritz Klein was placed in
the center. Klein was Belsen's camp doctor and formerly
SS physician at Auschwitz. A solitary figure standing among
the five thousand dead who lay in the pit, he stood with his
hands on his hips while British photographers recorded the
scene.

Before the dead were covered over, there were yet more

witnesses to the manner of their death, and of their burial: the mayors of all the surrounding towns were brought by the British to the site of the mass grave. To their left and their right were the SS men and women, standing dourly at attention. The SS men who had them kept their peaked caps on their heads, the rest of their ensemble being a variety of tunics and trousers that had seen better days. The SS women, who presented themselves in their thick bray skirts and jackets with the eagle insignia on the sleeve, were a uniformly burly and unkempt lot, which was not surprising given the work that they and the male SS had been required to do in preparation for the mass burial. But this was not so of the mayors who stood next to them. The mayors were, without exception, stately men; they had come to the mass grave dressed formally, in long topcoats, and all of them held their hats in their hands as they gazed into the pit.

One of them was a tall thin old man who looked into the excavation and, seeing what was there, turned away, his head in his hands, which were long and thin like the rest of him and seemed too fragile for the weight they bore. His colleagues beside him stared straight into the pit.

At the burial itself, the British Army chaplains presided. The Catholic chaplain, who had wept bitterly when he first beheld Belsen, stood dry-eyed next to the Protestant chaplain now and prayed at the graveside. At another corner of the pit, the Jewish chaplain recited the prayers for the dead over the great mound of bodies, mostly Jews, that lay inside.

The chaplain and the inmate rabbis of the camp exhausted themselves saying *Kaddish* over the dead all day long. The British had estimated, shortly after they entered Belsen, that ten thousand of the inmates they had liberated were beyond hope, and their estimate was being borne out: the death rate was three hundred a day for several weeks after the liberation.

The efforts to save the living required that the typhus epidemic, which raged through Camp 1, the women's camp, be brought under control. General Glyn-Hughes ordered the barracks burned to the ground, but first the side

of one of them was adorned with an enormous portrait of
Adolf Hitler, and another decorated with an equally large
Iron Cross. Hordes of survivors and soldiers stood packed
together behind the wooden platform on which Glyn-
Hughes and other British officers waited to give the command: clearly, burning the camp was a dire, practical necessity, but the burning was meant to have symbolic significance as well. At a given signal, the flamethrowers poured
their fire onto the buildings of the women's camp; the
enormous picture of Hitler curled up in flames, and within
minutes nothing could be seen but fire and smoke where the
women's barracks of Belsen had been.

With the pestilent camp burned, the British proceeded to
convert a nearby Wehrmacht barracks into a large hospital
for the thousands of starving and diseased Belsen survivors.
They suffered not only from typhus and advanced starvation, but from tuberculosis, dysentery, skin diseases, edema,
and a variety of other sicknesses, which were the products
of protracted starvation. To help care for them, Swiss
doctors and nurses, British Red Cross workers, and medical
students came in response to the emergency appeal of
Glyn-Hughes. A number of the medical volunteers who
were put to work under the direction of the Chief Medical
Officer of the 32 C.I.S., Lieutenant Colonel J. A. D. Johns-
ton, themselves eventually fell ill from typhus, enough so
that a wing of the makeshift hospital had to be set aside
for them. Several thousand of the liberated prisoners were
flown to hospitals in Sweden for more advanced treatment
than was available at Belsen. Departing Belsen, some of
them screamed upon seeing, and fought entering, the
ambulances that were to take them to the trains, remembering as they did that trucks with the Red Cross sign on
them had been used by the Germans to carry people to
extermination places. Then, necessity being what it was,
German doctors and nurses were pressed into service
despite the obvious terror of some of their patients. When
the doctors, now working under the direction of the British,
tried to approach them with needles and solutions for intravenous feedings, their patients cried out, recalling how
recently German medical men in Belsen had injected in-

mates with intravenous shots of benzol in order to kill them.

In one section of the hospital lay a blond girl of twenty, who might have been interred in a mass grave with the rest had it not been for a British Army photographer who noticed that an arm moved in the stack of the dead that he was trying to film. She had lain unconscious for two days and the women in her barracks had carried her out to the death pile. After her discovery, British soldiers decided they would have to go through the entire mound of bodies that lay outside one of the barracks, to check for those who might still be alive. The blond girl, a Viennese Jew, was one of several discovered to be still breathing. Though closer to dead than living, she was brought to the hospital with the others. Before her arrival in Belsen she had been a prisoner at Auschwitz where, time and again, she had vowed to kill herself. Some Auschwitz prisoners threw themselves across the electrified wire fence to commit suicide, but the easier way to die was to touch the corpse of someone on the fence, in which instance the shock was less but the current was still sufficient to kill. Having decided to kill herself, she recalled later, she discovered each time the opportunity came that her courage failed her with the result that, in addition to having to live, she lived loathing herself for failing to die.

It was, at the end, in a place like Belsen that others like her who had managed to survive the worst of the death camps were broken. There was no selection to stand for, and no gas chamber here—nor was there food or water, for in the month preceding the liberation the administration, such as it was, had broken down entirely, leaving only the SS guards operating at full capacity. The inmates knew that the end of the war was near, and that the Germans were defeated, but to many, so reduced by torture and starvation that they no longer thought about survival, it had ceased to matter. Hunger was what they knew; bread was what they wanted. People who had lost all other reasons to live but the hope that some member of their families might still be living lost that hope, too, finally. By the last weeks of captivity, there were those to whom the memory of their kin no longer had meaning, those who thought they might still find a husband, child, parent, and a number, greater even than these, who understood by that time that they were the only ones left alive of their families.

Early in 1945, the Russians began to disseminate news of certain camps in the territories that they had liberated in the East: Oswiecim, a marshy backwater of Cracow in Poland (later known to the world as Auschwitz); and Maidanek, near Lublin, the first of the killing centers that was reported on in detail.

The pattern of what the Germans had "achieved" had already begun to emerge clearly in the spring of 1945 when Jodl signed the documents of unconditional surrender in Rheims. The German National Socialist regime had established, in addition to forced labor and concentration camps, six killing centers to facilitate the mass extermination of Europe's Jews: Auschwitz; Maidanek; Treblinka, in a remote village near the Warsaw district; Chelmno, near Lodz; Belzec, near Lublin; Sobibor, near Lublin. These centers had, with the exception of the enormous I.G. Farben division of Auschwitz and some smaller slave labor divisions at Treblinka and Maidanek, no function but annihilation. After the Jews, the primary targets of the killing centers and their reason for being, came the gypsies and Soviet prisoners of war, who were put to death in Auschwitz by the tens of thousands, along with political opponents of every kind and creed.

At the first Nuremberg trials, begun in the fall and winter of 1945, the International Military Tribunal received the information, including affidavits from SS statisticians, that four million Jews had been killed in the extermination camps, and two million annihilated elsewhere, mostly by the *Einsatzgruppen*, the mobile killing units that moved in as soon as the Germans occupied a territory. The *Einsatzgruppen* were, indeed, the primary means used to annihilate the Jews in the Nazi-occupied Soviet territories.

In their reports on the extermination centers that they had uncovered, and in all their references to the mass killings, the Russians invariably described the victims as "citizens of Russia" or "citizens of Poland" or "of France," taking care that these "citizens," as the Russians called the objects of the Final Solution, were never identified as Jews. For pragmatic reasons of their own, the British—who had the problem of Palestine to contend with, which the existence of so many homeless Jews would surely complicate —referred in their dispatches from Belsen to "Polish, Russian, and French nationals" or "nationals of every country." The English abandoned the practice soon enough, though not until the British policy was explained, with some primness, as being an effort to avoid Germany's sin of singling out one group, and not until the Jews in their zone had made clear their unwillingness to receive this answer patiently.

The overwhelming compulsion of those who were left was to discover what had become of parents, husbands, wives, brothers, and sisters.

Many survivors, knowing that there was nothing for them to go back to, and therefore unwilling to be repatriated to the countries from which they had been deported, settled in the nearest displaced persons centers. Others of the liberated Jews, having every reason to know that they would find no relatives there, nevertheless undertook to go home once more: they made their way back to Poland, Czechoslovakia, Hungary, and Rumania, from every corner of Europe and from the interior of Russia, an army of searchers propelled to the cities and towns from which they had been deported by the hope of finding someone left. For weeks they straggled by foot and hitchhiked to return to the places whose streets and houses they had known all their lives. One of them, a former Maidanek inmate who had hidden in the forests and then found shelter with a Polish farmer in a remote village, emerged from months of solitary hiding in the belief that she was the only Jew left alive in Europe.

For so complete and efficient was the machine of obliteration that the Germans had deployed, particularly in the occupied Eastern countries, that the Jews returning to their former homes from the camps and from hiding places were met with expressions of amazement from the Eastern Europeans who saw them: "What, still alive?" and "What?

Still so many Jews left?" These singular expressions of greeting soon became familiar ones to the survivors. Some Polish neighbors thought they saw ghosts, they confided to the Jews who came back; and most of the time the ghosts came back to their apartments to discover that they were now occupied by the neighbors and that all their possessions and property were in their hands for good.

Those who had been driven homeward once more found no reason to stay: they had returned to a graveyard, one that now threatened to hurtle them into the same oblivion as had claimed their relatives. The seeds of the Final Solution had taken root in hospitable soil in Eastern Europe where, upon the liberation, the atmosphere was thick enough with the hatred of the returned Jews that in the first year after the war almost a thousand more of them were killed. In July of 1946, a pogrom in Kielce, Poland, which claimed the lives of forty-six Jews, caused a representative of the recently formed Polish Communist government to observe that there was more anti-Semitism in 1946, after the Germans had been driven from the country, than in all the long history of Poland; the life of a Jew was not safe in any small town now, he declared after the pogrom, which was but one of a series of violent outbursts against the Jews that burned across the whole of Eastern Europe. And in turn the Jews who went back to their small towns in Poland, Hungary, Slovakia, and the Ukraine confirmed for themselves what the experience of the past several years had told them all along: that their homes and the homes of their ancestors, of the generations that had for better or worse been born and bred in the small towns and cities, were obliterated, with no trace left of the teeming and abundant Jewish life that had flourished there.

The Jews were gone: their survivors saw it in the neighborhoods now empty, in the sight of the townspeople digging under the Jews' houses for buried treasures, in the houses themselves where once they had lived, three generations together, of which nothing remained. And, having seen, they turned and left again, before the political borders could freeze and they found themselves locked for good in the charged and hostile atmosphere of Eastern Europe—the graveyard of their families—and under Communist rule. Their plan, like that of most survivors, was to get to Eretz Yisroel—then called Palestine—or to America. By one means or another, they made their way to Czechoslovakia, the nearest crossing point to the American zone of Germany, and from there to the displaced persons camps, now the site of the sole large community of Jews left in Europe.

ELENA

My husband and I didn't have what you would call a wild romance before we married. He had been in love with a girl who did not survive, and I with a man who did not come to the United States. I wanted time before we married, I wanted to think for a while, so I went to stay with my relatives in the Midwest while Stefan was getting himself settled in New York. My cousins were American-born Jews: very Middle-Western, kind, generous people, who also shrank from me a little. You understand, the concentration camp experience is nothing that endears you to people. People who came to my cousins' house used to ask me such things as whether I had been able to survive because, perchance, I had slept with an SS man. And if I had, did they think I would tell them? There were difficulties all around in that visit, what with my cousin taking sick and me feeling very uncomfortable, so before the summer was over, I packed up and went back to New York, where Stefan and I were married right away. The truth is he was much lonelier than I was, and so he wanted the marriage more.

My husband came from the same city as I did, Lodz. They were people of means, his family, assimilationists. Stefan grew up thinking he was a Pole, that Poland was his country, because they had sent him to private schools from the time he was small. He was a patriot like all the rest of them in his classes—his heart pounded just like theirs when they sang their patriotic songs, and he never learned a word of Yiddish until he was in a concentration camp. My family were not people of such great means, not like Stefan's family, but we were comfortable. My father was an educator and a leading Zionist in Lodz. Stefan's father was a Zionist, too, a complete assimilationist and a Zionist; he had settled it all in his mind, somehow, these two things were compatible. After the Nazis invaded Poland, someone informed my father that the Jewish Agency in Palestine had sent some certificates for Poland's leading Zionists, to get them out of the country, and that the Germans were allowing it; and that set off long discussions at home. Getting out of Poland meant going from Lodz to Warsaw, and that meant going by train and taking off the yellow armband, because Jews were not permitted to travel anymore. My mother and father debated and argued, but my mother was better at it than my father. She didn't want to leave her things, her furniture. Had she listened to my father, we would have been out of Poland long before the Germans invaded. I knew people who had much more to lose than she did, people who fled. But my mother was devoted to her possessions, to the kind of life she had. It was already October, 1939, and Mother and Father debated should they take off the yellow armband and go on the train, should they or shouldn't they go. They took two days to debate it, and they were no closer to an answer after two days, when it was too late, than they were when they began. There were five certificates of exit sent to Lodz. Of the five, two were for elderly men in their seventies. They could not flee, they said; whatever happened to all the Jews would happen to them. One was a younger man, in his forties, the same age as my father. He left; he was the only one who did. And when we were in the ghetto in 1940, and everywhere around us there were people dying of typhus and dysentery, we got a postcard from Trieste. It was from him, the one who left; he and his family were on their way to Palestine. When my mother read the postcard, she cried. "It's my fault," she told us. But by then it was too late to think about whose fault it was.

Two days later, my father received a summons from the Gestapo. It happened that the Gestapo offices were located in the *Gymnasium* where my father taught. Over the years, the *Gymnasium* had collected enough money to build a great modern building for its students, not just classrooms but a gym and tennis courts, and a field for ball games. In September of 1939 our family was supposed to move into this complex. The perfect month and year: the Germans arrived in September, 1939. My father had transferred his office and safe to the new *Gymnasium* office already. In answer to the summons, he arrived at Gestapo headquarters, which was his own office, and was arrested by a Gestapo officer who sat behind my father's desk, with my father's papers in his hands. On the desk in front of him were the things from my father's safe. They arrested him because he was an intellectual.

We tried to keep our apartment, because the prison into which my father had been put was only two blocks away from it. Jews were only allowed to walk in the streets till five in the afternoon, and since food from Jewish women who had family in the prison was not accepted until four-thirty, you had to be very lucky to get to the gate and off the street in time. My mother was determined to stay near that prison. Because we had a very nice apartment, she was afraid the Germans would throw us out of it, so she made it as ugly as she could, and I helped her. We spread ashes on the floor, smeared the walls, and dirtied the whole place. By the time we had taken off the drapes and soiled the windows, it looked shabby, but it was still hard to hide the fact that it was a nice apartment. It was bleak, but it wouldn't pass for a hovel; there were too many windows, dirty or not, too much space. We were not thrown out until my father had been let out of prison, three months later, and then we had to go into the ghetto.

Before that, we saw very few SS. Mostly we were being pushed around and abused by the Werhmacht, though occasionally you might find a decent soldier, too. Food was the greatest problem for us. The Germans couldn't tell I was Jewish, but the Poles always could. I don't know why, since my Polish was much better than that of the average Pole; my eyes were green, I had straight hair—I didn't look Jewish at all. One day my friend Sonia and I stood in line to get bread. There was a separate line for Jews and for Poles, and since there was a much better chance to get food on the Polish line, Sonia smuggled herself onto it. She had just got up to the window, and had her hand on the bread, when a Polish woman yelled, "Jew! Dirty Jew! What are you doing in our line?" The German soldier pulled Sonia by the shoulders and threw her into our line. We looked at each other, and then Sonia tried to smile at me, but she couldn't.

All along I went to school in the ghetto. Occasionally we would read for a whole day, or sometimes only for a few hours, depending on how cold it was. It got colder each day. It was bitter winter weather. We met for classes each day and went wherever we found some room that had not been requisitioned. Then, the next day, teachers would find that room had been taken, and overnight they would set up a class somewhere else. I can't say that we learned very much.

All this time, our family was getting privileged treatment. Certain people in the ghetto, and we were among them, got a special ration, people in key positions. It was unjust and my father knew it; he knew our extra share came from the communal rations. Rumkowski, the director of the ghetto, was a friend of my father, a *chaver*. My father got a double ration for himself, my mother, and for me, and even with it both my parents were emaciated. My father's prewar suit hung on him. He was the kind of man who was ashamed of getting the extra food. I saw the expression on his face when he talked about it. He knew that other people were getting much less. But the hunger was so terrible, who was so good and brave as to give up an extra ration? And how could you be so good and brave for your wife and children, too?

My father became very thin and yellow, anyway. When you don't eat, the skin becomes like parchment. My mother was just as hungry, but somehow she looked better than he did; she needed less. And I—I was blooming, I was sixteen and I was blooming. My mother used to give me part of her bread. With the help we got from the Älteste der Juden, we survived the ghetto, but in August, 1944, they told us they were going to relocate us. The German in charge, Hans Biebow,* came in and talked to us all, and

---

* Hanged after 1945, for war crimes.

said they wanted us to go to our relocation peacefully. Biebow opened up his coat and pointed inside. "See, I have no gun on me." That was what he told us to prove that we had nothing to fear from the move, but we didn't believe him. We ran; we all started to hide, but it was impossible: you can't hide without food. The moment you come to claim a ration there is no more hiding for you; to have a hiding place you have to prepare it, be sure you won't be denounced by the neighbors or the workmen whom you pay to help you prepare it. You had to have courage to make a hiding place and my parents just did not have the courage to hide or to run—to do anything. I was much younger when I judged my mother for being devoted to her possessions. When I became middle-thirtyish, I saw what middle age does to you. You slow down, you're just not in the same fighting mood as you were when you were younger. You hate to give up the familiar. I begin to understand her a little. But she was wrong. I resented her, yes, I was mad at her. Because those that were separated from their mothers at Auschwitz were better off. An older person was a burden; my mother was only forty-eight, but that, for the camps, was old. The truth is a terrible thing to say, isn't it?

We were caught in the middle of August. We were hiding in my father's office, and the child of a neighbor, who was hiding with us, cried. They heard us, we were caught. It doesn't really matter. If we hadn't been caught then, it would only have given us another two or three weeks in the ghetto. My father tried to guess where we were going; possibly he even knew, but he only told me to stay with my mother because probably they would separate the sexes. That was all he told me. When we got to Auschwitz, I stuck to my mother; I held on. The men were lined up apart from us. I thought that the Germans would separate you if they thought you were related, if you were mother and daughter, so I let go of my mother and I walked with the mother of my friend Gina, and Gina walked with my mother. I thought, if I walked with my own mother, they'll see the family resemblance. Gina's mother was a tiny gray-haired lady, but my mother was young-looking and tall, a handsome woman. When we came up to the SS, Gina and my mother were in front of us. They were both waved to the left, where I saw mostly younger-looking people, and I wanted to go left, too; I didn't know what right meant, I had no idea. I wanted to go with my mother and Gina. When I came forward to the barrier, a blond, good-looking SS officer asked me, pointing to Gina's mother, *"Ist das deine Mutter?"* And I said, *"Nein."* I didn't have any reason to say she was my mother. *"Wie alt bist du?"* the German asked me. *"Achtzehn,"* I said. He looked me up and down. *"Das ist alt genug,"* he said, waving me to the left. Gina's mother went to the right. If I hadn't been stopped and asked about the woman I was walking with, I would have been sent to the gas chamber with her. We stayed in Auschwitz for five days, and then we were sent to a branch of Grossrosen, where they had an airplane factory. Five hundred of us from Lodz were put to work there, but there were also many foreign workers there, slave laborers and prisoners of war. By this time the Germans had taken over Italy, so Germany and Italy were no longer allies. In the factory now there were Italian prisoners of war working along with us. Such kind, courageous men, those Italians! They helped us, and brought food to us at work. And though things were very bad for us, though we were hungry and we wore rags, our spirits were not so low in Grossrosen because of those Italian prisoners of war. We saw them every day at the factory, and though, since we were Jews, they were strictly forbidden to help us and speak to us, they did help us, they did speak to us. They helped us with food; they kept us alive with hope. They would get to us quietly when the SS women guards were not looking, or sometimes they diverted the attention of the guards by flirting with them. Some of those Italian men were very handsome, too. While one of them would flirt and take up the attention of the SS woman, another would smuggle some food to us, or just whisper, *"La guerra finita."* Or they would just say to us, in broken German, "Don't give up hope." If you knew what the behavior of those people meant to us, what those words meant to us! In the camp itself, the SS woman in charge took a special dislike to my mother. Possibly it was because my mother was tall and nice-looking and you could see that she was a lady. One day, after her gallstones had left her in peace for seventeen years, my mother had a bad attack. The pain sent her to the infirmary—not that there was any medication there for us, but there was a Hungarian Jewish doctor, and at least, lying there, she didn't have to go to the factory. But I was young, and because I was young, I was shrewder and sharper; I knew it was no good to be in the infirmary. She stayed half a day, and I told her, "Mama, tomorrow get up, line up with us and go to work." But my mother still just could not understand where she was or what it was all about, and so she stayed there. The next afternoon, the SS Kommandoführerin who hated my mother came into the infirmary. She ran to the bed where my mother was lying and shouted at her, "I'm going to send you out on the next transport to Auschwitz! I don't need any rich lazy Jews here." And, in fact, the next day we were told we were being shipped out of Grossrosen. The Kommandoführerin said we were only going to another camp to work, but the other SS told us we were really going back to Auschwitz. They said that we were going directly to the gas chambers, that we were not even going to stop at the main camp first for a selection. Then the Kommandoführerin put me and my mother with a group of about sixty women who had somehow miraculously managed to escape the death selection before this. One was lame, one had a bad eye, the rest were emaciated; two or three of the women were past forty. I was the only one in the group who was young and in good health. I said nothing to my mother; I stood with her, and I went with her, but I resented it: I couldn't let her go alone, and yet I didn't want to die. What I wanted was for my mother to tell me, "You stay, and I'll go; you don't have to come with me."

But she didn't. I wanted her to tell me that. I don't even know, if she'd said what I wanted, whether I would have stayed behind. Perhaps, if my mother had known for sure we were going to die, she would have said something to me; she would have sent me away from her. In the end, it turned out that we did only go to another camp, as the Kommandoführerin said. None of us ever knew anything for sure, because they mixed you up deliberately. We came to Belsen at night after a day or two on the train, and there I knew we could not survive. There was no work. All we did all day was sit there and kill lice, and beg or steal water for washing and drinking. The lice were brought in by the Hungarians, who were completely broken people, physically and spiritually. They had been rounded up only in the last year of the war; they didn't have the hardening of the ghetto experience. I tried to avoid them; I didn't hate them; they were pathetic, just living stinking skeletons who kept crying to God in Hungarian. Pretty soon we all had lice, and from the lice came the fever. Spotted typhoid killed my mother after she lay unconscious for days. I had the fever but was conscious most of the time; I remember everything. In the end, I gave up on my mother; I couldn't even lift her head. Before she died, while she was lying there, she made me swear to her that I would go to my uncle in America when the war was over. She was many things, my mother, there were many sides to her, but at the end her last breath was spent on me. She was thinking of me; I couldn't mistake that.

STEFAN

I don't like to speak of the past. I had enough. Furthermore I wouldn't even go to a synagogue to say *Kaddish* for my father. It would be disrespectful to his memory. You see that synagogue there? People say, "Why don't you even go in and say *Kaddish* for your father?" Not a day passes, not a day, that I don't think of my father; should I go in there with those people and their furs and that atmosphere and pray for the memory of my father? First of all, I'm not a religious Jew, and if we had not had to have a bar mitzvah for my son, I wouldn't even belong to a synagogue. I was not bar-mitzvahed in Poland; we had an absolutely assimilated family. My father was a Zionist, and a leading one, too.

Oh, there are many things I cannot understand now. Why Father, who was such a passionate Zionist, wanted us to assimilate; not only that, many things. We never talked about it. Maybe he thought that assimilation is the way we would all survive in Europe. Poland was my country, I thought of it as my country; Polish was my language; Poland. I spit on Poland. Yes, probably that was what my father thought: assimilation meant survival. I know I was dead many times; I crawled; but I still wanted to live. If I could talk to each one of those six million Jews that died, and could ask them, Do you want to die as a Jew or live as a Christian, ninety-five percent of them would choose to live, wouldn't they?

An American captain saved my life, a doctor from Brooklyn. The last few weeks of the war, I was put in a barracks with dying people. It was a camp near Mauthausen. They had given us poisoned food. It was one of the last-minute efforts to eliminate witnesses—Himmler's orders. I got sick with everyone else, and by the time the Americans came, I was one of those put on a stretcher and made ready to be removed to a mass grave. Then this Army doctor from Brooklyn noticed that I moved my leg, and I was taken off the stretcher and brought to a field hospital. He watched over me for four weeks, but when I woke up, delirious, and saw this uniform, I ranted and yelled at him like an insane man: "My father would still be alive now if the Americans hadn't waited for the Russians to advance on Berlin!"

My father. In the camps, fathers fought sons for food, and brother fought brother sometimes; I saw those things. But between me and my father there was nothing like that. There had always been a great warmth between us. When I was growing up, I know I would rather have talked to him than anybody, and he felt the same about me. One day in the camp, he took me aside and told me that he had witnessed my brother's death, and that I now must stay alive. He meant it. Then he gave me his bread and I took it. I took it because he showed me he would throw it away and not eat it himself if I didn't take it from him. I didn't cry when he died, though. I don't know why, but no tears ever came to me.

In 1946, I came to New York. I was twenty-four then.

Those first two years here, I was so lonely. Sometimes it comes back to me now how it felt. I lived with my uncle, and almost every night after supper I would rush out of that house and into the street, because I couldn't stand hearing my cousins call "Ma" and "Pa" to my aunt and uncle. I had still never cried before that time, and the reason I cried then was my uncle found a letter written to him by my father in 1939, which he showed to me. It had been written during the time I was away in school. My father wrote about this and that in the letter, and then he wrote about me: "Stefan went to France and I don't have to tell you how lonely I am for him." He wrote how much he missed me, and when I heard that in my uncle's house in 1946, yes, I cried for the first time.

3 | Arriving

I

The summer of 1947 brought Abe Flekier to America, a
wiry tense-looking youth of nineteen on whom roaming
and brawling in the postwar displaced persons camps had
left indelible marks of toughness. Although the set of his
full curved lips was suggestive of softness, it could be seen
at once that the suggestion was a misleading one, since
the most obvious thing about him was a physical power
that seemed to spring from his skin with the potential to
inflict grievous damage on an opponent. Indirectly, it was
his quickness with his fists that had caused him to go to
Kansas when he arrived in America, for in Kansas there
was an older friend who had watched over him in the
displaced persons camp, had restrained him in his wilder
moments, and had acted on him generally as a quieting
influence. They had traveled to America together on the
same ship, but afterward, while the other went to his
relatives in Kansas, Abe wandered agitatedly around
Manhattan.

It had occurred to him often that sometime he might see
the young American soldier he had met after being liberated. He remembered how they had looked at each other
after he had staggered from the boxcar toward the first
American he saw, recalled every detail of the soldier's
face, boyish and tearful-looking under the dirty helmet as
he picked up the candy on the dashboard of the jeep and
gave it to Flekier: how then he had searched his knapsack

and every pocket of his uniform, putting everything he found there in the way of food into Flekier's hands. From time to time, the soldier's face came before Flekier, making him wish urgently that he had taken his name and address; but how would he have known how to ask for it? These thoughts distracted and briefly comforted him as he went aimlessly about the streets of the city, too nervous to find interest in any of it. The crowds and the buildings of Manhattan depressed him, and the people packed together at every street corner made his fists clench, as did the sight, which he saw on the run-down upper West Side street of his hotel, of two and three heads poked out of a single window. He hated New York immediately; walking about its streets, he felt suffocated by the bodies around him, an old physical feeling but one unendurable to him now that the need to suffer it was past.

Finally, fearing that he would get himself into trouble if he stayed in New York, he arranged to go and join his friend in Kansas City. In Europe he had been put into prison by the American military authorities several times, because it had been nothing to him to strike a German citizen passing on the streets if the German looked at him a moment too long, or if one had perhaps walked by too haughtily, not looking at all. At these times, he had brushed aside his friend's admonitions to be careful. All the same, the warnings were not unwelcome, just as restraint is not unwelcome to a child who senses that his wildness is bringing him closer every moment to danger.

Alone except for an older brother still in Europe, Flekier had been taken from his parents when he was thirteen to work in the child labor gangs the Nazis had gathered from Poland. His schooling had ended two years earlier, at the age of eleven, when the German armies entered Warsaw, closing all Jewish institutions of learning. Now, at the age of nineteen, he could read and write, but beyond that he was without training or education of any sort but for the admittedly broad schooling provided by the concentration and labor camps.

The sense of his ignorance added to the already great turmoil inside him, a general unrest reflected in his quick-

ness with fists and a darkening, cocky look about the eyes.
Usually those eyes were full of the one kind of knowledge
he had mastered, which concerned survival, but at other
times they were full only of the knowledge of his ignorance. Sometimes his lips would draw back into an in-
voluntary and not very charming grin, since it came from
shame and not from humor; the grin said, I told you I
don't know anything, and that I am ignorant, but you
went right on believing otherwise.

But moments like these did not last very long, and soon
his head would be thrown back, the competitive darting
look would come back into his eyes, and his rolling,
nervous prizefighter's walk would once again assert his
ability to handle himself. It was his dominant look, and it
was not unreasonable that he should have it, for, ignorant
as he was, he had been smart enough to keep alive and he
knew it.

In Kansas City his friend took him in hand and introduced him to people. Quite soon, Flekier was being invited
to Friday night dinner at the homes of Jewish Kansas City
people, and going out on dates with their daughters, who
seemed not to be discouraged by the fact that he knew
hardly a word of English. In his wiry way he was good-
looking; at least, both Jewish and Gentile girls appeared
to be drawn to him, though Flekier did not fail to notice
that the girls seemed also very drawn to his friend and to
another boy just arrived from Europe. The friend and
Flekier roomed in a kind of youth hostel and were known
generally to the local people of their acquaintance as "the
refugees," a description that was logical at the time, though
it became less so as the years went by. Nonetheless, to the
people of Kansas City and to the residents of similar communities where the survivors came after the war, the
refugees of the late forties would continue to be called
"the refugees" for more than a score of years.

Flekier began to go to night school, primarily to learn
enough English to enable him to earn a living. He managed to finish the eighth grade. His English was advanced
enough by this time to enable him to carry on a conver-

sation, but he still had great problems with it, because he had neither an ear for languages nor any need to speak consistently in the new tongue. Like many immigrants past and present, he had friends with whom he could speak Yiddish or Polish whenever he liked, a practice that did not speed his facility with English.

When the Korean War broke out, he found that he was a newly drafted private in the U.S. Army—one, moreover, without the advantage of the language facility enjoyed by native-born draftees. This disadvantage, he soon discovered, was not as great as he had supposed. He was placed in a company of draftees from Kentucky, southern Ohio, and Arkansas, and was, shortly after his basic-training period ended, made an instructor in Troop Information and Education, a development that filled him with amazement.

Respectful but suspicious and uncertain as he was whenever he was singled out for any reason, he rolled forth with his sidewise, prizefighter's walk to see the Captain and to inquire his reasons for the choice of a greenhorn, as he called himself, for an instructor.

"I talk broken English," Flekier had told the Captain.

"You speak broken English?" the Captain asked.

"I talk broken English," Flekier repeated doggedly.

"Well, you just line up everyone in the company," the Captain told him. "You line them up and see what I have to pick from." When he thought of this scene later, Flekier always saw the Captain staring aggrievedly at a space in the room where an imaginary line of men had been formed.

Of the hundred and fifty men who trained with Flekier, it turned out that forty percent of them had not passed the third grade, a fact that astonished him, and that permitted him to undertake the role of Troop Information and Education instructor with some confidence, since he himself had passed the eighth grade. His job consisted mainly of reading aloud and discussing current events, of gathering together all the soldiers who had not completed the eighth grade in civilian life, and of getting them to army classes every morning—in all, not very complicated duties, but Flekier took a serious view of them as he did all matters related to work.

Undoubtedly, the army saw that there were educational benefits to be derived from having men like Flekier around, for his commanding officers seldom missed an opportunity to introduce him to the troops as a man who knew something about war and suffering.

"You think you had it rough," the officers would tell their men somberly; "talk to this man." And all the men, who had seen nothing of war, listened seriously to the words of their commanding officers. The result was that Flekier became a figure of authority to them, particularly when fear of going into combat overwhelmed them, as it did in 1952, in the frozen hills of Korea.

Flekier had never been in combat himself and was as frightened as they were. Often, nevertheless, he found himself surrounded by soldiers as soon as the shelling began, all of them clearly under the impression that he would know what to do, that he who had been so close to dying had somehow learned how to escape death. Added to this absurdity was the conviction of the soldiers who clustered around him that, despite his protests to the contrary, Flekier did not feel any of the fear they felt.

He was at first uncomfortable in the role of authority, but as often happens to those who have had status thrust upon them, he began to feel that it was, after all, not so unreasonable. By the time he had finished training and had landed in Korea, the shamed grin was appearing less and less on his face as he absorbed the fact that there were a great many men around him who had even less than he did of learning, and apparently of many other things as well. When the shells flew overhead, and his fellow soldiers asked advice on how to stay safe, he would advise them, in still broken but confident English, that the best thing was to dig a hole and stay there; this information they received gratefully from the wise and experienced veteran whom Providence had put in their midst.

Flekier's relations with his fellow soldiers were not always so amicable, however, outside of foxholes. In the course of his army career he was to use his fists frequently. He responded, invariably and with speed, to insults aimed at Jews, none of which needed to be directed at him in order to send him forward ready for a fight; it never occurred to him that he might ignore it. In the army; there had been a few of them during basic training, and a number of others during the two-week troopship journey to Korea. It was Flekier's habit, as soon as he heard such a remark—though seldom directed to him—to prepare immediately for a fight; it never occurred to him that he might ignore it. Instead, he would stiffen and stand still, arranging himself before going over to the speaker and instructing him to repeat what he had just said.

These fights never caused him trouble the way quickness with his fists had in Germany, for at the end of his army service he had an unblemished record and a number of citations to his credit. By the time he had left the army and was on his way back to Kansas, Flekier was ready to find some permanent occupation. He had had, for years, a conviction that learning a trade would assure his future, and it did not seem to matter to him what trade it was. Before he was drafted, he had begun to learn cabinet-making, for no particular reason except that he had once been told by a cabinetmaker in Kansas City that it was as likely a trade as any he would find.

Craft or no craft, uncertainty about himself and his place in the world began to dog Flekier as soon as he was mustered out of the army. Though he knew friends awaited him there, as did his older brother, who had by then arrived from Europe and settled in Kansas City, he was seized by a fit of loneliness as he prepared himself to go back. In the army, at least, he had been busy every minute, too much so to think. A weight pressed heavily on his throat, a feeling by now familiar to him. These moments came to him invariably when he was alone and without other business to occupy his mind: times when, as now, he was traveling and the years in Europe flashed up at him while he stared, without seeing, at the flat countryside speeding past.

The first calm memories led undeflectably to the last,

which were not calm, for the order of those memories was that of a man who is impelled to reach the center of a whirlpool and who, knowing it, creeps up on it by stages. He thought of the mad noise during the selections; of the people he had known in the camps; of the liberation. Other memories crowded in on him in succession until he reached the final one, which was the memory of his mother; then, always, he was anxious to be up and about at some business, or talking to people, for her image in his mind's eye was clear and unbearable to him. It was also true at such times that, having reached the dark center of his thoughts, he could then turn from them.

II

Several months before the time that Abe Flekier came to Kansas City, there arrived in Manhattan a man almost fourteen years his senior and one as full of assurance and the experience of getting on in the world as Flekier was lacking in it. There were reasons for that assurance that were not alone the product of a greater maturity, for the man, Leon Jolson, was the son of a rich father, as Flekier was not. Because the family business was sewing machines, and because it was an extensive and prosperous one, Leon's father had seen to it that his son acquired an extensive technical education. By the time the Germans had marched into Warsaw in 1939, the younger Jolson was already well established and the head of the family business.

Nothing was left, after the war, of either his family or its holdings. Immediately after the liberation, he began to do some small business and trading, as did many survivors in the displaced persons camps in Germany. Peddling and buying was carried on at a great and successful rate in the areas in and around the displaced persons camps, partly because of the natural propensity of vacuums to get themselves filled—the lack of goods was such a vacuum in Germany—and in greater part because the survivors were shattered men with internal needs that required filling by every means available, including constant enterprise.

All of them had lost their homes and their families and the process of attempting to regain these forever irreplaceable things took many forms: they took new mates in the displaced persons camps; they bore new children; some set forth to extract a livelihood from the world in an attempt to reclaim losses greater than any livelihood had ever before been asked to replace.

Jolson sold needles in the displaced persons camp and surrounding areas, making a little bit of money, most of which was spent in the fashion that befitted a man just liberated. With his wife, who had also survived, he arrived in New York in 1947, virtually penniless. After settling her and himself in the Hotel Marseilles in New York, an establishment used by social agencies to house new arrivals temporarily, he began to look for a place to live, and to think about a way of earning a living. In all his efforts now, he was driven by the haste that was characteristic of many of the survivors who had seen years of their lives used up, and by a certain post-liberation buoyancy. He was, in addition, a methodical man, a believer in systems of success. When he was in hiding, he had created, as he called it later, a "theory of movement," which consisted of putting a stethoscope against the wall and listening to the sounds of the Polish residents of the apartment house where, unknown to them, he had secreted himself. His theory of movement consisted of not moving when he knew that they might be in a position to hear him, and of accomplishing necessities, such as flushing the toilet and the like, only when those residents were not likely to notice the sounds. A man who looked upon such relatively clearcut precautions as a "theory of movement" was, it could be fairly said, a man who put a certain value on the fruits of his mind, and this attitude was in fact evident in all enterprises he undertook.

Apartments of even the poorest sort were scarce in New York in the late forties, when veterans were returning home. Jolson spent his first week in America determining where the low-rent Jewish neighborhoods were in New York, and he went out each morning to haunt the local candy stores and streets of those neighborhoods for news of apartment vacancies. His busy, theorizing mind had yielded him a premise that he proceeded confidently to follow; namely, that death made apartment vacancies. That it was an idea which had already occurred to others, he was not aware; he considered it his own, one of the products of a theoretical mind. Every morning, he bought the Yiddish newspapers and scanned the obituaries for names and residences of the newly deceased. Armed with this information, he made his way to the Lower East Side or the Bronx, a tall brisk man with a crop of straight silvery hair which gave him, at the age of thirty-four, the appearance of one of those citizens produced in the South for the sole purpose of being sent to the Senate, an impression that was dispelled soon enough by the accents of Yiddish and Polish which dominated the few English words he knew.

His belief in the efficacy of death as a means of providing vacant apartments was quite soon justified, for after a week and a half of diligent inquiry he located a woman whose husband had just died, and who planned to go immediately to live with her children. He found himself thus in possession of a fourth-floor walk-up on Fox Street in the Bronx, a street that was to become notorious, a decade and a half later, as the worst in New York, a ruined, rat-infested expanse of burned-out buildings, an area so desolated it has been compared to a war-ravaged city. Fox Street in the late forties was far from what it is now, but it was even then a decidedly poor neighborhood, Jewish, with a small but growing number of blacks. Nevertheless, it was a source of joy to Jolson and his wife, exhilarated, after years in hideouts and crowded displaced persons barracks, by the possession of an apartment they could call their own. The mean, treeless street and the shabby exteriors of the walk-ups, he barely noticed, for beyond these was the delight of six rooms, full of the ugly but serviceable furniture whose purchase was part of the price one paid a former tenant for getting an apartment during the shortage.

Bounding forth from Fox Street in the morning with his accustomed vigor, Jolson first went to the neighbor-

hood that was the center of the sewing-machine trade, the
West Twenties in Manhattan. Here his problem with English was of small concern, for there was no lack of Yiddish
speakers among the businessmen of that area. Money was
the urgent problem; like other new arrivals, he was due
to receive from the Jewish social agency that had helped
to bring them over a monthly allowance of between forty
and fifty dollars until he could find work, but that, even
in 1947, was not a great sum.

On the first day's wandering through the center, he was
given a few dollars for carrying a sewing machine from
one location to another. He walked farther through the
noisy truck-lined streets, where he found traders and
buyers of old sewing machines, each of whom he approached to ask what he had to sell or needed to buy.
By the end of the second day, he had managed to earn a
commission of three hundred dollars acting as middleman
between buyer and seller. For a few days, he continued
his practice of wandering through the sewing-machine center, making contacts and earning commissions. It was a
time of great shortages, and needles were in particularly
low supply everywhere in the world. In recognition of
that fact, as well as the fact that there was no future in
making odd commissions, Jolson took a day off from the
sewing-machine center and visited all the foreign consulates
that had commercial departments in New York City.

Having acquired from the consulates of each country a
list of companies in the sewing-machine business, Jolson
went, list in hand, to the public stenographer he had found
at a Manhattan hotel. Making himself understood somehow, he dictated to the stenographer letters to most of
the sewing-machine firms in Europe, telling them of his
whereabouts and announcing that he was at their service
if they should need someone in America to obtain machines or parts. It was the act of a practiced and confident
businessman, one trained in the knowledge of certain
resources that would be at his disposal, even though he
was a stranger in a strange land. If he had come to
America almost as penniless as Flekier had, he possessed
in abundance what that youth had not begun to possess,

and what older survivors of a different background did not have either: the reflexes of the man who had once known success.

He had, in addition to those reflexes, the survivor's instinct for the short cut, the aversion to the standardized route. He had, above all, a self-regard that was part of the proceeds of survival for some. Not unfittingly, since the Nazis were at once the most consistent and arbitrary of masters, among the captives of the Nazis there developed widely divergent principles of behavior in the effort to stay alive. Some determined that when the Germans called for volunteers, they should always step forward, no matter what job the Germans might want them to do or where they might be sent to do it, on the ground that any movement in their condition was better than none; others determined never to step forward when the Germans called for volunteers, on the ground that a known condition was better than an unknown one. When they were herded from one place to another in large groups, or being lined up, many understood that it was important to reach the center of the crowd, since those in the front ranks of prisoners and those in the rear most often took the brunt of the beatings, or the attacks of the dogs. Others had an impulse to keep to the rear no matter what, to be the last, if possible, of any group being led by the Germans or being directed by them to do anything or go anywhere, an instinct whose point was reflected by one survivor: "I always tried to go back, back, back. I knew nothing good could be waiting for me; why should I be in a hurry to go first?"

There were people who believed instinctively that their survival depended upon doing the opposite of what everyone else in their situation did, and the opposite of what the Germans told them to do. In the ghettos before and during the mass deportations, it meant going into hiding if it was possible, and the capacity to sustain oneself in great and private danger without the comfort of others. It required isolation and audacity; it meant running alone to a forest, or a cellar, while everyone else went, together with their families and neighbors, to that destination which the Germans had chosen for them. It meant, too—the rare times when it was possible—such things as the decision to leave family members behind and jump from a train that might be speeding its passengers to their death, or that might, then again, only be going to a labor camp, which the Germans invariably promised their passengers was their destination.

Nothing less than their lives was at stake in making these decisions, and no more can be concluded than the bleak truth that for some few they had worked and for most others they had not. Despite the considerable role that caprice, chaos, and random chance played in survival, survival had its reasons nonetheless, and not a few survivors found those reasons in themselves. There were those who wanted to give the reasons a name, to define them clearly, as though, in identifying the technique by which they survived, they might find the logic for the fact that they—and, in so many cases, they alone of their families—had extracted themselves alive from the tragedy: for to find the logic for the fact was, in its way, to find the justice for it.

Those who emerged with an increased regard for themselves because they had lived often felt they were alive only because they had risked paths that others had been afraid to take, and so they were confirmed in this pattern of behavior in their later lives; or they believed, at least, that they should be, which often amounted to the same thing. Those who had knowledge of themselves as having made the instant crucial decisions that might have been the difference between life and death held on to that knowledge, and not without pride. Men and women who, when cornered, had plotted and contrived their survival successfully, who had, they saw, reached for it in the thin instant of possibility that presented itself, could not help turning such knowledge of themselves over and over in their minds afterwards, as they could not and had no wish to avoid the roots which that knowledge took in them.

When the Germans arrested Jolson for the last time, it was after a year of living in hiding places in which a man's body barely fit. He had, before going into hiding in Aryan Warsaw, put together and closely analyzed a list of Poles and other non-Jews who might be trusted to bring food and to act as contacts. Reducing the list to those he thought could be trusted never to betray him, he was left with two; their characters he had evaluated and mulled over again and again before asking their help. By the time the end came, and the Germans had rounded him up with the others during the Polish uprising of 1944, he learned that his judgment in the two had not been misplaced, that they had not betrayed him, though both, one a Pole and the other a Russian woman, had come into grave danger while serving as his contact, and one had been questioned by the police.

When he was arrested, the Germans believed him to be a Pole, and sent him off on a train with the members of the Polish underground whom they had rounded up after the uprising. This disguise had proceeded uneventfully until one of the captured Poles informed a member of the SS that somewhere in the crowd of prisoners on the train a Jew was hiding. The SS officers began to move through the cars calling for the Jew to give himself up, and ordering prisoners to unbutton their trousers, so that it could be seen whether they were circumcised. When the SS reached his car, Jolson presented himself as the first to show that he was not a Jew, planting himself before the SS officers with his hands on the buttons of his trousers; and this behavior, he believed, caused the SS officer to push him impatiently aside so that they might go on to check the others in the car, all of whom clearly had more to hide than the first man to leap at them tearing at the buttons of his trousers in his frenzy to show that he was not a Jew.

It was one of a chain of such memories that he carried about with him after the war. Hurrying home to Fox Street at the end of a day, he could reckon his progress as high, considering where he had begun: by the end of his first few months in America, he had accumulated some money, for within a short time orders had come in response to the letters of inquiry he had sent overseas. In addition, the apparently impossible orders for needles that had come to him from clients overseas had been filled. He had netted thousands of dollars in commissions the first month and almost as much in the second, but impatience drove him on: he had no thought of living by odd jobs and transactions.

By the end of the first year, he had begun to think of leaving the Fox Street apartment in order to live closer to the small storefront office he had rented in the West Twenties. During all that year, he had thought of little but work, for he was utterly in the grip of an effort to establish himself again. Older hands in the sewing-machine center showed that they were amused by his attempt to strike out into the trade for himself after just a few weeks in this country, for they saw him as he did not see himself, as a refugee with neither the language nor the experience of the new land. They were immigrants themselves; they had known the struggle of long, hard years before they reached the point where they could own their businesses.

He saw himself, on the other hand, as the man he had been and could yet be again, a man empowered by the experience of survival to be even more than he had been; for it was in the nature of the holocaust that it bred extremity, and those who survived it had absorbed that extremity in their bones. The experience had confirmed, and thus enlarged, certain traits of character, so that in some traits the survivors were what they had been before, only now they were more so. He had been a resilient man of action before the war; now he was a bold one.

Day by day, as the first hectic year came to an end, he strode the not very great length of his office, analyzing the way in which his customers bought, or thinking about the errors of his competitors. He noted that he made sales where they did not, and believed that it was because he operated on the principle that customers who knew nothing about the insides of sewing machines would respond decisively to the outsides of them. They disliked clutter, and for that reason he first polished and japanned the ugly secondhand machines before he tried to sell them. He had sold many of them, and had made, in addition, large commissions on the procurement of scarce equipment for European clients; by this time, he had earned a sum that would have been considered highly respectable for a man who had been in business in America many years longer. He had done well enough financially, then; but more and more he grew restive in circumstances that offered no opportunities for great leaps, or for the theories and hunches that heated his brain.

These two, Flekier and Jolson, were in almost every way—age, status, and education—at opposite poles of the society that the holocaust had carried to America. They were a wave of immigrants unlike any that had come before, for there was included in that wave a large number of the educated and the professional classes, those who would not have emigrated but for the catastrophe Nazism had wrought in Europe. There were artisans, lawyers, doctors, tailors; the highly educated and the barely literate; representatives of the upper and of the lower economic classes, and those that came from the middle.

III

In 1946, the SS *Marine Flasher* carried among its passengers to America a stern-looking young man named Emil Wolf,* who, in his mid-twenties, appeared to be ten years older. This impression was due to the heavy horn-rimmed glasses he wore, and also to his eyes, which peered out gravely and judgmentally at all that they beheld. At the time of his arrival, he already knew English quite well; he had been born into comfortable circumstances, of a sort that had provided him, before the war, with an English tutor, in addition to the Greek, Latin, and French lessons that were the standard educational fare for the child of a cultured German family. His parents, Berlin Jews, had had two sons close together in age, and on both of them they had lavished a loving and intense ambition that they should rise in the world. It was intended by their father, a successful merchant, that his sons should study law, but this ambition, like all plans and thoughts about the future, became lost in the events that overtook them in Germany.

Of the family, only the older son had survived, a lanky white-skinned figure who carried a battered suitcase under one arm when he arrived at the Port of New York. It must at moments have been obvious that he was young, despite the aged judgment written on his face, at least it was to the Port of New York customs guard who had singled him out for attention. When the guard pointed at the old suitcase and asked him what he had inside of it, he told the man that there were some old clothes in it.

"Take that bag and that junk, son," the guard told him, smiling, "and throw it into the river there. You won't need it; America's gonna be good to you, you'll see." Sensibly tightening his hold on the suitcase, which contained his other suit and several shirts, he stared at the guard. Then, overcome by the unexpected kindness of this greeting, he did not know what to say in return; in the end, he simply thanked the guard and proceeded on the hot July day to find his way uptown.

The social worker in the agency office called the number of an uncle who lived in New York. The uncle was elderly, a first cousin to Emil Wolf's father, and a prosperous man who had escaped Germany and come to America in 1938. After identifying herself, the social worker told the uncle happily that a member of his family had come out of Germany alive.

"Alle tot," the uncle barked at her.

"No, they are not all dead," the social worker told him.

"I tell you they are dead. *Alle tot,*" the man said fiercely.

"What would you say," the social worker persisted, "if I told you that Emil Wolf is alive and standing here in my office?" After grunting again that everyone was dead, the uncle said he would come and see for himself who was standing in her office. The object of this conversation was not destined to stop long in the home of his uncle, who recognized him and took him home with him, if not, as was amply clear, with great happiness. His aunt cried over him, and the fate of the family, but clearly the couple would have been happier without this emissary from the world of the dead, come to upset their patched-together lives. They wanted to think no more about the dark experiences they had known themselves in Germany, or the far darker imaginings they had of the things that occurred to those who had stayed when they had left. They were neither indifferent nor cruel people; merely ones who wished no more interruptions in the ongoing tide of their lives, people who had been cowed by upheaval, so that for comfort now they had always to clutch to themselves the familiar routine of their days, to hold with a tight fist to all that they had.

Emile Wolf passed the first week staring absorbedly at every sight he saw in Manhattan, which impressed him and which was precisely as he had imagined it would be from his reading. At the end of it, however, he decided that he would have to join relatives in the South who were expecting him—the ones who had signed the affidavit that brought him to America. Furthermore, the long lugubrious conversations with his aunt made him intensely uncomfortable. The two of them sat together in the living room of the large upper West Side apartment, with its enormous dining table the aunt and uncle had brought with them from Germany, its silver pieces, urns, trays, and candelabrum that shone brightly from the glass cabinets and tables, in glaring relief to the heavy dark furnishings.

After the first day, what passed between him and his aunt were not conversations, actually. The old woman would sigh and repeat the names of the dead relatives. Then a silence would come, followed by tears. Invariably, with the room thus filled with the sound of his aunt's crying, Emil Wolf felt restless and guilty; he had, he knew, brought these tears on the household by his presence in it.

The Memphis relatives were generous, kindly people inclined to worry much over him, and as poor as the New York relatives were rich. His aunt, a soft-eyed nervous woman, insisted that he needed rest, only rest; his uncle agreed. So far as his plans were concerned, an agency social worker in Memphis advised him that he could get a job and go to night school if he wanted. It was at the meetings with the social workers and the psychiatric counselors, whom the social agencies employed to deal with the immigrants, that a resentment began to grow in him. Neither their psychological queries nor the answers he gave produced anything useful for him; he loathed the probing, personal questions, and the superior air of the questioners, though he contained his loathing behind an iron stare. As far as he was concerned, they were not, these fat women and these officious men, entitled to hear everything they wanted to know about him, to treat him as though, beyond question, they were his superiors.

They did not look like his superiors. One squinted at him, and looked pleased with herself, as though she were doing him a great kindness, when she told him to take a chair. There was another, a man, who took notes and asked him questions such as whether he felt guilty.

"Guilty about what?" Emil Wolf asked the man, who looked thoughtfully at him.

"Guilty about surviving?" the man suggested. Emil Wolf regarded the man in silence for a time, and then shook his head no. The man, who was a psychiatric social worker of some kind, nodded acceptingly and wrote his answer down.

"I mean guilt about survival; you don't feel upset from time to time that other people in your family died and that you lived? That's what the question means," the worker explained in an encouraging manner. "Now, do you feel guilty about this sometimes?"

Exactly what answer he gave the worker, he could not later remember, except that it was a truthful one: that the thought of feeling guilty for being alive had never entered his mind.

The questions and the interviews produced only a bad temper and no practical proposals. A week after he arrived in Memphis, he wandered downtown alone and, over the protests of his aunt, got himself a job as a shoe salesman. He had given up the idea of going to school, and was driven now by an urge to be independent as quickly as possible. The Memphis relatives were poor, and in need themselves; he could not be dependent on them for money. He wanted to be dependent on no one: that was his obsession. His evenings, which he had at first spent in his room engaged in his old pursuits—reading the novels of his favorites, Mann, Conrad, and Dostoevsky, and listening to music—he now began to spend going about Memphis, sometimes to the movies, but more often wandering, looking at the shopwindows. The work at the shoe store was not hard, but the hours he put in were long, and he was glad of it, glad of the eighty-five dollars a week that he took home and that—partly, at least—put him beyond the reach of charitable organizations and their questions. Other people, of course, asked questions of him not very different from those the psychiatric social workers asked. He was not offended by these, particularly since they were not asked by agency workers, people he felt constrained to answer because they had authority. No refugee found it easy to dismiss the fact that agency workers were officials, and they might yet have the power to send him where he did not wish to go or to withhold what he wanted to receive.

Often survivors who arrived in America were asked, "Why did you survive?" The question meant, actually, "Why did you survive and not the others?" The implication, which was not subtle, was the result of stories Americans had heard of the tooth-and-nail fight for survival in the death camps, and of the efficiency of the Nazi death machine. As the facts about the concentration camps were revealed after the war, it became reasonable to conclude that amoral behavior was a technique of survival. From this conclusion there took hold, as a sort of common wisdom, the more simplistic idea that the only people who could have survived were those who would perform the amoral acts necessary to preserve life in the circumstances the Nazis created: those who could steal the bread from other starved men, those who could gain favor by reporting someone else or by performing other, more unspeakable deeds. In one of the more noteworthy manifestations of obedience to the common wisdom, there were survivors themselves, many years after the war, who had learned to say that it was true: "The best died; the worst of us lived." Invariably, such observations were uttered with that air of self-approval which always betrays the presence of an orthodoxy; and while there were doubtless many who believed in the truth of these remarks because of what they had themselves seen during the war, it is likely that as great a number believed it because of the things they had heard after the war—or, more precisely, they chose to believe that they believed it.

In the years just after the war, however, the survivors were not at all prepared for the questions that were asked of them, nor were they familiar with the idea of a survivor image, much less obedient to one—as, many years later, some of them became.

One learned that it was quite possible he would be asked, straightforwardly or otherwise, by what means he had purchased his life; and often those who were asked these questions learned that such questioning was a pattern, best to be stored away with other strange responses they had encountered, each new one a proof to them that they and their experiences were utterly incomprehensible to all those who had not been part of it. They soon learned that they might be asked, by friends and relatives, what it was like to starve, and after being told that starvation was very bad, the friends and relatives might respond that yes, they knew, because there had also been shortages of many things in America during the war, such as sugar. The survivors learned that they might be told to tell the truth: surely once they must have been given a dessert after the main meal in all the time they were in the concentration camp? Never even a piece of cake? There were also those whose friends and relatives were intent on hearing nothing, and asked no questions whatever, out of a kind wish not to bring up unhappy memories. This was a generous attitude, but one that also served to isolate those survivors who could not successfully pretend that they had been nowhere, and that nothing of significance had happened to them in the five years or more that they had spent in captivity or hiding.

Emil Wolf's southern Jewish society inclined to the last attitude, which was according to his wishes and not in the least disturbing to him, for more and more he wished not

to stand out in that society but to melt into it. Almost to
his own surprise, he found himself enjoying life in Memphis, and there were good reasons for it. After the day's
work at the shoe store, he hurried home, now not to sit
in his room and read, but to ride around the city with one
or another of his friends, people his aunt had introduced
him to, and particularly the girls, who were all of good
families. As the aunt pointed out to him, the effect of
these girls on him was tongue-loosening. One in particular,
a tall brown-haired girl, listened to every sentence he
uttered as though this were the last chance that would be
granted her to hear anything of interest to her in life. The
result was that the number of sentences he uttered was
greatly increased. Evening after evening, he took leave of
his aunt and uncle and jumped into the car in which his
friends waited for him. With them, he would hold forth
on whatever it was that interested them at a given time:
movies, music, or simply small talk. He never spoke of
the war, or his experiences, and no one asked him about
those things.

At the end of a year in Memphis, he seemed at his ease.
Though the stern judgmental expression of his eyes remained, other things in his appearance had changed; for
example, he had begun to smile often and quickly, a thing
that had come naturally to him in the company of his
Memphis friends, all of whom were cheerful people, who
smiled a great deal themselves; in fact, they smiled most
of the time, in company. His aunt and uncle were happy
that their relative no longer sat by himself in the evenings,
although his aunt was sometimes uneasy at the way he
rushed out of the house after a day's work, and at the late
hours he kept; she had never got over the idea that he
needed rest.

Then, at the end of a year and a half, he became in-
formally engaged to the tall brown-haired girl who listened
with such devotion to everything he said. The girl was
from a wealthy Jewish family in Memphis from whom the
young couple could probably expect financial help, but
even had she not been, people had married on far less
than the eighty-five dollars a week he made at the shoe

store. From time to time, he still thought of going to school as soon as he had made the money to do it. At work, surrounded by shoeboxes, he could sometimes catch a glimpse of himself in the store mirror as he emerged from the clutter, shoe in hand, ready to fit it on a customer's outstretched foot. At such moments he wondered how his parents would feel if they had lived, seeing him this way, on his knees, selling shoes: how unimaginable it would have been to them, at one time.

Usually, though, at work he would turn all his attention to making sales, at which he was very good. Indeed, he made more than any other salesman in the store, and when he fell ill with a bad cold and a cough that did not go away, his employers and his relatives blamed it on his zest for work. But the cough remained. One of the salesmen told him that he should go and have an X-ray, advice that he one day obeyed, with the result that he found himself having to go back to one of the hated social agencies to seek help in getting admitted to a hospital for the treatment of tuberculosis. The center for treatment in America was the Denver Jewish hospital, to which he was sent. He was, as it turned out, one of a good number of people whose health broke down a few years or more after the liberation, the result of damage done during the years in the camps or in hiding. Tuberculosis cases were common among the survivors, in some of whom the symptoms of the disease did not become evident until long after the war.

Miserably, he listened to the instructions of the agency social worker who had arranged his transportation and his admission to the hospital. The agency treated him well, even generously, in his illness, a fact that was not lost upon him. Later, he explained to himself that it was not when one was down and out that one had to worry about the social workers, but when one was up and independent.

He was worse than down and out when he left Memphis. For one thing, his girl had broken their engagement shortly after he told her the reasons for his trip to Denver. In addition, the prospect of leaving Memphis for a new and unknown place, and one moreover where he would be confined again, filled him with a depression more terrible than anything he had known since the war. It was worse, in some ways, than anything he had ever known, for the new beginnings he had made in Memphis, the friends, the girl, the independence he had worked so hard for—all had been swept away overnight.

In Pleasantville, Missouri, he had to change trains. All the way to Missouri, his depression had grown deeper; he thought of being locked up in a hospital, of the possibility of never being released, of being told to leave America. There was no energy in him to think of brighter possibilities; simply, the thought of new beginnings, whether it was the life in the hospital or the one he would have to take up if he recovered, was impossible to bear. On the platform where he waited, he saw the Colorado Eagle roaring toward the station. Just as the Eagle sped in, he moved to the edge of the platform and leaned far over it. He stood that way for only a moment before the engineer pulled the brakes, sending sparks high in the air, and brought the train to a sudden halt quite close to him. On the Eagle, he opened a bottle of whiskey he had put in his suitcase, and he began to drink. He drank all night, almost as much in one night and morning as he might put away in two years, so that by the time he was close to arriving in Denver, he was, as he had planned to be, very drunk. Stupefied and sick as he was, he nevertheless noticed the mountains outside of Denver blazing at him from the train windows. The sight was not a comfort, for it intruded itself on his depression. When the train came to a stop, he staggered off into the white Denver sunlight, where he was found soon enough and packed into a station wagon. The hospital driver, also a former patient, had a number tattooed on his forearm.

"Give it a chance," the man told him, and said no more. The silence between them was effortless. Looking greenish, and feeling worse than he looked, Emil Wolf closed his eyes and leaned back in the seat, every now and then opening them a bit to look out the window, thinking that he was now very far from Memphis, that he was now like his old friend Hans Castorp, going up into the mountains from which he might not return.

S. GORDON

Gordon owns a two-family house in East Rogers Park, a suburb of Chicago. He has rented the upper floor to a young couple with a child, whose cries periodically invade the quiet of his six rooms. Neat rooms they are, and none of them overly large: the living room especially looks packed with serviceable, highly polished, and inexpensive furniture, the kind that might have been chosen by a newlywed couple of modest circumstances until they could afford better. Its owner is not, however a man of very modest circumstances, but a successful small businessman, proprietor of a jewelry store; nor is he a newlywed, for the tall woman he appraises dourly from time to time— which is to say, whenever she addresses a remark to him— has been his wife for thirteen years. It is a dignified appraisal and, in the faintest degree, a surprised one, the sort of look a headwaiter might give an undesirable who had somehow found his way to a center table. The times he responds to her questions, however, his answers are short but polite.

He had married her in 1959, more than a decade after he arrived in Chicago. The cousin who introduced them had informed him somewhat sketchily of her history: that she came of a family of German Jews, that they had got out of Germany and come to the United States in 1937, and that she had recently been widowed. She was in her early forties when he met her, and was a German language teacher in a Chicago university, a position she had held until her retirement a few years before; she had, she explained, grown tired of teaching, for she was by then approaching her sixties, and wished to devote the time that was left to her to other pursuits, mainly her passion for travel. Whenever she could persuade him to go, they took trips to Europe and to South America, the tall bespectacled woman and her husband, a much smaller figure with the shoulders of a laborer, and a silent air.

He began his story with grave formality, telling how his town of Czestochowa, in Poland, had been no backwater, but a center of Jewish culture with a great many schools, theaters, and similar institutions; he could tell the exact number of each of these, he indicated, pointing to a box of file cards nearby. When the Germans invaded, he was thirty, a married man with three children.

"My son Samuel was thirteen. Sarah was eleven. Chaya was the youngest. Seven."

Their mother, his first wife, had perished with the three children in Treblinka, he added.

His present wife clattered cheerfully into the room. She had taken up needlepoint a few months before, and in a short time had learned to shape animals of every sort out of the thick, bright-colored threads; she was surprised, and not a little pleased, at having become an expert at this craft in so brief a time, she confessed when she showed visitors her work. Now, frowning, she searched the living room for the round frame and the cloth with its half-finished horse. Soon she spied it beneath one of the toss pillows on the sofa, and departed, frame in hand, looking relieved. Her husband, who had regarded her in silence as she searched, resumed his story.

In Poland he had owned a clothing factory where, as soon as the Nazis came, he had a hideout built for himself and his family. The hideout, which was on the upper floor of the factory and could be reached only by entering a trapdoor, was more than ample for his own family. When, however, the Germans began selecting people for deportations, neighbors who had learned of his hiding place begged to be taken in, and soon there were forty men, women, and children packed in the upper floor of the factory while the Germans were rounding Jews up and putting them on the trains to Treblinka.

"Then, one day, they were having another of the selections and I saw my son running, he was running toward the selection. I ran after him. And what he said to me. My son said to me, 'Papa, let me go. I am starving here!'

It was true, we were starving then. My son said, 'Papa I am young. They won't kill children. I'll go and work.' So he went on the transport, my son. I told him, I begged him to come to the factory with me, but he was too smart, my son."

"I don't know how this happened," said his wife, who had appeared suddenly in the living room. She wandered across the room touching the tables and chairs, repeating, since no one had asked her what she meant, "I don't know how this happened." Her husband appraised her calmly, whereupon she smiled, showing prominent white teeth and a dimpled chin, which contrived to make her look pleasantly girlish.

"Somebody put the old cups in with the good dishes," she explained. Then, as though bemused by this turn of events as by a charming conundrum, she moved an ashtray back and forth with her fingers, looking at it as though it might hold an answer to the riddle.

"The transport went. I couldn't stop him. My son," her husband resumed. "I went back to the hideout and my daughter wasn't there. She was outside looking for me. Then she came to the hideout and started to bang on the door. The middle of the selection, I heard her. '*Tata, Tata,*' I heard her crying to me. '*Tataschu*, open up and let me in!' I couldn't open the door. The other people were yelling, 'Don't open, they'll find us all.' They were forty people with their children. So I didn't open up the door, and she stayed there calling me. '*Tataschu*, open the door.' Then she wasn't calling me anymore." He covered his mouth with his hands and sobbed, while his wife glided into the room, sighing as she did, not ungraciously. "I am very much against this, this is not a good subject," she said. "If anyone asked me, I would be very much against it, but no one asked me. Very poor," she murmured, and departed, addressing a look of final reproach to the living room.

"My daughter went on the same transport as my son, the same day. I have pictures of them," he said, when he was able to speak again. He told how he paid a Pole to follow the train the children were on; how the man had returned after three days and reported that the train went to Treblinka; how the man had found out that no one—man, woman, or child—could emerge from that camp alive.

He lived in the ghetto with his wife and his remaining child until the morning the Germans rounded him up, along with scores of Jews they had seized that day.

"When I got to the concentration camp, the SS officer, I suppose, took a liking to me. I made him a saddle. I knew how to work with leather, and he wanted to express his appreciation. 'What can I do for you?' he says. 'Let me go back and find my wife and daughter,' I asked him."

"Oh, come, now, this is still going on?" his wife said from the doorway. "This is not at all the way to do." Though she spoke firmly, her incredulous air and the tilt of her head gave her a gay look. "It's lunchtime now—otherwise, this can go on and on, correct? And this is not the way."

"Of course, he would not let me go back and find my wife and daughter. But he offered me, instead, extra food. 'No, I'm not hungry,' I told him. Later, I found out my wife and my other daughter were sent to Treblinka a few days after I was picked up."

Dishes clattered faintly in the kitchen. "You see," he said mysteriously, rising. "I am like my son, too smart. I made an error being always so smart," he concluded, and led the way to the dining room.

"See how upset he is over these things," his wife noted at lunch. "Look at him, how uneasy he is; and it will be for me to soothe him later. Bad dreams, whatnot."

Her husband attended to his plate, deftly arranging cold cuts on bread. "It's snowing much harder," his wife ventured, looking out the dining-room window. "I love Chicago, but the winters—oh, my, the snow is piled up all the time," she observed raptly. "And he cannot shovel snow all the time, to get the car out."

"Because I hurt my back. During the war. An SS man kicked me when I dropped a shovel; my disk was ruptured."

"Yes, yes, so I myself shovel. I am quite athletic; I don't think it's so good the way Americans never do the physical. Exercise, exercise," she affirmed, "and more exercise. This is my belief."

Her husband was quite positive he wanted no more lunch. While she poured coffee, he excused himself and disappeared into one of the rear rooms.

"Soon we will go on a trip to Mexico," she observed. "I look very much forward to it. To me the Spanish culture in general is very interesting. This, what you see in the cities in America, is not the true Spanish culture. By no means."

"Here." Her husband returned, a brown envelope in his hands. Opening it, he removed two old photographs taken by a commercial photographer in Poland. One was of a youth of about twelve. The second picture showed a laughing woman with three children, the smallest of which she held in her lap, while the other two stood next to her, their expressions full of a grave formality for the occasion. "My son," he said, and drew his breath in. "My wife and the children."

His wife, who had been humming quietly to herself, began to clear the table in a fashion that testified to her love of the physical: she swooped upon the plates, her long arms reaching the length of the table; she spared no energy in her efforts.

"It is not possible to think about them all the time," her husband said. "But certain days. Certain days, when there is a bar mitzvah I go to, I think of him, my son. How he would have had his bar mitzvah."

"You have to go, no?" his wife reminded him. "An appointment. You said two o'clock; see how late it is."

"I have to go warm up the car," her husband answered, pocketing the envelope as he went.

"Oh, Chicago, I would never live anywhere else," she said. "The architecture is something perfect. But travel is essential to one, isn't it so? I have to coax him," she confided, "but he goes and he enjoys it. Not to talk about these things. What good is it?" she inquired, departing.

"Here are these things, see," she said, returning with two wood carvings. One was of an animal with tusks, and the other of a madonna. "These are from South America.

I will show you," she offered, a note of shyness in her voice now. "And here, you see, it is hand carved, and the name of the artist. And there are many, many more things I have here. Only one moment, and I can show the most interesting of all," she urged, her long legs carrying her out of the dining room and back in a few strides.

"This is a representation of village life centuries ago," she said, indicating a long strip of metal in her hands. "It is actually a frieze," she explained, "and here is, you see, a villager, and there his animals."

Her husband could be heard outside stamping the snow off his shoes. "And I have a number of other pieces equally interesting, I think. But the time is passing," she said rapidly, gathering up the carvings. "There are new things always to learn. To learn, to observe, to see," she concluded as, with a gracious smile and a tilt of the head, she made her final exit.

"This mistake I made is in one way irrevocable, in another way not," her husband said as he drove, eyes hunting busily left and right to assess the traffic ahead. "I made a decision after the war and it was a mistake."

He told how, after the war, he came to Chicago and took menial jobs, living in boarding houses. Then, by borrowing and by working hard for eight years, he got the capital for a small business. But all during that time he could not think of marrying again. Friends pressed him with matches but he refused to consider them, for he had made a decision right after the war: he wanted no reminders of the past, and therefore no new children. Furthermore, if he married, he wanted a woman who was not a survivor from the camps; most of all, he wanted one who would not bear children.

"It was a mistake," he announced. "I can't change it. I took an older woman for that reason. Deliberately. I had plenty of chances for young women, plenty of matchmakers. But I said no—to have these children around that you can't give love to, I thought, don't take that risk. I thought, I have no love for the new children in me; I felt I will not be able to give them a father's love. So I took this woman. A highly educated woman, I thought she would be a companion."

He drove in silence for a time. "Do you know what it is like to live with such a woman?" he asked suddenly, in a voice that still marveled at the facts, though they had been uncovered long ago. "That she only likes to visit places and to collect things made from wood and tin, and she hates people, that more than two people together in a living room is a tragedy to her, that she likes only to have no company? All right," he said fervently, "all this I am responsible for; I made this choice." A driver blasted his horn in fury because Gordon had cut him off.

"Life's not over yet. It's better to be alone than this way. Better than to hate it every minute whenever somebody comes into a room and this is a person who lives with you."

He calculated: he would not be lonely, with the many friends he had, and the Jewish communal activities in which he took a leading role; citations and plaques covered the walls of his living room, testimony to the community work he had done and the charity drives he had successfully led. He had associates, in fact, with whom he felt more at home than the woman he had lived with for thirteen years.

"So it's too late for some things. Not for others. I think my wife is not a bad woman. Something in her training, it's possible, makes her cold." He was calm; he had made his conjecture in the spirit of psychological inquiry, nothing more, his tone said.

"The best way to live a life of tragedy is to be always a rationalist," he mused. "This is what I did. Whatever it was. Once, after the liberation, a Russian comes up to me and he says to me, 'Here's a gun. Come on and you'll shoot some Germans.' I looked at him. 'I don't know these Germans, how can I shoot them?' I tell him. 'Maybe this one that I'll shoot didn't do anything,' I tell him. I'm not sorry I didn't go with him, either. It's other things."

He turned the car onto a boulevard flanked by rows of apartment buildings, in one of which he had a brief business appointment.

"I see them, how they are with their wives. Friends of mine that they came over from Europe when I did, and they got married again—some of them that they already had new wives they met in the D.P. camps, and they had new children. I see how they love the children and how the children love them." Gordon pulled up in front of an apartment house and turned his coat collar up in preparation for the freezing cold outside.

"Fifteen minutes only, I'll be back," he said, and, with eyes no less bitter than the winter wind, went off to his appointment.

4 | Settling

The survivors settled wherever they had friends or relatives already established in America, or wherever the Jewish social agencies that brought them from Europe had
found sponsors for them. They were sent all over the
country, a dispersion which seemed both necessary and
wise to those social agencies, whose representatives labored
manfully to get some of the new arrivals out of the great
Jewish population centers of the East, so that responsibility
for them was apportioned among as many Jewish communities in America as possible.

It was decided that New York would take half of them,
a number commensurate with the size of its Jewish population. Competition for jobs and business opportunities would
be very keen in the big eastern cities, some of the agency
representatives pointed out to immigrants reluctant to
leave New York for Iowa or Michigan; they would do far
better in a smaller town or city. On the whole, the newcomers went willingly enough wherever they were assigned,
largely because, with the exception of New York, one
place in America was as strange to them as any other.
Most of them were little disposed, furthermore, to argue
with the authorities who had brought them to the United
States and arranged homes and jobs for them. They went
forth and settled near their sponsors, local agencies or individuals who had signed affidavits saying that they would
be responsible for finding employment and housing for the
newcomers. To be sure, there were some who saw no reason to go elsewhere once they had set foot in New York,

and they could not be persuaded by the most strenuous advice or cajolery that California, for example, had anything to offer.

"They offered me a ticket just to go and see San Francisco," one survivor recalled of the efforts to dislodge him from New York. "A round-trip ticket, only to visit— I didn't have to stay there. But I would not take it. I said, 'Thank you, I'm not going anyplace.' New York was the Jewish capital of the world, because no Jewish state existed yet. What was the use of traveling to these other places— San Francisco—when I had everything I wanted right here? I did enough traveling."

Others made good their plans to move as soon as possible from certain places to which they had been sent. One couple debarked from the ship that had carried them from Germany to New Orleans, and were at once thrown into a fright by the signs designating "Colored" and "White" facilities, which they saw posted everywhere. "It was the first thing we noticed. I could read English, so I translated it for my husband. Some people could drink at a fountain and some couldn't. Some people couldn't be served. These signs were the greatest shock to us. They struck a terrible chord. Even long before we were arrested and taken away to the camps, there had been these signs forbidding Jews to sit in the park, or to walk certain places. My husband and I were frightened of the regime in the South the moment we saw this, and we decided, as soon as we could, to get out of there whatever we had to do. We left after six months, and came North; there was no use trying, we could never be comfortable, because racial laws meant only one thing to us."

Other survivors who came to the South were warned by their friends in the North that the Ku Klux Klan would bomb their houses or burn crosses on their lawns. A number settled in the South nonetheless, in places like Atlanta and New Orleans, despite warnings or such forebodings of their own as they may have had; they settled there for the usual reasons, either because they were assigned to those regions or because they had relatives there, the latter a factor that no survivor would disregard.

"I was newborn," survivors often said when describing the condition they found themselves in after the liberation. This meant that they were, of course, happy to be alive, that they were ready to take up the life that had been given back to them. But the phrase had a darker meaning, too, as the survivors used it. It suggested that those who had been left alive after the holocaust were not only without a place in the world and without possessions, but also had no past life; the roots and ties of that life—mothers and fathers, the husbands, wives, children and holdings—had been erased entirely. "It was as though I had not come from anywhere." The one link with the past were friends they had known in Europe; friends could remember them as they were, survivors often said, and as their parents and relatives had been. "It gives back a part of you that is lost, that is dead," and this was a gift without price for some survivors, who could never long put from their minds the knowledge that the entire world of their origin, not only their families, had been obliterated. They looked for confirmation of the past in the presence of friends, and when, as happened, necessity placed them in situations where the friends were far away, they were desolate—lonely not merely in the way people are who are new to a country but in the deeper way of those who have suddenly had withdrawn from them some elemental connection in life.

If they could not disregard relatives because they had so few of them, neither could many of the survivors disregard offers of jobs or other help from relatives, though to accept these things meant sometimes that they would have to leave the large cities of the East where they had initially settled. They made these reluctant decisions because babies were coming, because jobs for refugees were not easy to find, because the eastern cities were expensive and all but slum apartments came at a price too high for them.

The Jewish social agencies, HIAS and the United Service, were primarily responsible for obtaining visas and bringing the survivors to America, after which the job of seeing to the new arrivals fell to local Jewish community organizations. In keeping with the tradition that wherever there are Jews there is Jewish communal organization, there were to be found, where Jews lived in America, local branches of Jewish welfare agencies, such as the Jewish Community Service or the Federation of Jewish Philanthropies, whose task it was to sustain the new immigrants. When they arrived, it was necessary that someone be at the stations in the strange towns to bring them to apartments that had been made ready for them; afterwards they needed clothes, money, and jobs, language interpreters and guides. And just as the persistence and the bureaucratic instincts of the social agents had often made the survivors angry, it was, most of the time, the same persistence and the long reach of these agents that arranged each detail of their settlement in the United States.

While they were still in Germany, one couple learned from the papers given them to sign before their departure that their assigned place in America was Corpus Christi—a Texas town, they were told by an American official. In Bremen, they went from bookstore to bookstore in search of a map of America large enough to show Corpus Christi, and were rewarded, after many hours and many bookstores, with a map that showed Texas was enormous, and that the place they were interested in, Corpus Christi, was located near the Gulf of Mexico.

Their boat left Germany in January, a bitter month in Europe. However, by the time they had come to the end of their two-week voyage and docked at New Orleans, they had discarded, one by one, the layers of heavy clothes they customarily wore in winter. New Orleans was not hot to a Southerner, at 67 degrees in January, but to the couple, accustomed to the temperatures of a European winter, it was like midsummer—so they told each other several times in the first hours after they arrived.

They had met and married in a displaced persons camp in Germany after the liberation. The woman, Rebecca Spanner,* was twenty-four, two years younger than her husband, Arnold, a Berlin-born Jew and, like her, an Auschwitz survivor. She was a native of Lodz, which was the seat of the first Jewish ghetto to be established by the Germans after the invasion of Poland, and, next to the

Warsaw ghetto, the largest. She, four sisters, and a brother had lived and worked together in the ghetto until it was liquidated. A 1942 photograph, which had come into her possession after the war, showed her and her brother and sisters smiling gaily as they posed crowded around one of the machines at the ghetto factory where her brother was foreman. She alone had survived. A number of explanations had occurred to her about why, none of them firm or conclusive; she knew better than to say that such and such was the reason, and not something else. All the explanations, nonetheless, reflected a conviction that her survival was related to her behavior, to her point of view—in short, to her character.

She later decided that the aspect of her character that might have done much to save her was her independence, or, as she was sometimes inclined to view it, a capacity not to care too much about anything or anyone. The spoiled youngest child of a doting family, and still only sixteen when the Germans marched into Poland, she had learned early to do exactly what she wanted without worrying about anyone else. When, for example, the Germans rounded her up for deportation, along with the friends whose quarters she had shared in the ghetto, her brother raced through the crowd of people at the station calling her name, but she never answered. Again and again he called her, and she heard him—he had brought with him a member of the Jewish police, who could possibly have intervened and got her out—but she had decided that if all the Jews were going to be sent away anyway, she would be with her friends, the people she boarded with. Perhaps, so she later speculated, if she had not been so independent, if she had felt compelled to answer her brother, had got away that day and then gone with him or her sisters when their turn came to be deported, she might, like them, have been killed. In addition, when she was in Auschwitz, the Germans had one day come and selected two hundred and twenty women out of the hundreds in her barracks. Nobody knew where the women were going, and certainly nobody wanted to be picked to join them: no one ever wanted to be singled out or picked for anything. When one of the two hundred and twenty women selected ran, unseen, back to the larger crowd while the guards were counting the women off, Rebecca saw, and slipped into the woman's place. She had no idea whether the two hundred and twenty women were being selected for gassing, a new camp, or some special kind of labor, or whether she would be going to a worse or a better situation. Later, she supposed she had joined the group, destination unknown, because here might be a chance to be transferred out of Auschwitz. The two hundred and twenty women were, in fact, shipped to Belsen where there was no standing for selections, no gas chamber, no real regimentation, and where, further, at the time of her arrival there, she and the other women were housed in tents in the open air, not jammed as they later were, thousands upon thousands, into filthy barracks. Belsen was decidedly an improvement, a respite, and she might well not have won that respite, according to her conjecture, had she been the type to form quick ties. Alone in Auschwitz—she had soon been separated from the friends she was deported with from Lodz— she had had the impetus to try to get herself out; there had been no one to say yes or no to her decision, or "Wait for me."

Long after the war, she was to think often and deeply about these matters—ever more so, in fact, as the years went by—and to be sorry that she had not carefully preserved mementos of her experience, like her striped blue-and gray prisoner's uniform. After the liberation, she had gratefully put on the new clothes the Americans provided and, without a thought, had thrown away the striped garment and wooden shoes she had been wearing. Some other survivors, out of an immediate realization of their roles as holocaust witnesses or at least a keener sense of the future than she had at the time, had kept their uniforms. She did not imagine in advance the hold the past would later have upon her, or that one day she would wish avidly to have back in her possession some concrete evidence of it, such as the uniform she had worn, filthy and tattered, right up to the end when they had been liberated. "My beautiful striped dress," she would later call it when describing how she looked that lovely morning in late April, 1945, when the Americans surrounded her train. For an entire week before, the Germans had shuttled the prisoners back and forth in an effort to evade the advancing Americans, in all that time never moving farther than fifteen or twenty kilometers from the train's starting point at Dachau. She had jumped from a liberated boxcar, one of a horde of emaciated women who poured, tumbling and crawling, out of the train before the eyes of the appalled soldiers. Her face wild, she was the one who had found a Polish-speaking American officer and dragged him with her to the side of the road where the SS were being disarmed, whereupon she had then slapped a captured SS woman. It was not a hard blow, not well aimed; the SS woman had stared straight ahead and given no sign that she felt it. The thing she always remembered vividly about the incident was her own fear and trembling at the time, the way she clutched the officer's arm with one hand and hit the guard with the other. The American had let her do it; then she allowed him to lead her away (afterward the same officer had come almost every day for two weeks, until his unit left, to the temporary camp where the women had been housed, to bring her and some of the others gifts of fruit, crackers, candy, and cigarettes), and that evening, provided with clean clothes, she had discarded the striped uniform. The last thing on her mind at the time was to preserve it, or to imagine a future in which it would have value for her.

Not that she was entirely fearless, when that future arrived, about immersing herself in thoughts of what had been: the Lodz ghetto where SS men swung babies by the feet and smashed their heads on stone walls; the deportations; Auschwitz; Belsen; the beatings, the starvation, the screams and cries of suffering. At times, after thinking and talking about the past, she had nightmares: one minute she appeared to herself in her dream clothed, free, and apparently leading a normal life; the next minute she was naked and in Auschwitz again. In her contemplation of the past, bad dreams and anxiety would always be dangers. Still, the terror the past held was in no way equal to the strength of its spell: there was mystery in it, a seduction more powerful than all the dread it awakened, the mystery of self and personality, of events themselves.

After the liberation, to be sure, her thoughts were bent on the immediate future, not the past, nor was there any great mystery about the way she felt, or what she was then. Like many a survivor, she was not particularly fearful about such things as a journey to a new country, or taking up a new life among strange people. Like them, she had found after the liberation that she had lost the vulnerability to ordinary dreads and fears which had once been hers in a normal life. The attitude of these survivors, simply summed up, was that between the years 1939 and 1945 they had known circumstances more terrible than any they had ever feared or imagined, and now, they knew, it was over; what was there left in the world that was worthy of their fear?

Everything was comparative: compared to a fine feast, a plain loaf of bread was nothing, but after the liberation, when the survivors cut themselves slices of bread every two hours from the loaves they had been given, because every two hours, like clockwork, they were hungry again, they deemed the bread feast enough; no butter, margarine, or jam was necessary. In an attempt to provide balanced nutrition without fatally overfeeding the starved survivors, the Americans served them bowls of soup with meat and rice or vegetables in it* three times a day, but since the loaf of bread was entirely their own—food they might eat whenever they chose—the survivors placed a prime value on it, guarding it jealously in some instances, as though it were the sole source of their nourishment. Compared to an apartment, one room in a converted German Army barracks was nothing, but compared to what had been? Compared to the familiar, a new life among strangers in a strange land was threatening, but compared to the daily overhanging peril of death?

---

* Earlier attempts to feed newly liberated prisoners, particularly those freed by the British in Belsen, resulted in many deaths. Generous gifts of rich food, such as chocolate, fatty sausages, or even healthy portions of plain food were fatal for the long-starved survivors, who required extremely cautious feeding.

Rebecca married Arnold Spanner in 1946. Shortly after their daughter was born in 1947, their visas to America came, whereupon they moved from their room in the converted barracks to a transit camp in Bremen, from which point their ship would sail to the United States. Rebecca's feelings about the future were a mixture of mild apprehension and pleasurable excitement. She was quite clear, however, about some things: they were refugees, takers, dependents; there were certain attitudes one did and did not have when one was a dependent, certain things one did and did not say. Like many a refugee, needful, she was able to come to terms with the requirements of the refugee role, which included a certain amount of acquiescence and humility. She learned to deal with acquiescence perfectly well by viewing it as a matter of policy, a pragmatic choice, with herself in command of that policy at all times. She herself, years later, would observe that a clear attitude about what was required of her had been to her advantage.

Some survivors coming to America, she believed, would exhibit attitudes implying that they expected to be taken care of because of what they had endured—she had observed this outlook, and had heard much talk about it, in some people in the camps—and she had no doubt that such an attitude made a terrible impression. She set out for America with her husband and her child determined that they should act as though they expected nothing at all to come easy to them, and also actually to expect nothing to come easy to them, though the first, of course, was the concern of higher importance.

She remembered every detail of her arrival. At the station in Corpus Christi, the two men waiting for them had been able at once to pick out the newcomers, who were probably a conspicuous sight in the crowd of casually attired travelers getting off the train on a midweek afternoon. Clad in a dark suit and tie, Arnold Spanner cradled an infant in his arms, while his wife, Rebecca, stood next to him attired in a two-piece suit, hat, and gloves, all clearly finery, however rumpled their twenty-hour train ride from New Orleans had made it. The two men who greeted them at the station spoke warmly to them in a terrible pidgin Yiddish. With such as it was, however, they were able to inform the couple that they would first be taken to dinner at the home of one of the men's sisters, who lived in Corpus Christi. From there they would drive to McAllen, where they were to settle, and would be put up with a local family until the house that had been rented for them was made ready.

Between 1947 and 1951, the peak period in which the survivors were being dispersed and settled in America, it was sometimes possible for those in charge to choose the people for an area according to their idea of who could best adapt to the local conditions. McAllen, Texas, for example, considered that it required one young couple, not rigidly orthodox, who could therefore probably adjust to a place that was not, after all, one of the centers of Jewish life in America, a town where kosher food was not available around the block. McAllen chose the Spanners to live there, rather than Corpus Christi, and there, whether they wished to go or not, they went. Before the trip to their new town, they had first been taken to dinner in Corpus Christi, as the men who met them at the station told them they would be. The dinner—a silent affair, mostly, thanks to the language barrier—went off smoothly enough but for one moment when Rebecca Spanner had reached for a plate of small black things like miniature plums, and been repelled when she tasted, instead of the sweetness of a plum, something salted and hard that she could not bring herself to swallow. It had needed only this surprise to produce the rising tide of nausea in her which she had dimly felt coming on before. Thinking that if she swallowed the salted bits she would become ill immediately she kept them in her mouth—the first night in America, with everyone watching and judging you by your manners, you did not take chewed food out of your mouth at the dinner table—until it occurred to her to have a coughing fit under the cover of which, as delicately as possible, she transferred the stuff to her napkin. Later, she was told that the salted things were black olives, which she had never seen before and which, forever after, she could not bring herself to put into her mouth.

During the drive to McAllen, the hosts sat in the front while she and her husband sat in the back of the car and whispered to each other in Polish, on the off chance that the hosts might understand more Yiddish than they seemed to. Past eleven at night, they reached the town. In wintertime, McAllen's houses darkened early; furthermore, they looked to the couple as though they had no one living in them. No chink of light was visible; no sound came from them. Where were they being taken, Rebecca had asked her husband in a whisper. "A *dorf*,"* she answered herself, having received no reply from her husband, who was busy staring into the darkness, looking for clues in the outsides of the few shuttered houses they passed. "A *dorf*," she maintained again, whereupon her husband turned and whispered in Polish not to worry, no one would force them to stay if it didn't work out for them here. She had been ready to be settled anywhere in America, at least for the first few years, but now that the time had come, her heart sank to see how tiny and remote a place they were to live in, how far from cities and people. In the back of her mind, she supposed, she had all along seen herself coming to a city or, at the least, a large town. And why not, when she had been born and brought up in Lodz, the second largest city in Poland?

In 1950, McAllen had a total population of about twenty thousand, including sixty or so Jewish families. Rebecca, determined that she and her husband would look as though they expected to work hard for everything they got, found herself, from the moment of their arrival, in a position where this determination was neither practical nor relevant. You could not be given so many things so often, as they had right from the outset, and keep maintaining that it was all a great surprise each time or that you expected to struggle hard for every dress and pair of shoes you had when you were given these things and all other necessities regularly. Her sole role, and that of her family, she saw, was to be recipients of generosity; the people here were not concerned with her attitude toward inde-

* A very small village, a backwater.

pendence or anything else, only with the fact that their refugee family had to be taken care of. Once she understood that this was her role, which was a highly complicated and difficult one despite its many gratifications, she attended to it with as much dutifulness and attention as she would have expended on looking independent. She knew how to take and then to display, quietly, the usefulness of things given her—which was no lie, to be sure—to ask questions whose answers she knew, more or less, and to seek advice she did not actually require. She did not do these things consciously, always—though quite often she did—but out of a moment-to-moment apprehension of what it would be best for her to say. Nor did she say them only because she and her husband were practically dependent on the generosity of the people around them. Quite simply, she wanted to be a success in McAllen, even if it was the smallest and remotest town in America (which it was not), and they were going to leave it the next month; for the time being, it was the only world that mattered.

There were decidedly pleasant surprises. She had not expected, for example, when they got to McAllen, that they would be given a five-room house to live in instead of an apartment, which would, in fact, have been what they would have got if they had settled in a larger town or city where others like themselves had come in numbers. As it turned out, they had the full and uninterrupted attention of McAllen's well-to-do Jewish community. All the furniture in their house, the equipment in their kitchen, the clothes they wore were provided by that community's businessmen. If they did not receive the best and most expensive furniture available, it was new, and Rebecca was pleased with it, though not as pleased as she was by the handsome frame house that had been rented for them, with its high ceilings, its fireplace, the porch that encircled the house, and the large grassy yard in the front and back.

Money was not plentiful, but neither were expenses high: it was possible for them to get along quite well on their hundred and fifty dollars a month allowance, since virtually all of their expenses but food were taken care of. Every few months, for example, three new dresses and new shoes would be provided her by one or another of the local merchants, and a new suit given to her husband. Their medical bills were negligible, but such as they had were taken care of by the Jewish Community Service, which also paid the rent on the house. They felt far from pinched, in short, which was fortunate, since she had quite enough anxieties of other kinds to keep her busy the first months in McAllen.

She was disturbed, for one thing, at her inability to carry on a proper conversation in English. People were not forever patient, she felt; they would not expect you to know the language at first, but it would register with them how quick or slow you were to catch on to it. Rather than risk making dreadful errors, she retreated into silence while conversations went on around her, a solution that, of course, posed its own discomforts.

Among the sixty or so Jewish families in McAllen, there were very few people who knew Yiddish. There was, however, one person: a Texas born and bred local schoolteacher, whose Yiddish was fluent and impeccable, and who scoffed at Rebecca Spanner's hesitance at talking to people because she didn't know English. Almost every day the schoolteacher—retired by the time the Spanners had come to McAllen—or another of the ladies of McAllen would come to call for Rebecca to take her shopping or for coffee at someone's house. In McAllen, where nobody ever locked a door, visiting back and forth was impromptu, informal, and, above all, constant activity, a fact she was made aware of at once. Always willing, she went where she was invited, though her embarrassment at taking no part in the conversation made the visits less enjoyable than they might have been: and here the schoolteacher, Sarah, took a firm hand. "Just talk," she would tell her testily when she hung back. This would happen usually when other people were around, for in Sarah's presence alone she was not reluctant to talk. The older woman was blunt and aggressive—far more so than any of the other people Rebecca had met in McAllen—and these qualities made her presence a reassuring one to Rebecca, who was encountering so much graciousness elsewhere that it made her concern herself, even more than she was already prone to, with being on her best behavior. With Sarah—or Aunt Sarah, as she soon came to call her—she relaxed and felt she could open her heart. When they were alone, Sarah drilled her tirelessly in English. One thing that impressed Rebecca about Sarah, that made her want to learn English from her and to please her, was the fact that Sarah spoke such admirable Yiddish, of a pure, almost literary kind, which she had learned long ago from her parents and somehow managed to preserve, though there had not been anyone to speak Yiddish with in McAllen for many years. Rebecca was also grateful to have Sarah tell her, with her usual brusqueness, that since the people in McAllen spoke only one language and she, Rebecca, spoke three—none of which was English, it so happened—that it was not she but the other people who should be feeling self-conscious.

In a few months, under Sarah's relentless tutelage, Rebecca was able to carry on an English conversation quite acceptably. It was just around this time, too, that a Texas newspaper sent one of its reporters out to the Spanner house to do a story on the refugee family, an episode whose results Rebecca was not able to put from her mind for a long time to come. It was the period when stories about the European war refugees provided dramatic copy for the pages of newspapers now empty of war dispatches: a time, too, when America was proudly conscious of itself, of its strength, its democratic traditions, its difference in every respect from that Europe the refugees fled. There was a sense of celebration in every account of an arriving ship of displaced persons, in every story of the new Americans, as they were called, in every photograph of a survivor and his reunion with American relatives, and what was being celebrated principally, in addition to the arrival of the new Americans, was America itself.

Since Rebecca's English was still uncertain, Sarah took the burden of the interview for her, relaying to the reporter Rebecca's answers to the questions he asked. When the reporter asked what she liked about America, Rebecca answered truthfully that she valued its freedom. When he asked what she liked about Texas, and what particular American amusements she enjoyed, what foods she liked, she had no difficulty listing them for him. The questions were very simple, she thought; Sarah need not even have been there with her; she had expected far more complicated ones. Afterward a photographer came to take a picture of the family, and Rebecca, her husband, and the baby posed. Several days later, the interview was printed in the newspaper, beneath a headline that made Rebecca's cheeks flame: DISPLACED JEWISH FAMILY FINDS U.S. PARADISE WITH FRENCH FRIED POTATOES.

Though Sarah assured her it was nothing to worry about and that this was the way of newspapers, the headline was something she could not get over; for days she brooded over it, and blamed herself for having held the interview in such a way as to make her appear a fool. And anything that made her appear a fool in the eyes of McAllen was cause for worry, for despite the graciousness of the people she had met there, she believed that everything she did and said was judged, that the judgment was a strict one, and that the first impressions she made would be the lasting ones. This, she knew, was the reality the stranger faced when he entered any new society: and how much more so for one like herself?

From the beginning, she had understood the necessity of watching every word; one had to know when to talk, when to keep silent. Also she had determined almost as soon as they arrived in America that there were certain answers Americans expected to receive when they asked questions about the survivors' experiences during the war, and those were the answers she gave. She had determined, too, that there were certain beliefs about conditions in Europe which she should under no circumstances challenge. The nature of these beliefs was suggested to her when, during the drive to McAllen the night of their arrival, she had pushed the button on the car door in order to open the window, and one of the men driving them had asked her how she had known what to do to open the window. "I was lucky," Rebecca told him in Yiddish, instead of telling him, as was in fact so, that in postwar Europe modern cars with push-button windows had been available; that they had ridden in them; and that it was not difficult, if you had seen the insides of modern cars a few times, to figure out what the extra button on the inside of the door was for.

During the first week in McAllen, they had been invited for Friday night dinner, a sumptuous, traditional Sabbath night meal of fish, roast meat, and chicken, in the course of which their hostess asked Rebecca Spanner how long it had been since she had had any meat. "Ten years," Rebecca told the woman in obedience to her conviction that Americans wanted to hear such an answer rather than one which spoiled their notions, their sense of pride in America's bounty. "Ten years!" the hostess exclaimed, satisfied. "Ten years," Rebecca had affirmed untruthfully. Later, much later, she explained to the woman that great quantities of food had been brought into Europe, particularly to Germany, which had so many displaced persons, and that in the five years they had spent there after the war there had been plenty of meat. But at the beginning, when she was new to the country, she had been unwilling to intrude with these or other facts on what she considered to be the cherished beliefs of Americans. To her way of thinking, this was the polite—moreover, the socially practical—thing to do, and when she lied thus it was without a pang of guilt.

Once, some of the women friends she had made in McAllen took her to a movie about Americans interned in a Japanese prison camp. In the movie, which starred Claudette Colbert, the Americans were subjected to savage torture, and Rebecca's companions flinched and groaned with horror as they watched the screen. From time to time, Rebecca noted, the women looked at her from the corners of their eyes to see what her response was, and one or two of them were moved to tears by the film and kept wiping their eyes with their handkerchiefs.

Afterward, when they were walking toward the car, they talked about whether it was only a movie or whether the things they saw in it, such as clubbings and other deliberate torture, did actually happen. One of the women who had cried while watching the film was still quite upset about having gone to see it; another said that such things could have happened, but this was probably exaggerated the way the movies always exaggerated everything. When the women asked her for her opinion, she merely told them that what they had seen was not so terrible; more she did not say. In fact, of course, she had found nothing at all in the movie to make her flinch; the brutality shown on the screen was mildness itself compared to the reality she had seen in the Lodz ghetto and the camps.

"If they couldn't even believe that." she said to her husband, Arnold, that evening. In the night, she dreamed she was standing naked in Auschwitz, and woke from the dream gasping for breath. Calm soon enough, but unable to go back to sleep, she thought back to her actual arrival in Auschwitz: how she had been made, like the other girls and women, to strip and then stand in line naked; how the soldiers had looked at them, naked, as if they were pieces of garbage. Crying, she had undone her long braids while they stood there, and covered the front of her body with her hair, until her turn came for a *capo* to shave her head. And why was it, she wondered so long after that time, if you shaved a person's head she was unrecognizable to friends she had known all her life and even to herself? Why did that detail, and no other, the shaving of your head, have such power to change you? Other questions she had considered, too, which she never found the answers to; unimportant-sounding queries they were, but still they made her wonder. There was the question, for example, why no girl or woman she had ever known in the camps had had a menstrual period. After the liberation many survivors said that saltpeter or something similar had been put in their food, such as it was, but others scoffed at the idea that the Germans would bother with chemicals to keep the women free of menstrual blood, or otherwise concern themselves with hygiene, when they had packed them in to live in the filthiest conditions imaginable—not that such inconsistencies were unknown to the Germans. She herself imagined that it was probably because none of the women had done anything but starve in the ghettos and in the camps, and the lack of nutrition had caused their periods to stop, but she would have liked to know for certain whether that was the right answer; authorities had studied these things, she supposed, and written about them, but where she had no idea.

These were, of course, questions to be gone over when lying awake at night, or in talking to her husband, and not shared with the people she had come to live among in McAllen. For she took the movie incident as a sign that her instincts were right: unless Sarah or someone else asked her straight out, she intended to avoid talking about starvation, the ghetto, Auschwitz, selections, or any other such experience, convinced as she was that people could not accept what was incredible to them. To tell people what they could not or would not believe was to put yourself in a bad position one way or another: either they would resent it or they would feel that you could not be trusted in other things. Later, memories of the past began to crowd her mind more and more often, and she hungered to go over everything that had happened, everything that she had seen, to sort it out logically and chronologically (it was not unusual for her to spend an hour figuring out whether she had been in one camp before another, or deciding whether it had been winter or summer when something particular had happened), and to wish that she had kept her uniform, just to be able to take it out and look at it, instead of having to deal with recollections. At times, she felt the eerie anxiety of not being quite sure, suddenly, whether an incident had actually occurred or whether she had only feared it might happen, or whether something had happened to her or to somebody else. She was still not inclined to talk much about the past, unless she was asked. Proud, in later years she could tell a story, albeit not without a small edge in her voice, about how, after they had moved to Houston, a Jewish professor from the university had played cards with her and her husband every week for several years, and never known that they had been survivors or that anything special had ever happened to them, other than the fact that they had come from Europe after the war. They had discussed war, crime, politics, history, and issues of every sort together, but since it had never occurred to the professor or his wife to wonder what she and her husband—who were, after all, Jews—had been doing in Hitler's Europe during the war, she had never told them. When they found out, years after, that she and her husband had been in Auschwitz and gone through everything, as they put it, they were terribly surprised; not that they had learned it from her, even then.

She had not wanted to put herself in a bad position in McAllen for a thousand practical reasons. By the end of the first year there, however, her carefulness was rooted in something more than practical concerns. McAllen had, in short, captivated her, drawn her deeply into its small-town life and ways. The kindness of the people! The warmth they had shown so unstintingly! More now than before, she was determined that she and her husband should do nothing to spoil their standing; no more willing student, therefore, ever studied a society and its mores than she studied McAllen.

By that time, they no longer considered living elsewhere, and when, later, they had to move and there was really no alternative but to leave McAllen for Houston, she felt only misery. Leaving, she had, however, taken with her many of McAllen's ways, including the hospitality and the neighborliness which were such prime values there, and which she now considered to be her own. In Houston during the fifties, for example, a number of survivors were being settled, with more coming in all the time, and to these she opened her house, seeing to it that they were introduced to people, that they got lunches and dinners to welcome them, and that they lacked for nothing that neighborliness could provide. Later, when her husband bought a car and she learned to drive, she took the newest refugees around and showed them the sights, extending to them in those and more particular ways the manners that had been extended to her in McAllen, the gestures of friendship to a stranger which had eased her own first days there. There was much good advice she could have given the newcomers about their behavior, about what one did and did not say, had she deemed it polite. She could have told them, as she more than ever firmly believed, that attitudes determined not only survival but the way one got along in life afterward: one had only to be able to anticipate what was required.

THE ROSENS

Since their youth, in Poland, Menachem and Paula had been members of the Yiddisher Arbeiter Bund, the Jewish Workers' Organization, a fact that had been a source of sorrow particularly to Paula's orthodox family. To this day, because the Bundists had no enthusiasm for religion or religious symbols, there was no mezuzah on the door of the Rosens' apartment in the International Ladies' Garment Workers' Union project on New York's lower West Side. Before the war, the Bundists had no enthusiasm for Zionism, either, for they were Jewish Marxists, ardent secularists who believed that the Jewish redemption would come neither through the Messiah nor Zionism but through the redemption of the proletariat. But the holocaust had radically altered their old attitudes toward Israel: Bundists might never be happy with the idea of nationalism, but after they had seen two-thirds of the Jews of Europe destroyed, they could no longer set themselves against the existence of the Jewish state.

It was the second marriage for both: Menachem Rosen's first wife and children were killed in Poland, the oldest of them a girl of eighteen, who fell a combatant in the Warsaw ghetto uprising; Paula Rosen, her first husband killed, survived the camps with her five-year-old daughter and her niece. She was a small vigorous woman, a sharp contrast to her husband, who was frail and had the tentative slow step of an invalid. One evening, having taken his slow way to another room and back, Menachem produced Paula's daughter's photograph and she listened while he spoke of miracles; he did not like to talk of miracles, much less any in the Nazi period, but how could it have been other than a miracle that the child had lived? And the niece?

His wife committed herself less easily to the miraculous. "My husband was taken away at the same time as my brother. I worked in a labor battalion, and I had to have a place to leave the child. We were fairly well known in our small town, and I went everywhere looking for a place to leave her. I had precious things which I offered to pay the Poles. 'Take this child! Take this child!' I told them. A lot of them were afraid: it was dangerous for them; the Germans would take them out and shoot them right away if they found her. She was a quiet child, hardly five, but she knew exactly what she had to do. This one Pole said to me, 'I don't even have a deep enough river near my house to throw her in if the Germans come.' That's what he said: 'I don't have a river deep enough to dump her!' So I took this child and I found a Polish woman who kept her for me. I worked during the day, and at night, when it was dark, I crawled to the woman's house. I dug a tunnel with my bare hands under the barbed-wire fence around her house. This way, I entered the house from the rear, crawling on the ground. I wanted only to see the child, to smell her, to touch her. I didn't want to speak to her, just to touch her, to smell her. I didn't want to talk to the woman, either; I had nothing to assure her with. The woman yelled at me, 'Why do you come here, you are mad! Go away, madwoman!' It was dangerous. To her I looked wild, the way I was holding this child.

"One day, when I was at work, I learned that all of us were to be shipped away—no one knew where, whether it was Treblinka or elsewhere, we had no idea. I just ran. I ran to the house where I hid the child, and I grabbed her and I took her with me. Let them shoot me. What happens to me will happen to the child. I always had the instinct never to go forward. Always go back, back. When everyone went ahead, I lagged behind. That's what I did with this crowd. I kept myself to the rear. We were put on the trucks, and we ended up in a labor camp, Skarzysko. And somehow, that day, the Germans were not paying attention. They saw this child, but they just paid no attention. At the camp, I had my niece with me, a girl of twelve, Sarale. We said that she was fifteen, so that she would have the right to work. And she did work. My little girl was lying hidden on the top bunkers during the day while I went to work. My niece, who had the night shift, stayed with her, so she wasn't alone. We were fed at the factory. Whatever I had, some bread or some soup, I brought back to my child at night.

"My niece Sarale was not strong, and she was not good at the work. It was hard work, in a munitions factory, and here she was only twelve. One day, when I came home from my shift, I see that everyone in the barracks was crying. Sarale had been taken away. And my daughter was crying. Sarale had been reported by a *capo* as someone who was unfit for work, and was sent to the place where all the sick and old people were waiting to be taken away to be killed. I ran to this place where they kept these people. And Sarale is with them! And she looked so terrible because she was crying since twelve o'clock the night before. She knew what was waiting for her. Everybody knew what it meant when they took you away with the sick and the old.

"I ran back to the barracks and I poured water into a container. There was a little pot I had, and with that pot of water I also grabbed some things. I didn't know what I was taking in my hands; I picked things up and I just ran. With what logic in mind I couldn't say now. I was possessed. I ran back to Sarale. There were Germans and some Jewish police guarding the place where they kept her, and how I begged the guards, I pleaded, 'Let me in to see her, let me give her the last kiss! Let me give her the last kiss! This is my neice Sarale.' And somehow they took pity, they let me in to see her.

"And what I did. I took the water, and washed up her face. I combed her hair and I took a blouse I brought. It was a *shmatte*, but it had a little white here and there. I took a little paper that had red in it. After I put the blouse on her, I made her red cheeks and lips with that paper, I rubbed her face and washed her. All the time, I told her,

'They won't take you, they won't; don't be afraid, I'll save you.' I just could not let her go. She looked like the dead from crying. But after the red had been rubbed on her cheeks and she was washed up and dressed in the little *shmatte* of a blouse with the white on it, she looked so beautiful! She looked so beautiful between all those dead and dying people.

"I did not dream that I could actually save her. My idea was to cheer her in her last hours, to give her some courage. Only that. How could I save her? I knew they didn't give people back once they took them for death. So I stayed with her till the Germans came and they made a real formal selection. When they were putting the people in the trucks, I said to Sarale, 'Go talk to them.' I made her go up to one of the Germans and I went with her. I said to him, 'If you take this child, then take me too.' Then Sarale began to cry, and to beg this German. He was an elderly man, this German. And he looked at her and he yelled, *'Gehe mir los!'* which means, 'Get lost!' He pushed her to show her she should get away from there. So Sarale was saved. And we began to kiss and hug each other and to cry for joy! Another woman was saved from going to death with that group that day, too, a young one. I don't know what she did; I only knew my own instinct was that there was only one thing to do: to cheer Sarale up."

Her own daughter barely escaped death several times. Once, when the camp was being evacuated, Paula had stood for a selection, the child hidden in a rucksack on her back. Another time, when camp authorities discovered the girl in the barracks and placed her with a truckload of people who were to be taken away and put to death, her mother ran to the camp nurse for help. The nurse, with whom she was on good terms, put on her uniform and carried the child off beneath the folds of her coat in a moment when the truck was unguarded.

Now the child was a woman of thirty-seven, a devoted daughter and happily married wife, if a little high-strung. When her daughter was first married, she had lived in a Queens neighborhood where all the residents had fences around their lawns, Paula recalled. But the girl had refused to do as her neighbors did: she couldn't stand seeing fences around the other houses, to say nothing of seeing one around her own, because, she told her mother, the fences turned into barbed wire if she looked at them. A Queens neighbor, noting the absence of a fence around her lawn, concluded it was for lack of money and offered kindly to pay for one himself.

The niece, Sarale, had not married, having become instead a scholar wholly absorbed in her studies of art. Between themselves, the aunt and uncle sometimes pondered the mystery of Paula's niece, who had turned out to be, as it seemed, not greatly interested in anything other than her work—not family and not the ties of the past, either.

In 1974, Menachem died after a long illness in and out of hospitals; his wife had run back and forth taking care of him all the time, with her usual boundless energy. Some weeks after his death, Paula began to find she could not get up in the morning for exhaustion, a feeling entirely new to her; she simply wanted to lie there, she reported. A friend of many years' standing, the wife of a fellow Bundist, ventured a reason.

"You have no one to save any more," the friend suggested, and Paula agreed with her.

5 | Stella

On the last day of the Braunsteiner deportation hearings, two new witnesses waited outside the courtroom for the proceedings to begin. One, a bespectacled woman, sobbed, surrounded by several modishly dressed women of about her age, the middle-to-late forties, most of them former inmates of Maidanek. The witness, a Queens housewife like Hermine Ryan herself, was one of a small number of Jewish women who had jumped from a train taking them from Maidanek to the gas chambers of Treblinka. The inmates dispatched on that train were among the few survivors of "Harvest Day," so called by the Germans, the day of November 3, 1943, on which an estimated 18,500 Jewish prisoners of Maidanek were driven into a trench on field five, the women's camp, and massacred. Since Hermine Braunsteiner had claimed during the hearings that she had not been in Maidanek in November, 1943, the witness Henrika Mitron had come to give eye-witness testimony that the Vice-Kommandant had in fact been on field five at the time of the mass extermination.

The other witness, a merry-eyed blond woman, hovered nearby, waiting, she said, in the hope that she would encounter Hermine Ryan entering the courtroom. In this she had been disappointed: Mrs. Ryan, her husband, and her attorney had either come very early or somehow got by the door without being seen, and now they sat by themselves, waving off everyone who came near. The blond witness, whose name was Stella, explained that she waited for Mrs. Ryan because she wanted the chance to walk up close to her and say something to her that she would hear. What it was she would say when the moment came, she did not know in advance; and she was not concerned about it.

"Something would come to me," she said with assurance when asked what it was she would want to say.

Clearly torn between her desire to stay and talk with the other women, and her desire to keep an eye on Mrs. Ryan and the inside of the courtroom, she divided her attention between them. Now she turned to the group in the hall and exchanged whispers with someone, now she turned to canvass the small entryway to the courtroom, now she returned to murmur a word to the woman who wept; now, while she murmured, she flicked a watchful eye toward the door.

Like the others who waited in the hall, she came of a Polish Jewish family. But, unlike them, she herself might, with her light hair and fair skin, easily have passed for a non-Jewish Pole, even among those Poles who had shown, during the war, that they were experts at detecting the Jews among them. It was true that her fluent Polish and her non-Jewish looks had helped to save her more than once. Nevertheless, it was as Jews that she and her sisters had been brought to Maidanek and as a Jew that she had encountered Hermine Braunsteiner there. In general outline, her experiences during that period were like that of the other witnesses already seated inside: those who had also known Hermine Braunsteiner thirty years earlier, who now stared across the room at her, who sat up very straight in their chairs, who sometimes stood up and turned their faces toward her, so that she might see them if she looked.

A tall black-haired woman, who never took her eyes off Hermine Ryan, said, "I want her to look at me once." But Mrs. Ryan looked nowhere except to the right of her, where there was a wall, and to the front of her, where her husband and her attorney stood talking in hushed voices.

"She looks very little changed," a witness said.

"The same legs."

The tall black-haired woman kept her eyes on Mrs. Ryan's back and said nothing. The time was long since past when the session should have begun, an irregularity of the sort to which all the participants in the Braunsteiner case had become accustomed; and when it did begin, it was only to announce that the hearings would not continue. The West German government had, the day before, requested Hermine Braunsteiner Ryan's extradition, an event that effectively brought the Immigration Service's deportation hearings to an end.

The tall black-haired woman inside the courtroom, the blond fair-skinned one who waited outside, the witness who wept in the hall, and those who surrounded her all had much in common beside the experience of the concentration camp. They had all been born in comfortable, if not wealthy, circumstances. They were young when they were taken to the concentration camps, none of them more than seventeen, and they had had the attractiveness and the resilience of youth, a resilience that more than anything had helped to save them.

The difference between themselves and Braunsteiner, which they had been strongly conscious of some thirty years earlier when they were prisoners and Braunsteiner was Vice-Kommandant, was not less a part of their consciousness now. It was well known to them that the SS women whom the Nazis put in charge of the camps had been drawn from the lowest class of Germans, that many of them had been released from prisons for this work. "Prostitutes," the SS guards routinely called the girls who were their prisoners, a fact that was not without its irony, inasmuch as there was a fair number among the guards who had themselves served time in German prisons for prostitution. To those who confronted her in the hearing room, the details of Hermine Braunsteiner's life before she became Vice-Kommandant of the camp were neither known nor necessary. They knew what the guards were, and they knew what she was. They probed and measured her with their eyes; they looked from her to her husband. One wondered aloud what sort of man would want such a woman for a wife.

"Someone who couldn't get any better," another answered. "Someone just like her."

They knew that they were different from all Braunsteiner was now and had ever been. It showed in their bearing, in the unashamed and self-possessed look they had about them, in their clothes—a sense of difference that neither the concentration camps nor their former servitude had erased. Unlike Braunsteiner, they were women who knew the possibilities of glamour in themselves, and had always known it; their groomed, lustrous, piled hair told it as much as anything. On this occasion, their expressions were cold-eyed, stricken, or grave, but these things did not hide the high consciousness on their faces that they were women, desirable women, that they had been admired and loved in their lives, that if they were not the most beautiful and desirable women in the world, they were nevertheless beautiful and desirable enough to satisfy themselves.

They had been brought up to think well of themselves. Daughters of good families, they had spent the formative years of their lives securely. Their parents were strictly orthodox Jews or moderately secular ones. Whichever it was, their children grew up certain that they belonged to the society around them, that they met its social and ethical standards, and that by those standards they and their families would in no way be found wanting. The time came that they were abased and degraded. They had survived it, and though they had lost everything, though their experience had left them innocent of no evil, they did not lose the core of their early lives, which had taught them that they were worthy.

The prospective witnesses who appeared in the hearing room that day were known to one another. They were, with the exception of one of them, who lived in Connecticut, part of the large community of survivors who lived in the Kew Gardens—Forest Hills area of Queens. The detached or semi-detached private houses in those pleasant neighborhoods were a far cry from the apartments in Coney Island or the Bronx where most of them had begun their lives in America. They had worked their way slowly over the past twenty-five years, moving as their economic state let them to better apartments, safer neighborhoods, until they were able to afford a house in Kew Gardens.

Stella, the blond woman who waited for a chance to say something to Mrs. Ryan, lived with her husband and their two children in one of those pleasant, quiet neighborhoods in Kew Gardens. She was, to all appearances, the most girlish of the witnesses who appeared at the Immigration Service hearings that day, though she was roughly the same age—in her mid-forties. Even as she stalked the halls in the anxious atmosphere outside the hearing room, keeping a watchful eye on Braunsteiner and her party, it could be seen that she was one of those people who would never bring the proper face to dark occasions. Her feelings about Hermine Braunsteiner were colder and harder than those of anyone present; yet as she pursued her quarry with her eyes and waited, her natural disposition asserted itself and she looked—there was no other word for it—sunny. She might have been waiting for a friend to come and carry her off to a picnic, so amiable did she appear, so blue and doll-like were those eyes fixed watchfully on the hearing-room door, and so empty of grimness. When once or twice she smiled at someone she knew, the smile was that of a hostess for a guest of honor, a face-wreathing flash of light that made anyone who saw it feel how preposterous was the idea of her connection with the matters that were to go on in the hearing room that day.

All the same, she belonged there, and no one was more aware of it than she. The moment Braunsteiner's picture appeared in the *New York Times*, Stella said, she had run to the phone to call a friend, a girl she knew in Maidanek.

"Remember our *Aufsehrin*, Hermina?" she had asked the friend.

"Who could forget her?"

"And do you have the *Times* today? Go look at it."

The friend returned to the phone. "You are damned right. It's her—you are damned right."

It was all, apparently, that the friend was able to say for some time.

"Not only that; she's living right here," her caller pointed out.

That night she had not fallen asleep at all, but had lain wide awake figuring out what she should do, and thinking about Maidanek. She did not have to face a traumatic rush of memory, as some others might have when something made a buried aspect of the past suddenly rear up at them in the midst of their postwar lives. She was used to thinking about Maidanek and the other places she had been, used to talking with her friends who had been there with her. Each had obtained certain kinds of information about life and people from her experience. One had learned, and she was deeply interested in the fact, that if you asked a person to kill you, he would never do it; that asking for death robbed people of the will to kill you—people who otherwise could have killed you with no trouble at all. Another had learned, and it was an observation every one of them heartily agreed with, that if you had to ask an enemy for mercy, it was better that the enemy should be a man than a woman, because there was no chance at all with a woman; the women they had known as captors had invariably been crueler than the men.

For years they had pieced together the details of the past; what one forgot, another remembered. The number of friends who had survived with her was small, but they were close; and when they talked about the time in the camps, it was not entirely horror that drew them back, but also the memory of their youth, a part of which was recalled to them vividly in the shared memories of the camps.

The prospective witness who had stood weeping in the hall recalled, some time later, that it was ridiculous to believe that none of them had ever made a joke or laughed in the death camp. They had made jokes about their appearance, about their shorn heads, which made them look like plucked chickens; or they told one another, laughing, "Tomorrow you'll be soap." They did these things, as they sang songs, to keep their nerve up, and they were able to do them, she observed, only because they were young.

One day the group from Maidanek gathered in a kitchen in Queens. The purpose of the meeting was to settle a dispute over the ingredients of a soup the Germans had given them on occasion. Once in a while, in the camp, they had received a mysterious soup all of them remembered. Because it had a slightly sweetish taste—the reason they remembered it all these years—they had devoured it, and had looked on the days that soup was distributed almost as holidays.

Each of the women had her own ideas about what might have gone into it. The one thing all of them remembered was that there had been a few grains of rice floating around on top; they supposed, too, there must have been some sugar in it. But by the end of the afternoon, after following all their notions, after stirring, throwing different things in, and trying new mixtures, they had collectively failed to achieve the taste of the concentration camp soup. During their captivity, food, only food, had obsessed them. Starved, living on a diet of ersatz coffee and bread twice a day, or water and potato peelings with worms floating around (which they ate with the rest because of the protein), they talked and dreamed food. They planned elaborate menus; they listened to fantastic recipes full of rich ingredients, and even invented their own, though some of them had never cooked anything in their lives. Now, years later, the long hold of that obsession took another turn, and in the midst of plenty they tried to recreate the one food that, in those days, had been the object of their greatest desire: the soup with the sweetish taste.

It had to be something chemical, they concluded after they had given up, because they had never tasted anything remotely like that sweetish taste after they left the camp. Stella, who had been one of the organizers of the experiment, was of that opinion herself.

It took some knowing her to see that there was sometimes calculation in the great blue eyes she turned to the world. All the same, she showed less of it than was usual in women of conspicuous good looks, looks into which there had gone a certain amount of work and planning. She had a strong bent toward the flirtatious, and just as strong a bent toward straightforwardness, tendencies that did not, in her, rule one another out. It was the first that accounted for the inviting smile that hovered about her eyes and mouth, the frequent faint flutterings of lashes, and the many confidingly uttered "I don't have to tell you why"s that punctuated her conversation. The second accounted for the conversation itself, in which there was usually no artifice, except as circumstances required it, and then it was an artifice of such a frank sort that it did not seem to differ very much from straightforwardness.

Her lips, full almost to thickness, were always slightly parted; it was the mouth of a voluptuous child, emphasized by a slight gap between two of an otherwise perfect row of small white teeth. From that mouth, much to her annoyance, there issued a heavily accented English, a condition common to most of her friends; for, unlike the survivors who lived in places in America where few spoke their language, these lived in a neighborhood, and in a city, where there were plenty of others like themselves. Since necessity had not decreed it, they continued to use Polish; consequently, though their English might be precise and idiomatic enough, their heavy accents had never left them, while others had lost them almost entirely.

On the street where she lived in Kew Gardens there were nine houses together, and no less than eight of them were owned by Polish Jews who had survived the war and the camps. Around the corner stood six more houses similarly inhabited by families of survivors. Cohesive Jewish neighborhoods are, of course, no rarity in New York, but in the Bronx, Brooklyn, or, formerly, the lower East Side of New York, such cohesiveness was based simply on the propensity of Jews of every variety to make their homes where other Jews lived. In Williamsburg and Crown Heights, Brooklyn, Chasidic and other orthodox Jews lived in tight neighborhoods to protect a religious way of life. But in Kew Gardens, parts of Forest Hills, Bayside, and the upper West Side of Manhattan, small Jewish communities had been formed entirely on the basis of the fact that its members had once shared a common fate.

The builder of the houses on her street was a Polish Jew himself, who had come to America after the war. In addition to the houses in Kew Gardens, he had built in Bayside twenty more blocks whose houses were also largely inhabited by Polish Jewish survivors. In part, this had come about because these survivors had reasoned, when they were ready to buy houses, that they were best off dealing with one like themselves, particularly if there was trouble about repairs or some other problem regarding the house. There still lingered in them, years after 1949 and 1950, when they had arrived, something of the sense they had had then: that the connection between American Jews and themselves was only slightly less remote than the connection between themselves and American Gentiles. But beyond the practical reasons, there was another, perhaps more important factor dictating their choice: that in buying a house from such a builder, they stood an excellent chance of living next door to, or across the street from, people who had shared their experience, people who could not quite be strangers to them, though they had never laid eyes on them before—neighbors the crucial facts of whose lives they knew before they were even introduced to them.

Though Stella lived in such an enclave, she was of two minds about it. On the one hand, there were certain comforts to be derived from the arrangements. On the other, they spoke Polish too much, a fact she disapproved of, though she did it herself; and they all stuck to one another too much. Her heavy accent made her unhappy, but that was not the main reason she disapproved of the way her circle of friends clung to one another and to their old language.

She was devoted to America, a feeling that had grown deep and prideful over the years. The devotion was one that all her friends shared without exception, and there was irony in the fact that in this, too, they felt they had only each other for understanding. As far as they could see, Americans did not have such feelings, or if they did they were not displayed. It was their dilemma that they had come upon a time when hatred of America seemed to be in the air—particularly on the college campuses—if not in the minds of most Americans; when a reference to American democracy brought a glaze to the eyes of their children's friends, if not to the eyes of the children themselves, or, at best, a stare of disbelief. The worst they had not yet seen, perhaps, but the upheavals of the late 1960s with the flag-burnings and rhetoric had given them a strong hint of it. They had seen how not just the young but whole universities, including their presidents—to say nothing of faculty members, teachers obedient to the wisdom of those they taught—had, under the flags of the anti-war, anti-racism movements, displayed their moral outrage on these issues by showering a generalized contempt on American society and its institutions, a contempt that became, at its peak, quite fashionable even among Americans who normally concerned themselves little with issues of war or racism. American democracy was a lie, the survivors had heard from other American citizens, and American society was a destroyer not only of individuals and freedom but of nature itself; one had only to look at America's polluted rivers and her air to see what a rapacious system had wrought. As for the government, its designs and operations were in no significant way different from those of a Fascist state.

Like most survivors, Stella and her circle of friends were astounded by these views. That they should hear America called a Fascist state! America! Of all countries! Yet they had heard it quite often in the 1960s; they continued to hear it in the seventies, and invariably, when they listened to this description of America, they became enraged. Nor could the Vietnam War change their feelings, though the news of the My Lai massacres tormented them, and the photographs of the victims—old peasants and children—burned their way into the survivors' hearts; the meaning of this news and these photographs could not be avoided.

"How sad. How bitter that the sons of our liberators should now be the ones to do something like this," one Belsen survivor said of My Lai. For many days after the story became known, the prospect of watching the news on television sent her from her living room in despair, just as, a moment later, the news drew her in again. She could not watch the film clips, and neither could she turn her back on them; for whatever their political opinions, survivors were always to be one in this: they were compelled to know the news of atrocity, and to believe it. To turn away from these things in order to avoid disturbing themselves was in their view a luxury not permitted, especially to them. It was too close in their minds, some of them declared bitterly, to the indifference that had prevailed in the world while they and their families were being herded away to be killed. Indeed, while it could hardly be said that the holocaust experience had made the survivors more virtuous or humane than other men, and it was likely true that the darker capacities of some who survived had been hardened and enlarged by their experience, still a great many of them were incapable of certain kinds of unconcern characteristic of other people: the ordinary man's indifference to the tragedy of those far away, for example. They could never quite attain to the onlooker's mentality, and they tended to respond viscerally to that most difficult of things to respond to: tragedy in the mass—Biafra and Bangladesh, massacre and famine. It was not a choice of good over evil in the survivors that made them thus incapable of indifference; it was often not a choice at all, but a condition: whether they wished it or not, they would see what they might have wished not to see, and feel what it was most comfortable not to feel.

But, they pointed out, My Lai had been uncovered and punished, however imperfectly, and America had shown its shame over it. Watergate had, in a lesser way, disturbed them, though to some the whole affair wound up only proving to them, as it had to a fair section of the American public, the power of a democracy and its free press.

But to some, Watergate represented a thing that came too close to certain of their memories for comfort. "Haldeman and Ehrlichman, Ehrlichman and Haldeman—these were exactly the same types in Germany, and they felt exactly the same way—that their leader's power must be preserved at any price."

"Children," others said of the Watergate stars, and waved Haldeman and Ehrlichman and all their aides away. "This is all child's play, these spies. The Germans were experts."

Nevertheless, while some thought it was child's play and others shuddered, Watergate, with its band of zealots and its spy machinery, was no minor event to them. The zealots had put loyalty to party and to their chief above the law, above any other consideration; to some survivors, these were familiar—and dangerous—portents of a future they had seen before. Others felt, instead, that the government they took pride in had been sullied, and this, too, was no minor event to them.

Still, none of these issues had the power to change their view of America. America had its problems, they conceded with pursed lips, and not the least of those problems was her citizens, who were so spoiled and indifferent to her.

"Come here," Stella summoned her daughter once. "Tell me what you did in school for Memorial Day celebration." A picnic, the daughter replied; the teachers had taken them to a park for games and sandwiches.

"A picnic," her mother sniffed, with the satisfied air of one whose worst suspicions had been borne out.

That was not the only thing. She herself had seen the local Memorial Day parade. "Who was marching in this parade? Three people: one man with crutches, one old woman who could hardly stand up was dragging herself along, and one person from the Salvation Army."

It was a disgrace, really, when you thought about it, because one thing about Poland, rain or shine, everybody had come out to show respect for the patriotic holidays. And what was Poland to deserve such treatment? Smart Poland had been, though, and right to make its people care in that way. And what there was to care about in Poland you could imagine; but it was the right attitude.

"Only to knock America," Henrika, the other prospective witness at Hermine Braunsteiner's deportation hearings, said bitterly another time. "To spit on America. To call her such things: Fascistic, repressive—whatever they say. The blood runs up in my face when I hear these words." And her hand flew to her face to contain the blood there now when she thought of the words. What did those who spit on America know about these things? About Fascism or repression?

She did not say there was nothing to criticize in America —not at all. She herself had not cared for it so much the first year, for other reasons. Brooklyn had been dingy and disappointing, and the people she met there so narrow and uncomprehending of the things that went on in the world.

But these things that were so difficult for her at first had nothing to do with the way of life she perceived here. Not once to have to be afraid or to account to anyone for what you read; to say what you like; not even to have to go to a police station to register when you move to a new place, or to carry an identity card. Had she realized in advance that there was actually such liberty here, greater than any they had dreamed of, had the habits and fears of Europe not still been with her, she certainly would never have chosen to give her children, born here shortly after she arrived, the Gentile first names she had given them. She would dearly have loved to give them Old Testament names. Her own first name, Henrika, had been given her by her parents because it did not seem particularly Jewish—not that it had helped. Even in her childhood, the teacher in the Polish school she attended had pointedly told her that Henrika could not be her real first name, and had asked her every day, "What is your real first name?" Fortunate she was that though in a number of ways her son with his assimilated name had grown up like any American youth and had followed all the current fashions with his hair and his music, he had not become political, so that she did not have to hear from him at least all the talk about "Fascistic" America one heard from the others, the self-satisfied ignorant talk that made her blood boil.

Stella, whose blood did not show quite so much when it boiled, always concluded grandly when this subject of America-haters came up, "It's a pity," a phrase of many uses, one that she had a talent for employing in the particular way which conveys that the speaker intends no charity whatever toward the object of pity. It was her way to look on the bright side. She was not one to brood long over anything either. What was the use of it? So much had happened to brood over; to begin the job would leave no room for living and enjoying the life she had.

It was true she was sad sometimes, and worried, most often about the safety of Israel; for her, when the State of Israel was threatened, everything in life was threatened, and this response was true of her friends as well. When Israel was at war, when things went badly, as they did in

October, 1973, when the enemies' promises of annihilation would seem to be about to come true, she hung by the radio and could not eat or sleep. Jumpy and despondent, she would try to make phone calls to friends in Israel, though she usually failed to get through on the phone lines to the Middle East, which were always jammed in such times. It happened that in the midst of such a crisis she would receive letters from friends in Israel, survivors from the camps. Sometimes the letters promised that Israel would win in the end, they had no doubt of it; they said that morale was high, despite everything, and they implored their friends in America to keep their own morale high. When she received such a letter, she breathed easier. Other times, particularly when the casualty lists were being published, and the number of dead had taken its toll of almost every family, the letters were depressed, as all Israel was, and she in turn was as depressed as any Israeli.

Otherwise, she seldom became depressed about anything. If she found that she was feeling sad too long about something, she would soon find a way to make herself stop. At such times she would reflect on her life, and how she had come through everything. What was it all for? Was she alive so that she could make herself miserable over some little thing or other? She knew what was and was not important, and in her opinion the things that made most people depressed were not worth thinking about, really. Perhaps other people had room in their lives to be thinking always about little things; she did not. Perhaps their lives were richer for it, perhaps little things were as important as great ones, but she could not think so. She did not believe it.

People liked her and she accepted it as natural that they should. There had been, of course, in her circle of friends those who took offense at things she had said or done, but they were few, and she liked to think she paid no attention to them. Injured feelings, imagined insults—it was precisely these unimportant things people were forever thinking about. She seldom quarreled with anyone, though she listened at some length to the quarrels of others, and was interested in the details. Once, one of her friends had made it clear that she was angry with her. Jealousy was probably at the root of the anger, Stella reasoned. The friend, who had been given charge of a certain guest list, had failed to submit Stella's name, with the result that she did not get to attend an event that she was supposed to, and that she wanted to attend. There were other signs of hostility as well. Of the friend's behavior, Stella remarked only, "It's a pity," in her usual way. If one person took a dislike to her, it could not be helped. If one person was of a jealous disposition, ther was nothing to be done. There were other friends. It was, again, one of those things certainly not important enough to dwell on.

The facts of her life were these, if she wanted to dwell on them. She had been born in Warsaw, of fairly well-to-do parents, the owners of several shoe stores and a tannery. When she was sixteen, the Germans sent her, along with her two older sisters and their father, to the Maidanek camp in Lublin; her mother several months earlier had been deported to Treblinka. It was in Maidanek, in the women's camp, that she had met Hermaine Braunsteiner. One day in Maidanek, she was caught trying to throw a piece of bread to her father in the men's camp, with the result that she was brought before Hermine Braunsteiner. Braunsteiner had ordered twenty-five lashes, and watched while the guard administered them with a bullwhip. As a result of the whipping, she was unable to work, and her name had been automatically put on the list of those destined for the gas chamber. After the whipping, she had been carried back to the barracks, bleeding and semiconscious, unable to stand for two days much less to report for work. But her older sister Rutka, who was among those just then being sent out of Maidanek to work at Skarzysko, a labor camp, contrived to change places with her. The two hundred women selected for work at Skarzysko first passed a body check to determine that they were fit and healthy, and then they received clean uniforms, with different markings from those worn by the Maidanek inmates. In some way—Stella never learned how—after passing the body check, Rutka had exchanged numbers and clothes with her. With the help of other women in the barracks, she pushed Stella, still stupefied, into the center of the crowd so that she would not be noticed, and sent her off with the group leaving for Skarzysko.

There Jewish inmate doctors were able to salve her wounds, and it was not many days before she was up and around, able to work, though she was still in great pain. About ten days after she arrived, she learned the outcome of her sister's plan to save her. Rutka, being strong and healthy, believed that she could safely take her younger sister's name and number; that when the day came that her sister's name was called, as it was clear it would be, and she was summoned to go with those selected for the gas chamber, she would be able to show herself as she was—fit and healthy and capable of hard work—to convince the SS that her death selection was an error. Rutka knew the risk and took it, friends later reported to Stella. The week after Stella had left Maidanek and her name was called as expected, Rutka took her place in line among those selected for death. But neither her healthy appearance nor her arguments of fitness persuaded the SS that her selection was a mistake. She was marched off with the others, to the gas chamber and death.

Stella remained in the labor camp for a year. Skarzysko, in 1944, was a hotbed of rumor. With the Russians coming nearer every day, word circulated that either the Germans planned to take all the inmates to Germany to work or they planned to kill them.

The camp had no crematorium or gas chamber, but a small forest nearby was used as an execution place. As the Russian guns came nearer, the Germans began to bury some of the bodies that were exposed in the forest. The guards were becoming nervous, and the more nervous they became the more the rumors flew among the inmates. One night, the camp Kommandant assembled them and told them that the next day they were to be evacuated to Germany. Each person would get two days' food, the length of time it would take them to get to Germany. In Germany they would be housed and fed in comfortable quarters, he promised, and given jobs that were not very hard. Few of the inmates believed him. Despite the curfew, they ran about from one barracks to another, discussing what the Germans really intended, whether they would dare to kill them all with the Russians coming so near, or whether they would do so just because of that fact.

Late that night, she learned that the inhabitants of the White House, as the white-painted barracks of the *capos* was called, had escaped. If the *capos* had run, she reasoned, it was because of what was going to happen the next day; they usually had excellent information. Her friends among the inmates were of the same opinion; but as night came on they began to shout to one another, "Quiet, quiet!" If they didn't have a few hours' sleep, they said, they would not be able to move in the morning.

She could not sleep for trying to figure out how the White House inhabitants had got out, and why. Then, in the midst of her figuring, she quietly got up and made her way to the outhouse at the end of the camp. There, behind the outhouse, she saw how the barbed wire had been stretched, and that this was how the others had escaped. The barbed wire of this camp was not electrified; there were two fences, six feet apart, between which the guard patrolled the camp perimeters.

A moment later—without knowing in advance what she meant to do—she walked from the outhouse and plunged through the stretched barbed wire to the other side.

Hearing the voices of the guards as they made their rounds, she ran straight into the forest. There, almost at once, she stumbled over the bodies of the *capos* who had made their "escape" from the White House. Years later, after the war had ended, she learned that the White House inhabitants, including the chief *capo*, had paid a German to get them out of the camp, and that the German had taken the money and shot them all as soon as they entered the forest. One of them, called Ulrich, was still alive when she fell over him, a young man her own age who lay gasping on the ground. At the same time, she could hear the voices of the Germans, now there with her in the forest. Unable to tell the direction of the voices and thus decide on which way she could safely run, she dropped down on the ground next to Ulrich and pretended to be dead. When the Germans came, they kicked the bodies. Lying under her arm, Ulrich made no sound. A German guard pronounced them dead and walked off.

She lay there a long time, until she heard shouts and screaming from the camp and the noise of the trucks, which told her that the evacuation of inmates had begun. Ulrich was dead; she had felt his body shudder underneath her as he died. One hand and the side of her face were covered with Ulrich's blood. She wiped the blood with the underside of her skirt. Then she smeared spittle on her face and pressed it to the ground to wash with the moisture of the morning dew. In vain she searched the floor of the forest for leaves to clean the blood off with, but she was in a forest where there were only pine needles.

Having wiped her cheek as clean as she could, she walked in the forest until she could see that she was close to a highway of some sort. On the highway she met two small girls, who showed her the way to a nearby railway station. In the railway station lavatory she found a small cracked mirror, which nevertheless showed her clearly enough that her face was still smeared with blood and that her earlier washing had only lightened it and spread it all over her face. After cleaning her face and combing her hair with her fingers, she entered a train, which had just pulled into the station, and made straight for the lavatory. From time to time, people who wanted to use the toilet banged on the door, and then went away grumbling when it did not open; she had locked herself in, so that the conductor could not ask her for a ticket. But after a while—she had no memory, later, of how long—when she heard the train slowing down for its next stop, she knew she could no longer stand to be locked up there, whatever else might happen. No one challenged her when she opened the door. A man looked briefly at her as he paused in wrestling with a suitcase to let her by. Then she was out of the train. It was dark, although the station was well lit and she was able to read clearly a sign that said Czestochowa.

As others found who had escaped, she was to discover that impulse and improvisation alone would carry one far, so long as the danger was great. Any deception was feasible and any loneliness bearable when necessity demanded; it was when the external dangers seemed to lessen that the inner ones began to make their claim. In Czestochowa, she was, without knowing it, still at the beginning of the tangled set of circumstances that began with her escape and would not end for many months—circumstances that became more complicated and dangerous at each stage, right up to the end. But already, in Czestochowa, she had begun to feel less afraid.

At the station she saw a nun. "I have a problem, Sister," she whispered to the nun.

"Tell Jesus your problem; he will help you," the nun told her.

"Jesus cannot help me in this," she replied. Then she pointed to a trainload of Polish civilians that had arrived in the station. It was just at the end of the abortive Polish insurrection of 1944, when the Germans were arresting Poles and transporting them to concentration camps. She told the nun that she had escaped from the train and was afraid of going to the German concentration camp.

The nun took her by the hand and brought her to a cloister, where she was fed and clothed and shown a place to sleep. Then, in the morning, she was brought before the Mother Superior and questioned about the insurrection in Warsaw and what she had seen there.

She was able to draw on her memory of an earlier uprising she had witnessed, the April, 1943, revolt against the Germans by the Jews of the Warsaw ghetto. She told the Mother Superior about the burning buildings and the people jumping from them, how the Germans had flushed the Polish fighters from their bunkers and shot them down. The Mother Superior told Stella that her convent had sheltered other Polish girls like herself, that she would be able to stay and work for her keep without fear. She was given a rosary and sent to prayers with the sisters and the other girls who had found shelter there. Remembering bits of the Hail Mary, which she had sometimes heard the family's Gentile maid recite, Stella moved her lips silently and said morning prayers without anyone noticing that she barely knew the words. Afterward she found a prayer book and memorized the Hail Mary. In the next few days, she fell into the convent routine, which consisted of hard work in the kitchen run by the nuns, and frequent prayer, which was no problem once she knew the words.

She had begun to feel safe, and the effects of that feeling showed themselves at once in the overwhelming urge she then had to confess to the Mother Superior and the others that she was a Jew and not one of them. The need to tell this particular truth was to arise each time she found herself in sheltering hands. The strength of the need was great, coming as it did from the urgent wish to end her isolation, from a craving to be comforted by those who had comfort to give: the ultimate comfort they could give her being that, though they knew the worst—that she was a Jew—they would still keep her in safety. It was a test of herself, and of the friendships she formed with the people who sheltered her, albeit while she was disguised as a Gentile. It was in part, too, a search, and she was not alone of her kind in making it, an effort to uncover some final proof in refutation of what the Nazis had said and experience had shown must certainly be true, which was that everyone, not only the Germans, wanted the Jews dead. Later, she learned to fight the need to share her secret; but in the convent at Czestochowa she had given in to it. She had been moved to do so by an especially beautiful painting of the Virgin Mary that hung in the chapel. Staring at it, she was able to talk herself into believing that the soft smile of Mary was really intended for her, that it was meant as a sign of reassurance, and willingly she took the promise of the Virgin's smile to heart. She decided to tell the priest she was a Jew during confession. As soon as she made the decision, she felt enormous relief, as though the weight of a stone had been lifted from her. The confession she had to make was not a little thing, she had first whispered to the priest.

"Jesus can hear anything, my child," the priest told her.

She did not know if Jesus could hear this, she said.

"Whatever it is, it is between you and me and God," the priest assured her.

"I am a Jew, Father," she then confessed quickly. She explained how she had run away from the camp, and gone to the nun at the station. When she finished, the priest told her in a kind way not to worry, that he would speak to the Mother Superior and tell her about it. In the meantime, she did not need to continue praying with the others.

Later, the Mother Superior summoned her, and, looking quite stern and unlike the Virgin Mary in the painting, told her that she might stay only until she found another place, but that she should bear in mind that they were short of food in the convent and that by staying there she was putting others in great danger.

The next day she left the convent. After a while, she made her way to another city, Cracow, and another shelter. This time she found employment with a German doctor and his wife. So kindly a couple were they that the doctor, who was attached to a German military hospital, came to her boarding house to take care of her when she fell ill, and his wife worried over her as any mother would. Again she felt the impulse to tell these people—who were as humane and loving as any she had ever met—that she was a Jew, but she could not do it, quite. After the war, she tried to trace the couple in Germany and failed. Thirty years after her escape, she still wondered about what might have happened had she told them, and was almost certain now that they would have accepted the truth, she had such a clear memory of their kindness. But at the time she said nothing because the doctor and his wife were, after all, Germans. Then, too, she bore in mind that once, feeling secure while walking about the city of Cracow with the excellent pass the doctor had provided her, she had almost been arrested for throwing food to some emaciated prisoners marching by her under German guard. The guards turned her over to the police, who held her for several hours until the doctor came to identify her. When the doctor had extricated her from this trouble, he asked her why she had done it.

"I felt sorry for the people, Doctor," she told him, adding untruthfully that she did not know who the people were. Patiently, he explained that she must not go near them again, because the prisoners were Jews. Still, despite this, she knew him well enough to believe that she might have told him she was a Jew, and that he could probably never have brought himself to betray her—not her. Had she found him after the war as she wanted, she would have told him the truth and been able to judge for herself what he would have done.

After this episode, there began a final series of mishaps that took her from Poland deeper and deeper into Germany.

This turn of events began when, as seemed ever to be so then, the Russians were advancing; with the hospital and its wounded having to be evacuated, the doctor got her, along with himself and his wife, on a German troop train, which took them to Dresden just at the time the British were bombing that city into an inferno. When the train arrived at the station, she slipped away from the doctor, for protective as he was, he would, she knew, only take her farther into Germany. Alone in Dresden, she pretended to have been driven mad by the bombing, and sat in a park under some trees while everyone else was in shelters and the British planes raked the city methodically, block by block. She saw that the planes were flying very low, that they knew where their bombs were going, and that they were not aiming at parks and trees. In any event, if she had to die, it would at least not be underground with Germans, but under trees in the open air.

Afterward she wandered through Dresden's ruins, passing herself off as a German, feeding herself at the emergency kitchens. In a matter of two days, however, she found that she could no longer wander alone. For that reason she attached herself to a line of Polish prisoners who had been marched past her near the outskirts of the city. So long as she did not go as a Jew, she did not greatly fear captivity.

Finally, in Leipzig, she had ended up in the hands of American troops. She and two hundred or so Polish prisoners had been locked into an underground bunker, when the Americans had broken in. One of them picked her up and carried her out, shouting something at the top of his lungs.

"*Schnell, schnell*, out!" the soldiers yelled, pushing and dragging everyone, and a moment later, after they were outside, there had been a terrific blast, which threw her and the soldier carrying her to the ground. After locking the prisoners in the bunker, the Germans had set time bombs to blow them up; virtually at the last minute, the Americans had learned of it, and had rushed the bunker to get them out.

The American who had picked her up and carried her had himself rushed away, after setting her on her feet. A little while later, he found her again, and gave her a loaf of bread. Ravenous, she stuffed her mouth with the bread and as she did so, there was a click behind her. She turned, and saw that an American was taking a picture of her just at the moment she stuffed the bread into her mouth. What did she care? Nothing at all. How like a monkey in a zoo she looked to them, and she knew it, and it did not matter to her at all. The American looked like a god. What more could you want of the Almighty Himself if he had come? He carried her in his arms, he gave her bread; he brought the war to an end.

Afterward she jumped on the tanks with some of the other girls, and rode with the Americans to Leipzig. And there in Leipzig she saw the sight that was to bring her joy for hours. The Germans had hung white flags everywhere, on all the doors and windows of the city. The next morning, as she walked about the streets, she was to burst into tears looking at those same flags, because now the catastrophe was all over, for certain, but only she was left alive of the whole family; just then, however, riding into Leipzig, she thought of no such thing. The Americans had directed them to go into any of the houses and help themselves to food and clothing. They were not to worry, they would be nearby, the G.I.s assured them in broken German; later on, someone would come and check, to see that they were all right.

The first house they entered was empty of people. Whoever had lived there had left everything—all the clothes in the closets, food in the pantry. It was a proper house, the first that some of them had seen the inside of in years, with its overstuffed chairs, its tables, pictures, and beds. She and the other girls ran to the pantry, opened everything they found, and ate it. Beans, sugar, cheese, butter—they mixed it all together on their plates and ate, and when they finished, the formerly neat kitchen looked as though banquets had been held there for several nights, with no one bothering to clean up after any of them. Afterward they ripped off the uniforms they wore, with the big "P" on the back, and rummaged in the closets to find skirts and dresses for themselves. Indifferent to the fact that none of the clothes they found fit them, they put them on. Then someone came up with currant wine, which was stored in the cellar, and Stella herself found some stuff made of fermented blueberries. For the first time in her life, she drank and was drunk, so that she ended the first day of freedom retching and throwing her insides up.

In the next days, they talked about taking revenge, and they heard talk of it. From whom could you take revenge? On the streets of Leipzig there were only old people to be seen. For a short time the Americans had quartered her in the house of an elderly woman. Once, she had let the woman see the lash marks on her back after the woman began, shyly, to ask questions about her: how she came to be there in Leipzig and what had happened to bring a young girl so far from home? After seeing her back, the old woman had run weeping from the house, and returned with several of the neighbors, elderly women also. The neighbors had had to see the lash marks, too.

"See—this is what our brothers have done?" the old woman asked them.

And this was what there was to take revenge on in Leipzig—crying old people, who were like her own grandparents.

It was justice, not revenge, she had always wanted. Now it was the same thing, she maintained, where Braunsteiner was concerned. So she had told her husband, too, when she sat with him and their children in the house in Kew Gardens and explained why she would have to go and testify. He could not have stopped her if he wanted to; but, as usual, he wanted her to do whatever she liked. He was a cheerful man, given to smiling fondly when he spoke of his wife in her absence, as though recalling all the things about her that pleased him, even though he might only be saying that he had to go and pick her up at the dentist, or that she was busy at home. They had met just after the war had ended, when he was an officer in the Polish Army. He had found her standing on a street, one bitter cold day, trying to sell some linens and sheets for her German landlady. He was a Jew, he had told her after inviting her for coffee—a fact that she was certain of, anyway, before he told her—and was, like her, the only one left of his family. Not three days later, he proposed, which was hasty even for the way marriages were made in those days of chaos and of so many familyless people just after the war; and three weeks later, after he had received official permission from his superiors in the army, they were married.

The ceremony was performed by a rabbi who arrived for the occasion half dead, because the groom, who had found him in Breslau, a great many miles away, had no alternative but to pack him onto the back of his motorcycle and ride with him at top speed for almost a day in order to get him to the wedding. For her wedding night the bride had nothing at all appropriate to wear, a condition her German landlady undertook to right by sitting up the night before sewing her a pair of pajamas out of a set of green silk striped curtains she happened to have in her parlor. As a final festive touch, the landlady had trimmed the low-cut pajama bosom with the green flowered border that until then had adorned the curtain tops. The wedding party itself —to which several hundred Polish Army comrades of the groom came bearing gifts, among them a goat and a cow that proved later to have been stolen from a farmer— lasted for three days.

Her looks were important to him, now as then.

"A woman should be glamorous," he pronounced once when his wife was not present. "I like to see her wearing jewels and furs, all these things, to highlight." With his great approving smile, his hand sweeping the air to gather in the highlights, he declaimed, "Glamour. Allure. Yes."

But beauty itself was not to be confused with glamour, he explained; by no means. Glamour was more complicated.

"Yes, yes, yes," the object of his approval said languidly, later. "It's very important to him. It's important to all of them."

She had no objection to this taste for glamour, her tone said. It was not something that she herself considered important; that he and other male creatures felt as they did was a fact of life; she did not blame them for it.

It was in her early thirties, just after the birth of her second child, in America, that tragedy almost struck her down. Because she had never looked more beautiful than she did then, and because once the war had ended she never gave any thought to other dangers that might come her way, she could not accept what the doctors told her. When her friend had gone to a doctor for an internal examination, she went along to keep her company, and was tested herself, with the result that she bled copiously for two days. After summoning her and her husband to his office, the doctor had told them that she had cancer, advanced to the third stage, when no cures might be expected from surgery. Possibly she might try radiation therapy, which would give her perhaps a year of life more; though she asked him to, he could not consider operating on her. "I don't like mortal cases on my operating table," he had explained to her.

That night, and for everal days thereafter, she told herself that the luck which had spared her thus far had finally run out. It was luck, and more than luck: it was Rutka, who had died in her place, and her own driving impulse to run anywhere, to do and say anything to stay alive. But mostly, being spared was a matter of luck; she said it often. Smarter people than herself had tried to figure out ways to stay alive; they had devoted themselves day and night to the task of planning how they could survive this way and that—brilliant people they had been, some of them—and they had been killed anyway. It was luck, because if you thought a thousand years, you could not have planned your way out of the situations she had been in; no planning could have devised the steps that impulse and accident had provided to save her. It was luck, yes, fortune, but it was her personal luck, for the fortune that saw someone through so much danger and kept her safe each time could not, she felt, be altogether without meaning, or accidental. In addition, the more experience one had of being saved, the more one believed in the possibility of being saved; the more one saw of one's good fortune, the less accidental it appeared; it began to seem bound, somehow, to the way in which one's life was supposed to go. At the same time, when your fortune turned bad, you could feel, as she did, that being spared so many times did not mean that it would all not catch up someday: and it had caught up. More than once, this thought occurred to her in the first few days after she learned of her illness; yet she could not believe it, either. She felt well; when she looked in the mirror, she saw how good she looked, how her skin glowed. It was impossible for her to imagine that a person who looked like that, so beautiful, could be dying.

Still, the fact was confirmed, by more than one physician. From one of them she had obtained a list of surgeons who did the sort of operation she wanted to have, and had gone methodically down the list, submitting to tests and receiving from five of them the same advice as the first doctor had given. Radiation therapy was the only alternative; they would not undertake a hopeless operation. A week or so before she was to enter a hospital to begin treatment, she had come to the last doctor on the list, an older man, named Taylor, with an office on Park Avenue. It was only logical to her, she had told the doctor when he asked why she persisted in her efforts to have an operation. To have a cancer cut out was better than radiation, which gave no hope at all, only a few more months.

"If you wish it so much," the doctor told her, "I'll perform it."

Her faith, the doctor had told her, was why he agreed to do it: he was a man of some faith himself. On the morning of the operation, her cousin Moshe had appeared in her hospital room, and all at once he had draped himself in his tallis and begun to pray over her, a sight that gave her a sense of doom, but was at the same time comforting. Then Dr. Taylor had appeared. So as not to interfere with the doctor's visit, her cousin Moshe halted his praying and began to take off his tallis.

"No, don't stop," the doctor told him. He had, he said, just come from praying to his own God. When they wheeled her upstairs, Moshe followed right behind up to the very doors of the elevator, leaving her with a last view of him standing there in his prayer shawl, saying the prayer for recovery as the elevator doors closed in his face.

After the operation was over, some six hours later, she learned, two nurses had supported the exhausted doctor when he left the operating room. He had cut out everything he saw, he told her husband, the rest was in God's hands.

And of course she had lived. In the days before she went to the hospital, she had occupied her mind by straightening out closets, cleaning and polishing the silverware, and she had understood that this was a way of preparing for death, this putting everything in order. The last weekend before she was to enter the hospital, her friends in Kew Gardens threw a party to cheer her. Included in the gathering were friends of her friends, people she did not know. One of these people came up to her during the party just as she had begun to cry, off in a corner of the room.

"Don't worry," the stranger soothed her. "Your friend will come through the operation all right." It was a reasonable error, as she had herself seen, staring in the mirror, it was difficult to imagine that anyone who looked as she did could be dying.

She had gone home after the operation, and a two-month stay in the hospital, with certain goals in mind. She would be satisfied to live, she bargained, just until the younger child started kindergarten, just until the older one had his bar mitzvah, events that were due in a year's time. After that, let come what may. When the year had passed, she bargained for another short time, and then another, resolving always that when she had lived to achieve them, when she had seen the younger one do this or that or when the older one finished school, she would ask no more. Let what would happen, happen. In that way, as a series of bargains, the years slid by; it was luck, it was destiny—whatever it was, she did not want to think. The crisis had only confirmed her way of looking at things. Her disposition was even sunnier than before, and in truth she had much to feel sunny about. Much time had passed, time successfully bargained for. When the Braunsteiner hearings were held, fifteen years had already passed, by which time she no longer found it necessary to make bargains—or short-term ones, at any rate. In all those years she had found little to complain about. When some unhappiness came to her, she shook it off as a dog shakes off water, partly because she did not believe in it: what right had she to unhappiness? In large part, too, it was because since the days in the concentration camp she had absorbed the idea that depression was the beginning of death; that was the reason they had sung songs—school songs, Polish songs, anything that came into their mouths.

It must have been surprising to her family and friends, therefore, when, happy and contented as she had been, a great restlessness took hold of her in the summer of 1974. Nothing would do but that she must pack up suddenly and go to Poland. This time, her husband was not at all willing that she should have her way, though in the end, as usual, she did what she wanted to do. It had been more than a year since the Braunsteiner hearings, a year in which she had lived, as she usually did, busily absorbed in every day's doings, in her family, her friends. Yet it had ended in a restless summer, which found her suddenly packing suitcases, deaf to her husband's objections that it was mad to run off to Poland, of all places. She had friends there still, she had replied calmly; she would stay with them in Warsaw.

In Warsaw the friends were happy to receive her. She and they had known one another since before the war, when they were schoolmates. Some were Jews, some were not. The former all had their reasons for staying in Warsaw, among them the fact that theirs were mixed marriages, mostly, as was so of the couple in whose apartment she stayed during the visit. Life was not easy for them, especially where money was concerned, but for a visitor, she saw, living in Poland was cheap. The day after she arrived, she had taken fourteen people to dinner, and discovered, to her astonishment, that the splendid full-course dinner for fourteen had cost the equivalent of just fourteen dollars.

To her companions the fourteen hundred zlotys that sum represented was more than the combined monthy wages of working couples like themselves. Then she had taken the friend she stayed with to a beauty parlor and treated her to a hair set and a manicure, which again had cost next to nothing by American standards. Afterward there were more meals and some sightseeing: Warsaw, which was devastated during the war, had been entirely rebuilt.

A few days after her arrival, she took up the real reason for her visit, and announced to her friends that she planned to go to Maidanek. They, as she had expected, were horrified. But they soon saw that nothing would dissuade her; and so, sighing, since she could not be permitted to go alone, they assigned themselves the task of driving her there. They themselves had never been there. It was an unhappy, unnecessary visit, a grim end to the reunion and the festivities they had all been enjoying, so far as they were concerned.

It takes three hours to drive from Warsaw to Lublin by car, and then five minutes more to get from Lublin to Maidanek. Along the road from Lublin to the camp, signs announce that the State Museum of Maidanek is ahead.

She saw, of course, as they approached the camp, that it was not as she remembered it.

First, an enormous monument, as tall and wide as any block in Kew Gardens, loomed out at them. Next to it was the office of the Maidanek Museum's Director, and there—with what intention she herself did not know—she went first. Leaving her friends outside, she presented herself to a woman who said she was the secretary to the Director. She wanted to see the Director, she informed the secretary.

"The Director is a busy man," the secretary observed, and then inquired what her business was.

"I have business," she told the secretary. "I am a former prisoner, a Jew. From America."

The secretary ran to the Director, and he at once opened the door and ushered her into his office. He was a slim, well-dressed Pole who looked to be in his mid-thirties, and he greeted her with a shy but hospitable smile. He himself would show her around the camp, he told her, and he did. Later, he explained to her approvingly that he wished to do this because he had never before met any Jew among the visitors to Maidanek—not one, at any rate, who announced the fact. There must have been many, he was certain, but Jews in Poland, he told her with some delicacy, were more assimilated than elsewhere.

"Therefore they are not very forward about these matters," he explained.

"Really," she said to the Director, marveling as though she had just heard of the behavior of some strange new form of life whose habits had till that moment remained unknown to her. Really. Well, in her own country, America, she assured him, the case was different. Well, to each his own, of course.

"In America if you are Jewish you don't have to be afraid to say it," she told him nicely, without malice. She saw how kind and interested the young Director was, that he had a humane face. He had, he told her, been a child during the war, and he believed very much in the work of the State Museum.

He was also an excellent guide, though he was clearly a busy man who was constantly interrupted by phone calls. First, he showed her and her friends the mausoleum, and explained that when the Russians had entered Maidanek, the fires in the crematoria were still burning. The Russians had collected part of the human ashes they had found as evidence, and left a quantity of them in the ovens, which the visitors could see clearly for themselves. He showed them the barracks, which were as she remembered them, except for the flowers that visitors had placed inside them, and he explained to them what the enormous monument was meant to represent. All the time he talked, she listened, but her mind was not entirely concentrated on what she heard. The Director then pointed out a group of students who had come to tour the camp, accompanied by guides. The students, who were in their late teens and twenties, listened somberly, their faces taut, their minds clearly concentrated on everything they heard, while their guide described the function of the hooks and the other torture devices on display. One group of twenty students stood before the whipping block while their guide explained something to them in Russian.

Stella went up to the group leader and said, in Polish, "I would like to introduce myself. I am a former prisoner here. A Jew. And I am from the United States." The guide translated her words into Russian, and solemnly, one by one, all the students lined up to pump her hand.

After Stella had rejoined her own group, the Director was called away to answer a phone call, and the friend's husband went off to take some photographs of the monument, which was fortunate for him, as it turned out. As soon as they were alone, Stella pulled her friend back to the mausoleum, and to the furnace where the ashes were.

The furnace was a little over five feet deep, not big enough to contain bodies of more than average height, shrunken though those bodies might be at the time they were shoveled in. To right this difficulty, a saw had been kept handily by, chained to a table at the side of the oven, where it still could be seen.

"Hold my legs," she suddenly directed her friend.

"What are you doing?" the friend asked in alarm.

"Just hold my legs, I want to get some ashes," she answered. Without further ado, she crossed the small space between the spectators' railing and the oven door, and crawled without great difficulty inside the oven itself, while her friend held her legs, too horrified to do more than obey. The ashes were quite deep inside the stove. Stella inched forward toward them until her entire body, all but her ankles, was inside the oven. The ashes lay underneath and around her, small whitish heaps in the darkness.

In one fist she had the vinyl envelope that had held her pocket rain bonnet, and with it she scooped into the ashes. When the envelope was full, she began trying to get out of the oven, but of course she found that she could not; that it was a lot easier pushing oneself forward through an opening than backward. The mouth of the stove inside was not as wide as it had appeared outside, so that for all her pushing, she could only get her legs out; the rest of her body was trapped in the stove. Up to this time, she had concentrated on what she was doing, entirely unaware of any feelings. Now she saw that she was trapped, and a great blind panic seized her; she closed her eyes, so that she should not see the walls of the stove around her, and began to kick her legs madly and shouted to her friend to help.

"What are you doing there? Jesus Maria; Jesus Maria!" her friend prayed, yanking at her legs.

Finally, she wriggled out, still with the envelope in her fist. Naturally, she was covered with ashes. When she came home to Kew Gardens a few days later, she told her friends how it had been. Here the Director would be coming to look for them at any moment, and here she, in the navy-blue pants suit she happened to be wearing that day, was covered from head to foot with ashes. To make matters more perfect, as soon as they left the crematorium, a rain began to fall, making a nice mixture on her suit.

"You could just imagine," she told them.

The Director was expecting her in his office, where he had invited her for coffee before she left. When she got there, he only stared at her a little and told her that she had some dirt on her suit.

Yes, yes, she told him; she had stumbled somewhere, and it had rained, but it was nothing; a good dry cleaning would fix it.

She must have given him that smile of hers, and confronted him with those blue eyes, which were so empty of grimness. Whatever it was, he was soon reassured, and became absorbed in their conversation. She told him how gratified she was to see that students were brought here, how happy she was to have a chance to talk to them, which was the truth. He, in turn, told her how happy he was to have met her, which doubtless was the truth, too.

In the car going back to Warsaw, she began to cry, and her old friend cried, too. For different reasons, she almost cried again, a few days later, when she got to the Warsaw airport and strapped herself into the seat of an American plane. Never, she importuned her friends later, should they fly on a Polish or any other but an American airline, if any of them wanted to go where she had been. What happiness when she entered the plane! How it embraced her! In fact, up until that moment she had not known how bad she had been feeling. The rudeness of the Polish customs guards at the airport put the finish on everything. One had even stuck his finger in a cold-cream jar—not hers, but that of the woman in front of her. On an impulse, she had decided that for them she knew no Polish, she who had been saved by her Polish, who had babbled Polish all her life, and throughout all the years in America. When the guard questioned her, she shook her head and told him in English that she did not understand. Let them prove she knew Polish: she had an American passport.

Once home, just as she expected, everyone she knew wanted some of the ashes. Other people might not understand why you would want something like those ashes from the oven at Maidanek, but to her and her friends it was natural enough: they had no graves to visit; the ashes were all they had for a memorial. Perhaps the survivors' group she belonged to might even one day build a monument to their dead, as had been done in other American cities, and the ashes could be kept there. For now, she kept what she had, little gravelly bits of uneven size, in a white envelope.

When people asked her why she had done such a horrible thing as to put her own body into the oven, she claimed that she did not know for certain; that, as usual, she did not know a moment before what she was going to do. But that was not altogether true. She wanted ashes, yes, but that was not the reason for such an act, she knew it very well.

It was obvious to her and to everyone. When one friend suggested that perhaps she was telling the ovens to claim her one last time, and another said that it was guilt, she listened with an attitude that said it was all possible. Instead of any of these things, the thought kept crossing her mind that she had wanted to put herself for one minute in Rutka's place, to feel something of how it had been for her in the end, to take it upon herself.

But that, too, was conjecture, not anything she knew for

certain. She had done many things in her life without knowing why. You did not always have to understand why you did things to get results, she informed a close friend.

It was true that she did not like to pretend she knew why she did things when she did not know, particularly since she sensed that not knowing gave her a kind of power. She considered that she owed much to her impulses; and she sensed that these mysterious forces which always rose up to direct and save her required that they remain just what they were—mysterious.

She herself looked the opposite of mysterious, generally, and never more so than when she came home from her trip, her usual good spirits even better than before. Her husband had long since got over his anger at her peculiar need to pack up and go to Poland suddenly, and was now, plainly, just glad to see her back. The man did look quite happy, as one friend remarked to her just after her return.

"And how," she acknowledged.

REVA

After the Russians bombed and shelled all night, the Germans left, and somebody opened the gates of the camp. I ran, with my brothers and sisters, without knowing where. Why did we run? I ask you. We knew somebody opened a gate and we just ran like fools. They were still bombing, and we ran along the roads anyway. As we went, I saw a lot of dead German soldiers along the road and, let me tell you, I don't know if it is in me to be so happy now to see a dead man as I was then. I saw all those dead Germans and I was happy, happy!

Now I am older, but I tell you, I still cannot stand the sound of German. Lately the Germans are traveling all over the world. Last winter we were sitting in a restaurant in Mexico City, after the ballet, and a whole busload of them came in. They started to talk. I wished I could yell at them, that I had the nerve to talk to them, scream at them. But then I looked at them; they were still young people.

What could they have been doing during the war? They must have been eleven or twelve when my mother was being killed, or my father.

I see it before me: I am standing on the Polish side, and I see my sister Masha standing in line with all the Jews going to Treblinka. When I was younger and busier and working, I was too busy to remember these things all the time, but last year I celebrated my forty-first birthday. My mother was only thirty-nine when she was killed. Sometimes when we are talking, my brother will say suddenly, "*Ach, der Tata und der Mama.*" Then he does not talk for a while, but just sits there. He is a very successful man but tense, and he longs for his father.

For me it is my mother, and what is it that we are all thinking when my brother says that? It is, If they could see us now, and be here with us, how good we could make it for them. They could have seen my children and my sister's children. Think of my mother's life: I look at my sons; I think how she must have felt when she watched us starving and crying for food, and there was nothing, nothing she could give us. I saw my grandmother die of starvation in the ghetto. Now I go to parties and I hear talk from women about diets, and how they are starving, and my blood boils; I burn inside. I think to myself, "You don't know the meaning of starvation! What are you talking about?" Of course it's irrational, how can they know? I blame them anyway. They think a diet is really starvation.

When my son had his bar mitzvah, I went up to the bima, the place in the synagogue where they call you up to read, and I blessed the candles. I closed my eyes, and suddenly they were both there next to me. My mother and father. They didn't say anything, they simply stood close to me, one on each side of me, and they touched my shoulder. They were there with me; I felt it. I can remember their hands. They were such good people, kind people, people who lived righteously. My father was killed on Rosh Hashanah and my mother was put on the train in Treblinka. I didn't see it, but I imagine how she died of suffocation on the train: that is how I imagine it.

RUTH*

My parents did not have the money to get out of Poland in time, but my father did beg his brother in America, "Take my oldest daughter; get her a visa." He wrote his brother a letter and said to him, "Save at least one of my children. Take my oldest daughter to America; say that she is going to be a bride of your son." We never heard from them. It's strange how that son, my American uncle's son, never did get married. Maybe not so strange. We had sent them a picture of my sister, who was charming and a beauty, but I suppose they were afraid.

In Poland, before the Germans came, my father and mother had a store where they sold stockings, men's shirts, negligés—a kind of variety clothing store. I can still see some of those shirts; I used to love to feel them with my fingers when I was a child. They were made of something like silk cotton.

When the Germans started the selections and the deportations, we wanted my nine-year-old-brother to hide with a Polish family, because children were taken right away. But Samek, my brother, was afraid because of what he had seen happen to a little friend of his who had been hidden by a Polish family. The Poles became afraid after a week or so, and told him to leave; it was very dangerous for them to keep him. Samek saw how his friend wandered the streets without any place to go, his family having already been deported. Samek refused to leave us, and so he hid on the roof of our house all by himself during the selections, and one of us would creep up beforehand to bring him food. My sister—my older sister—especially, was devoted to him. When the Germans took Samek, she went with him to Auschwitz to die, because she could not stand the idea that he should face it all by himself. He was nine, and he was so afraid.

My mother was sick the day before one of the selections. She couldn't go down there in the street; she would never pass and we knew it. But I had a dream that night where I imagined what to do to hide my mother. The next morning, my father left for work. He had a work permit, and a job to go to, and he just left. Everyone went to work, so he went. Just like that. I sound angry? I am angry, still angry. Why should my father have gone down? He asked no questions, just went, while my mother was lying there. I had a work permit, too, but I couldn't go and leave her. So I followed the solution I had come to in my dream. First I moved the washbasin and a table against the door of the room where my mother was lying. I filled the basin with dirty water. With that basin and table in front, it looked as though there was only an old closet where my mother's room was. She stayed upstairs behind that door all during the selection. And I don't know if the Germans searched the house, but if they did, they didn't find her, because when the selection was over I came back and she was lying there safe. I never said anything to my father about what he had done. What was there to talk about?

Authorities on the holocaust. Great thinkers.
Historians. Let them put this in their books:
that by the time we walked to the tragedy we
were already emaciated and enslaved. Hungry.
That it is human, not weak, not to want to
believe that someone is out to murder you, and
that on the way to the slaughterhouse he will
also drain you of your possessions, of your
strength, the gold from your teeth, and the hair
from your head.
Great intellectuals. Great writers. Jews!
— A survivor.

6 | Honor

I

On a cold gray winter afternoon, Jacob Korman, chief U.S. witness against Hermine Braunsteiner, paused abruptly in the midst of talk about the hearings to tell a story. The story had no apparent relation to anything that had gone before; it was plainly an eruption. He told how he had arrived in Rembertow, a town some ten kilometers from Warsaw where hundreds of Jews had lived. There was a factory in Rembertow, which produced bullets and other materiel for the German war machine, and there the Jews had been put to work until it was Rembertow's turn to become *Judenrein*. He himself had not yet been captured, but had wandered into Rembertow just after the roundup of the Jews.

"You think they let themselves be taken." It was not a question. "Peacefully. Like lambs. The world believes," he sang, in the falsetto he used for mockery. "One says. Ten more repeat after him." He told how Rembertow had looked, and what he saw there. The people would not go on the trucks when the Germans ordered them to; women had bitten the noses off the guards; men had been shot trying to pull the guns from the guards' hands. The dead filled the streets, and their hands—the hands of the women —were full of hair.

"Men's hair. That they tore from the heads of the guards. Hair everywhere. *A velt mit hor.*"*

He told that there were mass graves dug; that one could see the dead men and women lying inside, and right next to them the bodies of several of their guards.

"Not only in Rembertow. Other towns. The world knows, hah? What the world knows?" he demanded.

There was silence for a time. When he spoke again, it was in his normal voice. He added that the Germans had, of course, finally succeeded in taking the Jews of Rembertow away. The Germans had guns; the victory was theirs, naturally.

II

In Los Angeles, a younger man sat straight up in a chair, in an attitude of readiness. His name was Dimont, and he was just under fifty, with thick black hair and blacker brows, which arched high, giving him a perpetually inquiring look, even when, as now, he was only uncomfortable. It was the middle of a busy workday; he was not used to sitting idly around in hotel rooms at such a time. Regularly he lit cigarettes, smoked them halfway down, and put them out, hitting his arms against the high arms of his chair as he did. Now and then, he cast a quick glance at the stream of cars going past the window, and looked very much as though he would like to be in one of them. He should have pleaded a busy day, his face said at these moments; business was hectic, he worked twelve hours a day. It would not be untrue to say he was too busy, but he could not actually do that, as he well knew; he would have no peace of mind if

* A world, a universe of hair.

he did. So he had put his work and his busy schedule aside and gone where he did not want to go: to a place where someone had questions. As long as there were questions and people to ask them, he would find time, for there was a record to be kept straight, things to tell and to deny.

The thing he found strangest of all, he said when he began, was that there they were in Auschwitz, fighting for life each day, and the greatest fear of the people he knew was not just death, but the idea that every last one of them would die and there would be no one left alive to tell what had happened to them. That they should have had those concerns when they needed every ounce of concentration to worry about their lives was the greatest puzzle to him, he announced in a way which told it was not only a puzzle to him but among the things that he understood best of all on earth.

He had been born in Germany and deported with the rest of the family, all of whom—his mother, father, and three brothers—had been killed. After the war, he had gone back to Germany on five separate occasions to testify against certain Nazis, and the memory of those trials was bitter to him. The last and worst was in 1968, when he gave testimony against the German senior inmate who ran Buna.* The defendant had had two aggressive lawyers, and they had attacked every particle of testimony that he, Dimont, gave against their client. They had questioned him for hours on certain technical details, and had even asked him how many steps he could walk in a minute; unless he could make exactly ninety-five steps in sixty seconds, the attorneys argued, the witness could not have seen certain events take place. In the end, their client was convicted, with four years deducted from his sentence for the time he had spent in custody while the charges against him were investigated. But the witness for the prosecution had gone home soured by the whole affair, determined that this would be the last time he would go to Germany to testify. The defense attorneys had agitated him, but worse, there was the sight of the defendant himself, a man who was only

* The slave labor (I. G. Farben) division of Auschwitz.

in his mid-sixties but already had the look of senility: the dimmed eyes, the trembling head, the driblets that clung to the corners of the mouth. Dimont was repelled at the sight of the former *Lagerälteste*.* He would not have gone had he known, he reflected; he would not have gone all the way to Germany to testify against a vegetable.

The difference between the man he had known at Buna and the vague-eyed creature who sat before him twenty-five years later had startled his mind with a question; he had asked it of himself over and over during the trial, and the question was put plainly: "How could this fool command a camp of fifteen thousand Jews?" Perhaps fifty thousand Jews, Poles, and nationals of every kind had passed through his hands altogether: how was it possible that such numbers could have once feared the man who now sat in the courtroom looking so frail and confused, as though, if a fly landed on him, he would not have the nerve to brush it off?

Dimont had very good reason to know the *Lagerälteste*. When he had arrived in Buna, he was already a veteran of Sachsenhausen where, in two years, he had learned everything about surviving. But in the new camp there were different elements to deal with; you had to establish yourself again, to start all over again to find ways to get yourself out of the cold and the rain, ways to avoid getting the hardest work, ways to obtain a little more food, because these things were the difference between life and death.

Practically from the first day he had noticed the *Lagerälteste*'s meticulously clean, sparkling boots.

"Boots, that was his life," Dimont observed. "He knew one thing: that if he had boots like a German officer, he was in heaven." He recalled how, one day, he had approached the *Lagerälteste*.

"I see you have some beautiful boots. That you like to have your boots sparkling clean. I am an expert," he had told the *Lagerälteste*, who was, of course, pleased at the idea of having someone who would devote himself to the proper care of his boots. In that way he had arranged to go every night to clean the *Lagerälteste*'s boots with spit and anything

---

* Camp senior, appointed by the Germans.

else he could get his hands on. In return, the *Lagerälteste* had given him additional food, and then eventually promoted him to a job as a sort of private maid. He had cleaned the *Lagerälteste*'s room, made the bed, done his laundry, and cooked for him. It was a comparatively protected position, and one that had also enabled him to observe firsthand the *Lagerälteste*'s brutality: how he had murdered men with his bare hands.

That was why he had gone to Germany to testify; and then he had found, as he said, that the maniac had two Red Cross doctors at his side and two attorneys to defend him. The *Lagerälteste* was very well dressed, too, because a former duchess of the Hohenzollern family had bought four suits for him so that he would look presentable in court, a fact that the German newspapers had been quick to report. A vegetable the *Lagerälteste* might have been, but he had still recognized his former "maid" at the trial; that was clear from his suddenly increased vagueness as soon as he saw the witness. Nevertheless, Dimont recalled, the *Lagerälteste* had played dumb and pretended not to know the witness, after which his attorneys had proceeded to call the witness a liar.

"If you are going to call me a liar and question my veracity and insult me, I leave," Dimont had told them.

"We are a democratic nation now," the Presiding Justice had said, in turn. "No one wishes to insult you, but he is a defendant"—the Justice had indicated the former *Lagerälteste*—"and he is entitled to his attorneys."

The Justice had spoken politely, but the defense attorneys had immediately jumped up and demanded that the Justice resign from sitting in judgment on the case.

"The veracity of his testimony is not at all established *a priori*!" one of them yelled at the Justice. "You have no right to say that!"

The Justice appeared to give this charge some thought; then he apologized to the two defense lawyers.

Dimont had been furious. The business of the Nazi trials and the behavior of the lawyers were not, however, the most important issues on his mind; it was only that these were recent events and therefore they surfaced easily. More important, the trials were connected to another, more crucial matter, something that, he pointed out, people understood very little. He had noticed, in fact, that people were forever delivering opinions on things about which they had no conception. This was a discovery he had made particularly about intellectuals, for where had he found the foremost evidence to substantiate this discovery but among intellectuals?

"Isn't it ironic?" he inquired sadly.

The particular intellectuals he had in mind were those who had written learned works about the way the Jews became accomplices to their own murder: the intellectuals who decried the lack of resistance to the Nazis, the ones who knew—though they were not there in Europe at the time but safe in America—exactly how the Jews should have behaved to save themselves. In detailing these observations, his own tone was polite and full of the debater's graciousness, a tone that suggests the debater is willing to grant every argument its several sides; and, clearly, one of the first arguments he was prepared to grant was that since the intellectuals were the least equipped to do anything in the world, it was only natural that some of them should choose to busy themselves by explaining to others the way the world worked.

When he heard the talk about the Jews' failure to resist, when he read the works which explained how the Jews should and should not have behaved under the Nazis, he recalled how, in Sachsenhausen where he had been, inmates had often had to stand outside all day long in the cold, dressed only in the thin camp uniforms, in temperatures of 15 and 20 degrees below zero. To keep themselves from freezing, they had rubbed each other's bodies with their hands. At the same time, while they were standing there all those hours, one of the prisoners—an intellectual himself, it was true, a professor of philosophy and former Dean of the Faculty of Philosophy of the Dutch university in Groningen—gave lectures on Kant and Descartes. And the inmates listened: starved, their eyes jumping out of their heads with cold and misery, what were they doing? They were listening to lectures.

This was resistance, he wished to point out to those so concerned with the question of Jewish resistance. It was not armed resistance, but it was resistance nevertheless; and was it not remarkable, he asked, that nowadays resistance should be thought to concern only the physical and that those who held this belief were not simply people, but intellectuals—thinkers, social philosophers? It was resistance when, in Auschwitz, one of ten people loaded on a truck taking them to Birkenau to be gassed thought to take off his shoes, if he had a pair of good ones, and hand them over to some inmate who had not been selected for gassing, some stranger he didn't even know, because with a good pair of shoes the other prisoner had a chance of staying alive a bit longer.

If the historians and the intellectuals did not know that there were other forms of resistance than the physical, how could they understand what it meant to have men come together in a barracks on a Friday night in Sachsenhausen, secretly, in order to hear a fellow inmate tell stories from Peretz? Or what it meant for a group of people each to take a small piece of bread from his own slice to make an extra ration for one who was sick?

"Of course, if you have no conception at all of how anything was, it is understandable that you would make certain assumptions, and reason in a certain way," he said, in a voice innocent of irony. For a time he paused, eyebrows arching slightly higher as he contemplated the table on which a set of books rested, as though it were there that the historians had gathered to formulate their misconceptions.

He was, however, not surprised at the things those people could not understand—not any longer. He counted it one of the greater disappointments in life, the sight he had had of the way intellectuals behaved in the face of catastrophe. There were notable exceptions, to be sure; but he had observed that on the whole the intellectuals had very little moral stamina. He had not seen in them very often the humanity, the acts of selflessness that he had seen in simple, almost primitive people.

He was an educated man himself, if not what people would call an intellectual. After the liberation, he had chosen to go to Israel and live in a kibbutz, where he was happy—and where he would still be had his wife not rebelled against the hardships of kibbutz existence. But life outside a kibbutz in Israel made him as unhappy as life inside one had made his wife. As a compromise, they decided they would go to America. There he had worked days and gone to school nights for twelve years in order to take advanced degrees in business administration. Now he was a partner in a good sportswear house, but that would not be forever. He had plans for the rest of his life. He wanted to make enough money to retire soon, for example. There were things to be done; there might be lectures. He would know what to do with the time. Already now he was prepared to drop whatever he was doing in order to deal with particular issues. He could not be peaceful in his mind knowing that the history of his family, his comrades, and all of them, the survivors and the dead, had been written by those who had no understanding whatever of what had occurred, even though, as he said, he was in no way surprised by their incapacity.

III

Late or soon, survivors' talk turned to the issue of resistance. This was true whether they were sophisticates and intellectuals or people who, but for their recent history, might have been classed among the simple, unworldly folk of the world; for to be a survivor was to be removed for good from the possibilities of unworldliness. The most educated knew and the least educated had heard about the learned arguments that had been put forth explaining how the Jews should have done this and that or thus and so when they faced the Germans, how they might have avoided losing so many millions had they been wiser, better, more farsighted, and less trusting; the dry-goods-store clerk as well as the man of letters knew the names of the historians on whose authority the world had come to believe that the Jews themselves had been accomplices to their murder.

Having survived, they learned that there had grown up

around the death of their families and their civilization a
body of social theory which explained how it was that the
catastrophe was in large measure the fault of the victims.
The victims had not known how to behave in extreme circumstances, Bruno Bettelheim pointed out in *Individual and
Mass Behavior in Extreme Situations* and *The Informed
Heart*. In an impressive and influential holocaust work,
whose data on the behavior of the Jews in occupied Europe
were drawn exclusively from German sources, Raul Hilberg
explained at considerable length* how the Jews had acquiesced in the design to destroy them, how Jewish
psychology had contributed to that design, and the negligible efforts the Jews had made at resistance.

The idea that the victims are accomplices in their fate is,
at the core, a fascinating one to the modern intellectual, one
quite as appealing in its way as the connected modern,
liberal prejudice which holds that everyone is guilty but
the man in the dock. The fascinations of intellectuals have,
furthermore, always had a way of getting to the popular
mind and of being received there, if in simplified fashion,
as authority. Few were the survivors, therefore, who did
not one way or another find themselves confronting questions about Jewish complicity and the lack of Jewish resistance. The psychoanalyst Bruno Bettelheim had made
queries:† why had the Jews marched peacefully to the trains
that would take them to the gas chambers? There were
fewer soldiers than Jews; why had they not tried to overpower the soldiers? Why had they not seized their guns?
Why had Anne Frank's father tried to keep his family together in an attic in Nazi-occupied Holland instead of dis-
persing them, as their extreme circumstances dictated;
instead of trying to carry on business as usual, as, Dr.
Bettelheim explained, so many of the Jews were wont
to do?

He told how, before entering the gas chamber, a dancer
had been ordered to perform by the SS by dancing naked

* Raul Hilberg, *The Destruction of the European Jews* (New
York: Quadrangle, 1961).

† Bruno Bettelheim, *The Informed Heart* (New York: Free Press,
1960), p. 263.

before them; how, in dancing, she had become an artist once more and achieved a moment of selfhood, and how she had been able to reach for the gun of an SS man and kill him before being killed herself.

Why were there not more dancers and more moments of selfhood before the doors of the gas chambers? Why had Jews like Anne Frank's father not been wise enough to grasp the principles of behavior in extreme circumstances? Why had they selected a hiding place without an outlet, a place that was basically a trap, and gone underground as a family, rather than singly, which was safer? Bettelheim asked. And surely Anne Frank's father could, with his connections, have provided himself with a gun or two?

"Doubtless," retorted the holocaust historian Jacob Robinson, "the pages of the *Algemeen Handelsblad* in Amsterdam were full of offers of all sizes of hiding places for families and singles, with and without 'traps': *embarras de richesses*, come and select."*

Could not the millions of Jews of Europe "have marched as free men against the SS," Bettelheim asked, "rather than to first grovel, then wait to be rounded up for their own extermination, and finally walk themselves to the gas chambers?"†

Why had the dead not died fighting if they had to die anyway? Why did they not grab guns when the end was in sight? Why had they believed that the Germans could not possibly mean to kill them? Why were they so orderly?

Absurd questions, in the face of facts that had confronted the Jews of Europe, yet the survivors were not able entirely to treat them as such. The Final Solution had been the fate of ordinary men and women, not, in the main, heroes, poets, or dancers. Nevertheless, even if other people might wish to grant the survivors their ordinariness, it was not easy for them to grant it to themselves. For there was no one, it seemed, among those who had come through the gates of the concentration camps and the ghettos, lain

* Jacob Robinson, *Psychoanalysis in a Vacuum* (New York: Yad Vashem-Yivo Documentation Projects, 1970), p. 26.
† Bettelheim, *The Informed Heart,* p. 263.

in hiding, or been with the partisans in the forests who was not possessed of a sense of his uniqueness.

It was clear in the way they told the smallest details of their lives and in the confident manner of the telling—the manner of people who know the weight of what they have to say and need no assurance about it. Indeed, however humble or inarticulate they might otherwise be, survivors never said, as the inarticulate often do to defend themselves from the threat of expression, "I have nothing to say," "I'm not interesting," or, "I don't know how to explain myself well." They knew they had been participants in history, and the sense of that history opened their mouths not only about the specific tragic experience they had survived but about human experience in general. The holocaust was the central illumination and the authority for that which they knew about life, a sum of knowledge that was, in their eyes, considerable. The holocaust had tested and taught them: taught them to know the nature of men, as they believed, and to know it in ways and degrees it was not given other people to know.

If, by their own estimate, they were not ordinary, then they could not so easily dismiss charges, unreasonable though they might be, about their lack of resistance to the Germans, or answer, as ordinary men well might, that indeed they were no heroes and had had no wish to be: that they had miraculously survived and did not know how they had done it, and that, under the circumstances that had been, questions about resistance were absurdities. Instead, because life had placed them at the center of tragic history, they were inclined to judge themselves not as ordinary men and women might but in terms equal to the magnitude of that history.

It was thus that the subject of resistance churned with terrible frequency in the minds of the survivors. And whether they conceded wearily, as some did, that armed resistance had mostly not been possible, or whether they offered fierce rebuttals to the notion that there had been little resistance, or a combination of the two, the underlying fury of response was the same. It was a slander on honor, not a small thing in the hearts of men; it was a slander on the dead, a denial of the realities that had destroyed them.

The truth, as they knew it themselves, was that they had behaved in the way the armed might of the Nazis had dictated that an unarmed and helpless people behave; that there had indeed been bitter resistance and uprising,* and that most of those who had risen up had, in the end, been killed as had the unarmed and the helpless. Still, even with such knowledge as they had, it was not possible for the survivors to ignore the opinion—in the bitter words that had come into common use in the post-holocaust years—that the Jews had gone like sheep to the slaughter.

Thus the life-sized pictures of the Warsaw ghetto fighters hung on the walls of the survivor organization offices. They died with honor was the implicit theme of the posters, as well as the growing body of literature on Jewish armed resistance put out by various Jewish organizations—a theme about which one survivor commented tartly that it had always been her belief, and the belief of the comrades who had survived with her, that *all* the Jews who died had died with honor.

In 1960 there occurred an event that was to intensify questions and discussions regarding Jewish resistance and to be of considerable significance to the survivors. On May 23rd of that year, David Ben-Gurion, Prime Minister of Israel, announced that Adolf Eichmann had been captured by Israeli agents in Buenos Aires, Argentina. Eichmann had been living in Argentina under the assumed name Ricardo Klement. During the Nuremberg trials, he had sometimes been referred to as "the man in charge of the extermination of the Jews." The man thus described, however, was not among the prisoners in the dock at Nuremberg; he was hiding in a prisoner-of-war camp in Germany, under an assumed name. For four years after the war ended, Eichmann remained in Germany under assumed names, first as

---

* In addition to the Warsaw ghetto uprising, revolts against the Germans took place in the ghettos of Bialystok, Vilna, and Czestochowa, and in Treblinka, Sobibor, and Auschwitz.

an unimportant SS lieutenant and prisoner of the Americans, Otto Eckman—a name that was close enough to Eichmann so that in the event he should be recognized by another prisoner and called by his real name, the disparity between the prisoner's name and the one he had been called could be explained away to anyone overhearing it. But the news of the Nuremberg proceedings reached the Oberdachstetten camp in the American zone of Germany where Eichmann had settled into a peaceful routine. Along with the general news of the Nuremberg proceedings, there came the disquieting information that the name Eichmann had begun to figure ever more prominently in the testimony about the Final Solution, particularly that given the Tribunal on January 3, 1946, by Dieter Wisliceny, the SS captain who had been Eichmann's close confidant and assistant.

It had been Eichmann's exclusive concern to arrange the deportations of Jews from the German-occupied countries to the extermination centers and the various combination labor-extermination camps, a work which he undertook with notable zeal and a persistence so great that when Germany's armies were collapsing in the late summer and fall of 1944, and the wisdom of a more moderate policy with regard to the Jews had begun to make itself clear even to Heinrich Himmler, Eichmann would not be deterred from the task of getting the Jews rounded up and onto the deportation trains to the East. He had appeared all over occupied Europe to oversee the details of the deportations, a complicated procedure that involved a number of preliminary steps by now well known to history, beginning with the isolation of the Jews from the rest of the population, the requirement that they register and wear the yellow star, and ending with the roundups and the sealed trains whose destination was Auschwitz, or one of the other camps in the East.

In Hungary, in 1944, he had confronted the challenge of deporting the last great remaining body of Jews in Europe. This Eichmann set out to do in the face of grave difficulties, which had to do with the fact that by that time Germany was virtually defeated and the Horthy government* had begun to feel the effect of world pressure on the subject of the deportations; for in 1944 it was no longer possible to doubt their aim, or the fate of the deportees. In addition to having received the protests of the King of Sweden, the Papal nuncio, and the Swiss and Turkish governments, the Horthy government had also arrived at the belief that lists of Hungarian war criminals were being compiled by the Allied Powers.

The deportations had begun in May of 1944, and been carried out with extraordinary speed, under the personal direction of Eichmann and his men, the Sondereinsatz- kommando Eichmann (Special Operation Group Eich- mann). Without food, water, or sanitary facilities, the Jews were crammed onto the trains; on some days, five trains, with as many as fourteen thousand people on them, went from Hungary to Auschwitz. When the members of the Jewish Relief Committee in Hungary applied to the Sonder- einsatzkommando for relief of the conditions the deportees had to endure on the transports, they received from Hauptsturmführer Hunsche the following reply: "Will you finally stop bothering me with your horror stories." Hunsche told Dr. Kastner, of the Jewish Relief Com- mittee, "I have investigated. Here are the reports: There are at most fifty to sixty persons per transport who die on the way."†

For the final deportation of the four hundred thousand Jews of Budapest, which was to take place in mid-July, Eichmann had planned one great action. Virtually all of Budapest was to come to a standstill for a day, all traffic halted in its streets, while the Sondereinsatzkommando, the Hungarian police, and also the mailmen and the chim- ney sweeps of the city went about the work of rounding up the Jews, an affair that promised to be so public—and to draw yet more of the world's attention to the Jewish situation in Hungary—that the German Foreign Office

* Under Horthy, the Hungarian government had, up until 1944, more or less allied itself with Nazi Germany.

† Kastner, *Bericht*, cited in Hilberg, *The Destruction of the European Jews*, p. 547.

became uncomfortable.* That particular plan failed because, before it could be executed, Admiral Horthy decreed an end to the deportations and, albeit temporarily, had Eichmann's Hungarian assistants in charge of Jewish affairs arrested.

At virtually every other turn, Eichmann's determination won out over all obstacles in his path. When Wisliceny, his assistant, arranged the deportation of some fifteen hundred more Jews after the Horthy government had ordered that the deportations cease, the Hungarian police interfered and brought the train back at Horthy's express order. Eichmann was incensed. A few days later he summoned all the leaders of the Jewish Council to his office, where they listened to a long, apparently aimless talk about Jewish organizational life. When the talk seemed to have come to an end and the Council leaders tried to leave, they were ordered to stay where they were. Not until seven o'clock that night were the Jewish leaders permitted to go, whereupon they learned that in their absence the SS had entered Kistarca—the internment camp for Jews, outside Budapest, from which Eichmann's men had a few days earlier tried unsucccessfully to deport the fifteen hundred Jews—and taken everyone away.† By compelling the Jewish leaders to stay in his office until the train had got safely across the Hungarian border, Eichmann had made certain that no one with any access to Horthy would be able to alert him to the news—as had happened the first time—that a transport of Jewish deportees was going out against his orders. This time the train reached its destination at Auschwitz.

By October of 1944, the Germans had dispensed with the Horthy government and set up in its place a regime headed by the leaders of the Hungarian Nazi Arrow Cross Party. There was now no practical interference with Eichmann's efforts: though the Russians were at the gates of Budapest, his primary hope was still to get at least fifty

---

* Ibid.

† Testimony of Pinchas Freudiger, quoted in Gideon Hausner, *Justice in Jerusalem* (New York: Harper & Row, 1966), pp. 144–145.

thousand Jews out of Budapest and into Germany, with another forty or fifty thousand to follow. In short order, he concluded an agreement with the heads of the new Hungarian government, Szalasi and Gabor, that since neither trains nor trucks were available, transportation systems of every kind having by then broken down, the fifty thousand Jews would be marched from Budapest to Germany on foot. The march, the first of several, began on October 20, 1944, under the supervision of members of the Hungarian Arrow Cross, whose brutality was by all accounts equal to any theretofore shown by the German SS. The marchers received no food for the more than hundred-mile trek, and International Red Cross observers reported that wherever they went on the highway, the scene was the same: "The deportees marched in endless lines, ragged, starved, and exhausted, including old people who could hardly drag themselves along. The gendarmes drove them on with rifle butts, truncheons, and whips. They had to cover 30 kilometers a day."

After the war, while he was still at liberty, Eichmann related to his confidant Sassen—a journalist and former Nazi who tape-recorded many hours of Eichmann's conversations regarding the Final Solution—his reasons for ordering the Jews to be marched out of Hungary.

> . . . I wanted to show these allies my hand, as it were, to tell them: "Nothing will help; even if you bomb and destroy, I still have a way to the Reich."

In an autobiography written during his imprisonment after the war, Rudolf Höss, former Kommandant of Auschwitz, says that when he besought Eichmann's advice on problems relating to the Final Solution, Eichmann answered, "Without pity and in cold blood we must complete this extermination as rapidly as possible."

Eichmann's singular persistence in his role as deporter perfectly exemplified the priorities of the National Socialist program, in which the destruction of the Jews was second to no other goal. The head of Section IV-B-4, the Jewish affairs division of the Reich Security Main Office, Eichmann was eminently well qualified to be, as he was for all practical purposes, among the principal executors of the Final Solution.

After Wisliceny gave his testimony to the Nuremberg Tribunal, Eichmann no longer felt safe hiding in a prisoner-of-war camp in the American zone of Germany. Armed with new identity papers, he escaped—not a difficult feat in postwar days, when security at the prisoner of war camps was lax—and went to northern Germany. There Eichmann lived for the next four years as Otto Heninger. Then in 1950, with the aid of one of the underground organizations that had come into being after the war for the purpose of providing contacts, escape routes, and money for Nazis who had reason to worry about prosecution for war crimes, Eichmann made his way to a Franciscan monastery in Genoa which had been a secret way station for numerous escaping Nazis before him. Provided there with a passport and a new identity, Eichmann moved on to Buenos Aires where, as Ricardo Klement, he lived for the next ten years.

In the spring of 1960, Ricardo Klement's habits became the subject of close study to a team of Israeli secret agents. On May 11th, they waited for him to get off the bus that he took every night on his way home from work at a Mercedes-Benz plant, seized him, and hustled him into a car. Almost immediately upon his capture, Klement told the Israeli agents what they already knew, that he was Adolf Eichmann, and that he was aware he was in the hands of Israelis. Ten days later, he was flown to Israel and his capture announced.

As soon as the news of Eichmann's seizure by the Israelis became known to the world, there was heard a series of legal and moral objections to the manner of his capture. It was charged that Israel had violated the rights of another sovereign nation by going into Argentina and kidnapping Eichmann; that however terrible had been the deeds Eichmann was accused of, kidnapping was an act of lawlessness. "The rule of law must protect the most depraved criminals," a *New York Times* editorial admonished the Israelis. Argentina's representative protested to the United Nations Security Council, and her Foreign

Minister, after expressing his country's loathing for Nazi crimes, asked for Eichmann's return, as well as for unspecified diplomatic reparations for the affront to her; whereupon, after intercessions from the United States and France, it was diplomatically suggested to Argentina that she accept Israel's apology and content herself with the thorough airing of her complaint against Israel and with the discussions of the affront to Argentina's sovereignty, which had by then been going on at some length in the Security Council.

World response to Israel's seizure of Eichmann was complex and cautious but not, on the whole, negative. In Argentina, the newspaper *El Mundo* expressed its admiration for the brave men who had "during the years endangered their lives in searching the world for this criminal" and then delivered him up for trial by a judicial tribunal. In the United States, the Boston *Record American* stated editorially that it could not quarrel with the means used to apprehend Eichmann, and noted that there were more important things than protocol to consider in the case of Eichmann, an opinion that came to be heard more and more. Indeed, once the Argentina-Israel controversy was settled in the United Nations, with Argentina accepting Israel's apology, the rights and wrongs of Eichmann's kidnapping were no longer issues of public debate in the United States. But in their place arose the question that was to exercise legal experts, newspaper editors, philosophers, and social commentators of every stripe for the next two years: who should try Eichmann? Eichmann's crimes had taken place in Europe, it was argued, not in Israel, and he should therefore be tried in an international court or brought back to Germany to stand trial. It was doubted that Israel could provide the proper dispassionate background for legal proceedings against Eichmann. And again and again, those who opposed Israel as the place of Eichmann's trial objected that if Israel were to try him, the crimes Eichmann had committed might be perceived as crimes against Jews, instead of against humanity as a whole. "To define a crime in terms of the religion or nationality of the victim, instead of the nature of the criminal act, is wholly out of keeping with the needs of the times and the trend of modern law," Telford Taylor, American chief counsel at Nuremberg, stated in the *New York Times Magazine* (January 22, 1961).

It was a theme that was to be restated in many of the nation's leading liberal newspapers. "The case is not Eichmann versus Israel; it is Eichmann versus civilized man," the New York *Post* said editorially (June 2, 1961). The Washington *Post* had, from the beginning of the Eichmann controversy, bitterly opposed Eichmann's trial by the Israelis and stated that anything connected with such a trial was tainted by lawlessness (May 27, 1960). There were, to be sure, differing opinions. The New York *Herald Tribune* noted that there seemed to be no realistic alternative to having Eichmann brought to justice in Israel (June 24, 1960). The Sheboygan, Wisconsin, *Press* disparaged the importance of the legal niceties that had been thrown up around the subject of Eichmann's trial by the Israelis (June 16, 1960), and the New York *World-Telegram & Sun* observed that any court in the civilized world would be prejudiced against Eichmann. Problems of jurisdiction aside, there was little disagreement with the proposition that Eichmann be brought to justice, though in the course of the controversy surrounding his capture at least one newspaper, the Chicago *American*, took the opportunity to reflect on the Nuremberg trials, which it called a turn backward toward the Middle Ages whose purpose had been to kill the losers.

While a good part of the nation's press expressed its concern editorially over the problem of whether Eichmann could receive a fair trial in Israel, a Gallup Poll taken in May of 1961 showed that an unusually large number of Americans—some 87 percent of the national sample—were aware of Eichmann's capture by the Israelis, and that 53 percent of them believed Israel had the right to try him: a finding which proved, if nothing else, that ordinary Americans were, as usual when dealing with the application of justice, less troubled by higher moral considerations than were the writers of liberal editorials.

The response in the nation's press at all ends of the

political spectrum eloquently illuminated the atmosphere of the times in which the Americans viewed the Eichmann trial. Eichmann had been captured fifteen years after the war had ended and much had happened since, in addition to the simple passage of time, to bring about a state of affairs which made it appear that the light in which Nazi crimes were viewed in 1960–1961 was of a different order from the uncompromising sternness that was in evidence at Nuremberg just after the war. In America, there had passed long years of the Cold War, of McCarthy and loyalty boards, of security-risk designations and blacklists; and if these aspects of the war had wound down by 1960, the Cold War issues themselves had by no means disappeared. It was in 1961 that the doomed Bay of Pigs invasion was launched against Castro's Cuba; in 1961 that the Kennedy-Khrushchev confrontation over Berlin had taken place; on August 13th of that year that the Russians put up the Berlin Wall.

Again and again one read in editorials and heard from political commentators that while Eichmann was being charged and condemned for his crimes, the present-day embodiments of totalitarianism, the Communists, were scot-free and victorious. Pastor Otto Dibelius, Evangelical Bishop of Berlin, told a German audience that when the deeds of Eichmann were discussed, the whole world would be able to say, "That is the way the Germans are," and, he warned them, "We will not be able to answer, 'It was only a handful of Germans who in their insanity forgot all the commandments of God.' They were men from our midst, of our blood, our kind, our people. Such a thing cannot be shoved aside."

Pastor Dibelius, not having taken into account factors that rendered indelicate precisely such judgments as the one he supposed the world would make about the Germans, might say to his people that the mass of murderers were men from their midst, their blood, their kind. In America, however, it was possible to hear a different kind of caution from religious leaders concerning the Eichmann trial. The Catholic *Pilot* declared, "The Germans themselves were, of course, the victims of the Nazis. . . . Now this vigorous friend of freedom is one of the bulwarks of the West. . . . It would be a great disservice to the friends of liberty in our world if Eichmann was in any sense made to appear a German symbol or even a German type" (April 15, 1961).

Once Eichmann's trial began, criticism about the circumstances in which it would be held lessened dramatically, the result partly of the obviousness of Israel's intention to provide a trial that was scrupulously fair; but more, perhaps, because the drama of the testimony soon overshadowed arguments about where Eichmann should have been tried. Editorial writers and other political and social commentators began to say that their fears with regard to the trial had been laid to rest; but there were other issues, clearly, about which the critics' worries were never to cease, and the symptoms of these worries were found in the peculiar language which political and social commentators used in describing the trial. They reflected an odd combination of American political attitudes, of Cold War sensitivities on the one hand and of liberal, enlightened sensibility on the other. It had been a worry that Israel should try Eichmann lest his crimes be thought to have been committed against Jews, rather than against humanity as a whole; in addition, it was a worry that Israel should try Eichmann because in Anglo-Saxon law the victim does not try the accused, and the chief object of the Nazi extermination program, of which Eichmann had been so crucial an officer, was in fact known to be the Jews and not humanity as a whole. It was a worry that the trial of Eichman would embarrass Germany; that attention would be diverted from the threat of Communism by lingering on the subject of the Nazis; that Americans, who had never been Nazis—who had in fact fought and defeated Nazism—should consider themselves superior to Eichmann without reflecting adequately on their own sins.

In consequence of these and other concerns, Eichmann's crimes and all the workings of the Final Solution with which he was connected became, in the language of the editorial writers, "crimes against humanity." "Totalitarianism," not Nazism, was on trial; the subject of the Eichmann trial was not the implementation of the Final Solution, and the mass murder of European Jewry, but "man's inhumanity to man," "racism," and "bigotry." It would, in addition, have been difficult to learn, from the abstractions that commentators were given to using when discussing the trial, in which country Nazism had been seated, references to Germany being remarkably rare in this connection. Regularly, when editorial commentators did speak of Nazism, readers were reminded that the world at large was to blame for Hitler's rise to power.

In 1961, the subject of the holocaust had not achieved the status that it was to have years later, after the histories had been written, the studies compiled, and, among other things, the ecumenical seminars held on the Christian church's role in the holocaust. Indeed, certain sectors of the nation's religious press took a decidedly superior tone in discussing the manner in which the Jews attempted to bring Eichmann to justice. As the trial came to a close and Eichmann's sentence was about to be meted out, there appeared a considerable number of commentaries on vengeance in the Christian—notably the Protestant—press.

> Whatever is done to Adolph Eichmann by way of punishment will be ashes in the mouths of those who thirst most for vengeance.
>> —*Fellowship*, magazine of the Fellowship of Reconciliation, quoted in the *Mennonite Review*, May 25, 1961.
>
> In the ethical sense I can see little difference between the Jew-pursuing Nazi and the Nazi-pursuing Jew.
>> —Paul E. Killinger, Unitarian minister, in the *Unitarian Register*, October, 1969.

A few of the religious newspapers reflected the unusual opinion that the trial of Eichmann could be compared with the trial of Jesus. An article in a Protestant Episcopal magazine conceded that the comparison might be scandalous, but that the writer would proceed, nonetheless, to make the parallel between the trial of Jesus and the Eichmann trial.

The defendant in the earlier case was rather different from the present defendant, but nevertheless, he was accused as Eichmann was of subverting the Jewish nation. The authorities, as in Eichmann's case, had apprehended him by trick, and there was a dispute about who had jurisdiction to try him. . . . The difference in the two trials is that Eichmann's condemnation does not save a single man from bondage and service to death, while the condemnation of the other defendant set men free from death and from the power of death in their own sin. In both trials, Israel has been confounded in her longing for righteousness.
—William Stringfellow in the
Witness, March 8, 1962.

To be sure, the incidence of such comparisons was not high in the religious press, though there could be found in that press not a few commentaries alluding to the difference between Judaic vengeance and Christian forgiveness. "Vengeance in repayment for sins committed is 2,000 years out of date," an article in the *Lutheran* noted pointedly (June 7, 1961).

Despite the stated unhappiness of some of them with Eichmann's trial by the Israelis and his sentence, however, a number of Christian religious publications—*Commonweal*, the *Catholic Sentinel*, and the *Unitarian Register* and *Universalist Leader* among them—turned their attention to the failures that had made possible the extermination of Europe's Jews. "Six million Jews would not have died under Eichmann if our doors had not been held fast shut against their immigration in the 30's," the *Christian Century* noted. "Where, I wondered, was the Christian church?" asked the executive editor of the *Christian Herald*, in describing his feelings when he attended the Eichmann trial and heard the testimony of the witnesses. "Save for isolated examples of sacrificial courage, the church was either uninformed or preoccupied, or unfeeling or cowed. . . ."

Editorialists' cautions and abstractions notwithstanding, the hard facts about the Final Solution reached a vast audience with the advent of the Eichmann trial. In America, the coverage in regular news accounts was complete and vivid—too complete, some survivors had reason to attest—and, in one way, familiar: just as correspondents entering the liberated camps had done in 1945, reporters covering the Eichmann trial wrestled in their columns and their newscasts with the inconceivable nature of the events they were required to write about.

For a great many American Jews, the trial was a galvanizing force, bringing them face to face with emotions theretofore repressed, with events whose full scope and reverberations had been kept, rumbling, beneath the surface of consciousness.

The trial constituted the first in the series of shocks that would periodically, but with ever-deepening effect, close the distance between American Jews and their awareness of the holocaust, the others being Israel's wars of survival, particularly the Six-Day War of 1967 and the October War, 1973. Some years after the Eichmann trial, in addition, circumstances arose that greatly extended holocaust consciousness among non-Jews as well as Jews: in the anti-war movement of the middle and late sixties,* particularly in America, the destruction of the European Jews by the Germans was widely, if erroneously, utilized as a parallel for U.S. involvement in the Vietnam War and the destruction by bombing and napalming of countless Vietnamese. Mistaken as the parallel was between America's intervention in the war and the unique, state-ordered, elaborate, and deliberately executed program of genocide which the Germans perpetrated on European Jewry with such singular success, it was nonetheless given wide currency, with the result that the holocaust became a reference indelibly engraved on the consciousness of a generation which could otherwise have been expected to ignore it as a piece of ancient history. The signs the peace marchers carried referred as a matter of course to Auschwitz, to Himmler, and to Eichmann; and even here, in a sense more

* See Lucy S. Dawidowicz, *American Jewish Yearbook*, 1968, vol. 69, pp. 203–204.

complicated than the mere invocation of his name, the issues of the Eichmann trial loomed large, as large in the late 1960s as they had at the time of the trial—if not larger. For prominent among the themes debated during and after the Eichmann trial was the issue of individual conscience: whether the individual had a duty to refuse obedience to a system which perpetrated crimes against humanity. It was the issue of the Nuremberg trials, in short, but more recently and dramatically posed in the Eichmann trial, in a single figure and, by far the more important factor, in a trial whose focus was on genocide. This was a fact of no small political relevance to the constituency of the peace movement, a good part of which was disposed to connect the U.S. military intervention in Vietnam, particularly the massive bombing raids that were taking an enormous toll of Vietnamese lives, with American racism.

The debates that originated with the Eichmann proceedings had, besides widening the impact of the holocaust, other effects. In the single most controversial work published on the trial, *Eichmann in Jerusalem: A Report on the Banality of Evil*, Hannah Arendt explained the way in which Eichmann—in her portrayal a humdrum figure—had been caught in the totalitarian machine. The number of words written about totalitarianism during and just after the Eichmann trial is not known to history, but it was unusually high, and *Eichmann in Jerusalem* contributed a considerable portion of them.

It was not due to her concern with totalitarianism, however, that Hannah Arendt's study of the Eichmann trial became the source of controversy and of bitter response, particularly from other Jewish intellectuals, for years to come, but her contention that the Jewish Councils in occupied Europe—and indeed organized Jewry the world over, the Zionists prominent among them—had actively aided the Nazi design for political reasons of their own, and that without their complicity the Nazis could never have succeeded in killing so many Jews. It was another and highly complicated form of the proposition that the victims were accomplices in their fate: that it was the perfidy of their own organizations and leaders, not the determination of the Nazis in implementing the Final Solution, which had doomed millions of Jews.

IV

The survivors, of course, took no part in the extraordinary outpouring of opinion produced by the Eichmann trial about such things as jurisdiction or Eichmann's place in the totalitarian scheme. They could not claim ever to have laid eyes on Adolf Eichmann, or to have had contact with him of the sort some of them had with the SS at whose trials they testified, or to have received any direct injury at his hands—as witnesses could, years later, for example, testify they had from Hermine Braunsteiner. There was, furthermore, nothing they learned from the testimony of the Eichmann trial that they did not already know; nonetheless, to a great many of them the Eichmann trial was a profoundly liberating event. For almost overnight the publicity surrounding the trial had put an end to the years of postwar public silence in which their experiences had been submerged. The proceedings provided, as the Israelis meant it should, a complete and detailed documentation of the extermination program that had been carried out against the Jews of Europe, and the details of that documentation were heard around the world. For the survivors, most of whom were in displaced persons camps during the time of the Nuremberg trials, the Eichmann trial was the first experience they had of seeing the facts about the holocaust widely disseminated and talked about, and of witnessing public response to those facts, the latter being a concern of no small importance to them. For they were uneasy in their relation to the entity they called "the whole world," "the rest of the world," or what, in a term harking back to their experience of entrapment and utter isolation under the Nazis, they still sometimes referred to as "the outside world." "I thought the rest of the world didn't know anything about what was happening to us;

otherwise it couldn't happen, it wouldn't be allowed. Afterward I found out the world knew plenty." "I thought, Nobody knows; that's why I have to live—to tell the world. Of course, I found out later I didn't have to live just for that; the world knew."

But their sense that "the world" knew coexisted side by side with their perception that "people" rejected the facts about the holocaust, which had been widely published after 1945. The Eichmann trial came at the end of the first decade of the survivors' lives in America, a period of great busyness and adjustment, during which some of them had learned to use a frigid caution in discussing the past. Among native Americans, both Jew and Gentile, one could find, a great number of years after the war's end, many who believed that the stories of what had happened to the Jews of Europe were greatly exaggerated, if true at all, or who knew nothing whatever about the details. Shortly after her arrival in America in 1951, one survivor had the experience of being told by her American-born Jewish neighbor in Brooklyn that she ought to write stories. "You have a terrific imagination," the neighbor told her on hearing a tale about selections and gas chambers. Soon after, the neighbor had told other tenants in the apartment house that if they wanted to hear good stories they should spend an afternoon with the refugee, that "she has some imagination."

One middle-aged New Orleans survivor, proprietor of a small haberdashery, told how, one steaming hot afternoon in the late fifties, a truck driver had come in to buy a cheap extra shirt to replace the soaked one he was wearing: "I told him, 'Here's one for two dollars,' and handed it to him. He looked at my arm with the numbers on it. 'Oh,' he said to me, 'I see you got your souvenir. Well, don't try to tell people here what happened over in Europe; forget about it,' he told me. 'I was in the American army,' he said; 'I walked into those camps and I saw all those things the Germans did, and people here don't believe it when you tell them.'" He had, the truck driver told the haberdasher, given up mentioning the sights he had seen in the camps when he talked about the war to anybody but people who had been there and seen for themselves; he advised the haberdasher to do the same.

During roughly the same period, a survior living in San Francisco had attended an alumni dinner dance at her husband's law school, her husband being an American Jew whom she had met after the war. In relating the incident, she said that she noticed one man in the room staring curiously at her from time to time; finally, he came over, introduced himself, and confessed that he had seen the numbers on her arm. "I was wondering," he said, "why you were wearing your laundry numbers on your arm?" What were they really, he wanted to know, some sort of decoration? "I told him no, that's my telephone number. He was the dean of the law school, I learned from my husband later on."

After the Eichmann trial, though there were still to be found in America people who, for various reasons—not excluding anti-Semitic ones—continued to believe that the wholesale annihilation of the Jews of Europe was a story, or an exaggeration, their numbers were not great. So far as the question of resistance was concerned, the trial had, in addition, illustrated details of the carefully planned and unyielding vise in which the Jews of Europe had been caught, and thus it had, in a measure, provided answers to the questions of how the Germans could have succeeded in their extermination program without being hampered by wholesale armed uprisings on the part of their victims. In the end, however, the trial could be said to have enlarged, rather than diminished, the controversy about Jewish honor with which the survivors in particular were so concerned, and of which the question about resistance was but a part. The talk of Jewish complicity in the Nazi exterminations and about the role of the Judenräte would soon become, thanks to the literature that came out of the trial and particularly to the influential *Eichmann in Jerusalem: A Report on the Banality of Evil*, a fixed theme of all holocaust discourse.

The questions about resistance showed, further, that they had a life of their own, especially so far as the survivors were concerned; that they would only grow in intensity over the years, and not be quieted with answers provided by the Eichmann trial. Nonetheless, the trial was of immeasurable importance to them: Jews, acting in the name of a Jewish state, had caught, tried, and punished Eichmann, an event which underscored how far they had come from their former condition of helplessness. In addition, the trial of Eichmann had caused the details of the Final Solution to be broadcast everywhere in the world, and in this elementary way lightened the twin burdens of silence and cynicism that some of the survivors had carried since the war's end.

ELIZABETH K.

An apartment building at Madison Avenue and Ninety-third Street, where the long shining stretch of fine shops and galleries ends and the streets begin to take on the drab look of Spanish Harlem a few blocks uptown. Inside, in a fourth-floor apartment, are the remnants of households in Vienna and Holland, odds and ends of furnishings old friends in Europe reclaimed for their owner and sent here after the war's end. Their owner, however, conveys a grand obliviousness to furnishings: sufficient that they are there, they are useful. She has no particular feelings about them; these old things, as she calls them—she could get rid of them tomorrow and get new ones if she had to.

Many a holocaust survivor learned to assume an airily dismissive attitude toward belongings. How, after the losses they had endured, could they pay the smallest heed to material possessions? Worlds had been taken from them, flesh and blood: should they ever again lift a finger of desire for things? So some of them reasoned. One could admire things and enjoy them, but one would attribute no importance to them beyond that. For they felt that they knew, from their experience, what was the proper and true relation to one's possessions, and it came down simply to this: that one should be able to turn one's back on them and leave them all behind without a thought.

"I care nothing for possessions," the woman, Elizabeth

K., said. (One had heard those words often from survivors; they had been uttered, too, in lavishly furnished houses and in cramped lower-middle-class apartments full of hard-earned things on proud display—strict avowals, nonetheless, that the lessons of the past still endured.)

"When the Germans came, my husband and I walked with our silverware in our hands to deliver it to the Gestapo as all the Jews had to do. I suppose some people might have thought this was humiliating, to walk down the streets carrying these bundles; I suppose it was. My husband and I took this bundle to the table where the Gestapo sat, and delivered our silver to a man who had been a guest at our table many times. He was in charge of the delivery of jewelry and silver, and he didn't blink an eyelash when we walked in. People were then afraid to acknowledge any social connections with Jews."

Her voice was deep, its Viennese accent thick. When she stopped to take phone calls, as she did a number of times, her basso filled the room with hellos and endearments. It plummeted to an improbable depth to express concern, and rose in curiosity: there was more plummeting than rising on the whole, and always and everywhere in that voice was certainty, and the promise that all would be well. She was seventy-three now, and a widow. She and her husband had lived in their native Vienna until her husband, an executive with an oil firm, was transferred to Holland. There they had had, by every standard to which they were accustomed, a good life, giving dinner parties and going to them; their house became in short order a center of social activity. There was no reason for them not to have found such quick acceptance in upper-middle-class society in Holland; her husband was an extremely cultivated man, she noted, in a complicated tone of voice. Quite often she used this tone when speaking of her husband.

"My husband, he was an aesthete," she explained. "He was so noble: a thinker and a nobleman. He hated ugliness so. He suffered from ugliness. I was not so sensitive, which was quite fortunate, in a way, for all of us.

"In Belsen, he suffered twice as much as I, because I

could be with that ugliness without being destroyed by it. You know, I think his highest dream, his greatest ideal, in life was cleanliness. *Ja.*"

Out of respect, her voice had turned low; out of an irreproachable face, she flashed hooded eyes toward his photograph, and blinked rapidly as she explained her husband's sensitivity to a speck of dirt, a soiled collar. The husband thus described gazed out of a prewar photograph, a slender, youthfully bald man with solemn eyes, dead ten years after their arrival in America.

"We were arrested quite early in Holland. My daughter was thirteen at the time, and by the time she had her sixteenth birthday we were in Belsen. She asked me, 'Mother, do you think that on my seventeenth birthday I will be free?' I told her, 'You will see, you will be.' Hope gives tremendous courage; you had to give that to the child and to yourself or you could not live. I think that the worst thing I saw was the wagons, the trains—beast-wagons—arriving with little children to face this death all alone. What if my child should have to face this death alone? And these were babies, babies of two and three. I am very grateful that I was spared, that I did not have to see my child or my husband choke to death by gas. Where there were no gas chambers, there was still not a day without fear, and one could see the result in the children. Some, like my daughter, escaped into childhood, and some were violently and boldly grown up.

"I think even before we were arrested I knew our destiny, as my father did. He was the most brilliant man, an economist. My brothers are very intelligent, but not compared to what he was. When he saw what was going to happen, he wanted just to die. This was when the family was still in Vienna. As soon as he saw to it that my mother had a passport for Holland and my brothers had visas, he chose death; he refused all medication for his heart because he saw everything annihilated that he had worked for all his life.

"In camp I had a job ripping up soldiers' torn and bloodstained uniforms, and working side by side with me was a tiny woman who told me recipes all day long. Jewish and Viennese recipes, the fanciest and the most complicated—you know, kreplach and cakes and other things for which you needed all those rich ingredients, and so and so many eggs, and so and so much cream. And here everyone was starving for just some bread. Many of the women did this. All day long they exchanged recipes in the greatest detail: they would tell each other, you put in this and you put in that and you let it stand for a while. I must say, about this cooking in the mind, that I never did it. One day we were marching back from work and this little woman who had done all this cooking in her head quite suddenly said to me, 'Tomorrow morning I don't want to wake up. I am so tired.' I said to her 'Nonsense! Tomorrow you are going to wake up and be at the *Appell* just like me, at six.' But she was dead in the morning. You can't anymore, so you die. But for myself I had this child; you had to live for this child. I adored this child; how could I die before she died? And if you gave up, it was very easy to die.

"If you are a believing Jew, you will not like what I say. That when I was in this camp it filled me with the greatest anger that my family had not converted to Christianity four or five generations earlier. I had been given a completely assimilationist background—we got this from my father—but why then couldn't I have belonged to a family who converted? And then we would not have been taken to a concentration camp and lost those years. Often in the camp I told my husband this, and that we would never have been in there if our families had done the right thing. Since we were never practicing Jews, why should we belong to this chosen group? I tell this to no one now, because everyone I am friends with who went through all this, they are all terribly Jewish now. Oh, I couldn't tell them this! It is true, though; being a Jew was never any matter of the first importance to me, and I can tell you something, after all that has happened: when my daughter married a Jew, I was even a little disappointed. Anti-Semitism is not dead, you know, and especially in Europe; it raises its head all the time, it does not die.

"Jews in America make a bad mistake, too, I can tell you. It is not good that people put themselves in the foreground so, that a minority should be in so much possession of all the theaters and the arts and especially in the television. Of course, let us admit it, they are more gifted; they have been trained in intellect for all those generations. But even if you know these things, is it not better instead of being so prominent, is it not better to push yourself back, a little out of sight? It was the same way in Germany; this is what the Germans talked about—Jews were everywhere in the arts, in literature and the banks.

"I did go to visit Israel after the war, and I started to admire them. A fantastic country! But even there I was so angry to see little children with the side curls and those black hats. Little children! I say, Why do the Jews have to look different? If they are different inside, why do they have to be different outside? If you are a minority, you must assimilate. And you, don't you think something terrible will happen if you drink milk with meat? No? I know many such people here in New York, and of course you can't tell them such things as I feel. But do not mistake me, I am not an unbeliever. I always had faith in a Superpower. But not a Jewish God. If there was one, how could this have happened? You see, I cannot get it through my head that God would try to punish six million Jews. A Superpower, yes, without that I could not have survived. It gave you a will to play certain games with yourself. When I was marching in a line with all these huge black dogs the Germans had that were trained to jump on us if we got out of line, and I passed by the SS man who was leading the dogs, I said to myself, 'He is already dead.' I undressed him, I made a skeleton of him in my mind. I said, 'I am going to survive, and he is going to die.' These were only games, little games, to bring back your courage; perhaps they had really no effect, but I played them anyway.

"Think of yourself being put with a stranger in a bunker. If you are lucky, you are on top. Excrement was all over.

All night, if you had to get up, you fell over that frozen shit, as I must call it. You are always terribly hungry, terribly cold; you must protect that piece of bread. I have heard that many mothers abandoned their children, rather than follow their babies to death. The animal instinct to protect the child is so strong, but I don't know how it would be if there is a gas chamber in front of you and you can see the smoke and know what is ahead. Where I was, there were no gas chambers—either in Westerbork or Belsen—and I saw only mothers who protected their children with the last ounce of their strength. For a long time we did not know for sure about the gas chambers. We heard things, but we never understood what they meant, till afterwards. Once, we were being transported and a line of us stopped at a barracks. There was something like a bathroom in it, and the walls were scribbled all over with writing in Hebrew, in Yiddish, and in Polish: 'There are no Jews in Poland.' 'Everything is a lie.' 'We have been murdered.' But we did not know what it meant. There were no Jews in Poland? How come? But a year later, when the war ended, we understood, just as we understood what the French Jews, who had come to Belsen straight from Auschwitz, were telling us when they called across the fence to us, 'They have burned our babies!' We had never understood what they meant by it.

"The transports came, the transports left. The smell was something you could not forget toward the end, in Belsen. And then there was this mixture. There were Jews from Benghazi, who actually came to the camp in their Biblical clothes. Proud Jews these Benghazi people, and completely uncultured. After the liberation, they went around and exchanged chickens, live chickens, with which they had lived in the barracks! Or they roasted them, right in the barracks! Absolutely wild and uncivilized Jews, we had nothing in common with them. There was every kind in this conglomeration: beautiful Jews, ugly Jews, educated ones, ignorant ones. Ah, yes, and I have also seen ladies who had been very spoiled, of very old, very educated Jewish families, who died as no criminal in a prison has ever died: lying on straw so foul it could not be cleaned.

The dignity, the *noblesse* with which some of these old ones died—without a whimper. I saw one old woman who was dying in great pain: she spent all day holding a book up to her face, reading; then, at night, she would try to read by the light of this one candle we had for the whole barracks. Her pain was so terrible. She lay in filth, never complaining, but only she kept on reading these books with the greatest attention. It was a noble death; there was such a thing. She had a noble death, though she lay in excrement. I saw it. She knew, as my mother did, and most of these old ones, that they would never live to see freedom.

"When the liberation came, we were filled with the greatest happiness. There was excitement in the air, that we had survived, my husband and my child and I, and we were full of this joy! And there was this feeling, after we had come through all this, that no harm could ever come to us again. Of course, it took some time afterwards for me to understand how there could ever be a luxury greater than bread: but most of all, to have this liberty. I cannot tell you what it meant to us to come to America; this was the freedom we had never known before. To speak freely, to be without fear, to think as you like. It did not take us long to see what this country was. Americans do not know, they cannot understand, what they have here. Yes, we have had some hard times, some varied times, but I am telling the truth: we have been happy from the day we came here.

"We came straight to a small apartment in Queens, and we had nothing. I worked, my husband worked; our little apartment was like an inferno in the summer, it was so close to the roof, and we could not afford such a thing as air conditioning. We lived as we had to, very modestly, and I will not say that we had an easy time.

"Now I still live on a modest scale. My daughter, it so happened, married a fairly well-to-do man, and she did not want me to work from then on. I don't need much. Sometimes when I crawl into bed at night, I think about the pleasure of these clean sheets. And the freedom: I have not taken it for granted yet. But it is all bought with a terrible price: my poor parents, my poor husband. I suppose if it had not been for this tragedy, I would have been living the old life in Europe; I would have been the average, middle-aged woman playing bridge in Holland or Vienna, with the same circle of friends, and gone on vacations mostly to the same place. The holocaust saved me from this, which is a terrible fate, too, to grow old among the bourgeoisie of Europe."

Her daily life was a busy one. During the day, she had errands or it might be that her daughter's children needed to be taken to the dentist, or to school; her daughter, who lived nearby, was a career woman with a heavy schedule. In the evenings, the telephone rang constantly with calls from friends and acquaintances who required advice on their personal lives.

"I suppose I attract people," she conjectured once, without apparent curiosity. Her callers, indeed, seemed innumerable and it could be understood why: her optimism was unfailing, her assurance such that it might raise the lowest hopes.

"Yes, yes. You will see, it will be all right. My dear child, what nonsense; there is nothing at all to worry about, I promise you."

Of late, however, her own nights have become uneasy, her sleep restless, she says, as it never was in the years just after the war, with dreams now of Belsen and terror. Waves of sadness come on her now, too, reluctant as she is to confess it. Her weapons had been optimism and energy against hardship and mortal danger. "These things, sadness and depression, are saboteurs," she observes; still, from time to time now, depression and sadness overpower her.

"There is always this sadness inside you, underneath everything," she concedes once, unwillingly, and in the instant her posture is weary. But, like the commission of sin, the moment passes quickly. The phone rings and the guttural buoyant voice sounds a hello, head inclined, listening, all energies restored as she waits by the phone, poised, cunning, ready for the moment to begin her declarations that all will be well, that it could not possibly be otherwise.

7 | Particular Paths

I

Jolson, the dealer in sewing machines, was among those who attended the Eichmann trial. He went not as a participant but as an observer; and though spectator seats were not easy to come by he had no reason to be concerned on that score. By 1961, he was a wealthy and successful man. He had friends: if he wanted to attend an event, it would be arranged; if a ticket was required, somebody would find one for him. He was in a position now to do what he wanted whenever he wanted. As to money, that would never again be a worry.

Jolson sat quite close to the glass booth—"Eichmann's cage," as he called it. He watched how Eichmann scribbled constantly, making notes on everything that was said; how he looked always alert, and screwed up his eyes to show that he was taking everything in, that every word he heard on the earphones was of the greatest significance to him, that his mind was bent only on analysis. He knew what Eichmann was trying to do, the kind of face he was trying to show the world. Here, by pushing all these pieces of paper around in front of him as he was doing all the time, by scribbling—getting notes ready for his lawyer, probably—Eichmann was trying to say that he was the same important person he ever was, that he took part in these historic proceedings as an equal: as a judge of events, a contributor to the record, an authority—as every one of these things, but only not as a defendant. He

watched Eichmann turning his head this way and that
while he listened to the testimony, nodding his head in-
telligently sometimes, or pursing his lips as though there
were some great intellectual ferment going on in his mind.

He had wished to see Eichmann sitting in an Israeli
courtroom—only to look at him there in the glass booth.
At least, before he got there he had no other explanation
to give for the necessity that had made him drop everything and fly to Jerusalem. That he gave an explanation at
all surprised no one who knew him; for though he could
now afford to do what he wanted with his time, that was
only a practical fact, not necessarily the rule by which he
was governed. It was no less his belief now than before
that a man's time had to be a hundred percent productive.
It was an important idea for any man; but if the man was
one who had lost six years of his life, as he had between
1939 and 1945, it was an imperative. Whatever he was
able to achieve, he was always six years behind; a man
did not start out six years behind and look for success
unless he knew how to make his time productive. He had
based his career on that assumption; it was not something
to be adhered to only when one was struggling, and
dropped as soon as one was a success.

His career and his life were inseparable. Furthermore,
he found that he could apply to life the lessons he had
learned in business, just as he applied to business the
lessons he had learned in life. A survivor, he had learned
the value of taking risks, and after the war he applied that
learning to every enterprise he undertook. In short, life
had taught him to take chances in business; business, on
the other hand, had taught him not to take too many
chances in life. For example, he had learned never to lose
his temper so much or say anything so final to anyone,
friend or relation, that the door was permanently closed
on a relationship, with no possibility of mending a quarrel.
This was a lesson he had taken from business and applied to life; in business he had learned that there was
always a way to strike a bargain in the end, if only one
had left the door open a little way. What useful purpose
would be served by irrationality and stubborness? These

things closed off all hope of making a bargain that could be as beneficial to oneself as to the other party; and this was the reasoning he liked to apply to all relationships. It was, he liked to observe, not healthy and not productive to burn bridges.

He had this attitude with regard to the past, too; also with regard to such touchy matters as Germany and the question of Jews doing business there. This attitude set him apart from most of the survivors he knew. His philosophy—and he was inclined not to talk about it too often, except to certain close survivor friends who were not likely to take offense—was simply that healthy men could not live in the past: that feelings of revenge and hatred were, in his favorite phrase, "not constructive." Whatever had happened to them, men had to lead constructive lives. Survivors had to exercise control and keep from being obsessed by the past. Remember, yes, but not be obsessed: this was his firm belief, and, like many of his beliefs, the rightness of this one, too, he could say, was borne out by his own observation.

He had seen how the people who had least been given to thinking about the past all the time, to recalling who they had once been and what they once had, were the quickest to recover after 1945, and to prosper once more.

You could not come to America with nothing, for example, and go to an employer for a job and tell him that in the old country, before Hitler, you had been in charge of fifty or a hundred men, that you were in a position of the greatest importance. What would the employer say to himself? Only that here was a man he could not hire for an ordinary job, because he was used to much better and would never be satisfied with a lowly position such as the one he had to offer him.

One had to be willing to start all over, and to have patience: this was wisdom, so far as he was concerned. And starting over meant also to bury hatred. For example, there were Americans—Jews—to whom nothing whatever had happened during the war, who still refused to buy German goods, and he sighed when he thought of this, which he considered childishness. He believed himself in the sincerity of the new Germany, in her strivings toward democracy. To turn one's back on every German forever, to continue not to acknowledge them or do business with them—particularly a guiltless younger generation—was against reason and logic, the lights by which he lived: nor was it constructive or just. For these reasons he sighed when he heard how some people still refused to do business with Germany, to buy German goods, to have a German car. He himself would have done business with Germany if it were possible. The difficulty was that against all the lights by which he lived, against reason and constructiveness, he could not bring himself to buy German goods, a German car, or to do one penny's business with Germany. Instead, he had made many visits there, he had talked deals, and looked with interest at what was shown him, all to no end. And this was clear to the German businessmen, too, one of whom told him in a moment of frankness that they knew he would always come, he would look, and he would never do business. Nor did he try to; for it was one of the cardinal principles by which he lived, also, that a man should not argue with himself.

With the exception of Germany, he did business with countries in the four corners of the earth. He had, it will be remembered, arrived in the United States in 1947; thereafter, even by his own reckoning—and it was the reckoning of a man bent on making up lost years—his success had been accomplished with dazzling speed. No sooner had he settled into the small storefront office where he sold secondhand sewing machines than he began plotting ways of getting out of it. He had not come to America to establish himself again in order to end up in a secondhand business; it was not in his plans. One did what one had to do as long as necessary; all the time, one looked for the way out, the way up, the chance opportunity.

He heard, soon after he settled into the store, of a new sewing machine that was being manufactured in Italy, a machine with a number of features that were a vast improvement on anything American consumers had seen before, including a device for crisscross stitching. Consumers would want such a machine, he reasoned; one had only to present it properly. He believed in analyzing consumer response, for one thing, and had always studied his customers' tastes, even if they had only come in to buy needles. However small or great the enterprise, one applied to it the principles one had learned; he knew no other way.

He demonstrated the machine to every customer who came into his store. Invariably, the response was enthusiastic. Then he began looking for investors, going first to a clipping service where he got the names of three hundred people who were in the market for sewing machines. In the next few days his wife had the laborious job of typing out three hundred letters to the people whose names were on the list, informing them about the new Italian machine that did crisscross stitching. The letters had all been sent out on a Thursday; on the following Monday morning when he arrived at the store, he found twenty people lined up waiting to place orders, to ask questions about the new machine. In addition, a merchant he had met in the area thought that his brother might want to invest. In the end, he had investments and customers' orders for the purchase of two thousand machines. He wired the order, locked up the store, and took a DC-4 to Rome, a journey that in the late forties was a twenty-four-hour affair. Then, arriving in Rome to oversee the transaction, he made the alarming discovery that the Italian company was barely capable of producing four hundred machines in a month. He responded to the news by throwing himself into frenzied arrangements for new plants and vastly stepped-up production, spending countless hours in DC-4's between Rome and New York until arrangements for production were completed.

The Nechi, as the Italian machine was called, was soon a success in America; just as soon, he was on his way to becoming a rich man, and others who had invested in the machine were on their way to becoming rich, too.

A year after he arrived in the United States, he incorporated. But even earlier than that he had begun to pay off his debts—an ability that had, at least in one instance, notable consequences. A few months after he had arrived in America, when he had desperately needed money to finance an order for some equipment, he was told that a Jewish agency, the United Service Fund, would sometimes grant refugees loans to help them get started in businesses of their own. Having got a loan of two thousand dollars from the agency, he found, some five months after, when the equipment deal had yielded him a handsome profit, that he was in a position to pay the loan back and in addition to offer the Fund a donation of a thousand dollars, a circumstance that clearly took the Fund personnel by surprise when they were confronted with it. Check in hand, he had gone to the office to pay the debt and to offer his contribution, but the officials who received him that day concluded that this was not a matter so easily disposed of; it required further consultation, and the best thing for all concerned, they gave him to understand, was that he should go home, taking his check with him. He was told to return in a few days, by which time, presumably, the news would have got to higher officials that a penniless refugee, who had just come to the country and had had to borrow two thousand dollars to get himself started, had in five months' time come to return it, with a donation.

He took pride in the speedy discharge of the debt, but neither pride nor anything else in his experience had prepared him for what he found when he returned to the agency office a few days later: he was ushered into a room swarming with reporters and photographers, where United Service Fund officers and the president of the United Jewish Appeal, Lessing Rosenwald, waited to greet him— a refugee fresh from the displaced persons camps of Europe who had made good in so brief a time. The story was not only proof of the man but also of America as a land of opportunity. Not surprisingly, in weeks to come the possibilities of this theme inspired the interest of newspapers and magazine editors all over the country. Nor was it less interesting or important to the Jewish agencies— who, even after 1945, had had to labor long and hard against restrictive immigration clauses—to have in one of their refugees so perfect an example of all the qualities Americans were thought to prize: grit, enterprise, and independence, the ability to strive and win against odds and, not least, the determination to pay one's debts.

There were articles about him in *Look, Fortune, Reader's Digest*, and a number of other national magazines, so that quite soon he had got used to giving interviews. Not that he didn't enjoy it all: it was simply that this was the first aspect of American life that was entirely strange to him. "This, I have to say, completely overwhelmed me," he said in later years. He read about himself for months; for months drunks called him from bars to ask him for money.

When, as was his habit, he analyzed the new circumstance for future reference, his findings were not very unusual or complicated. He determined, simply, that this was a particularly American thing, that it could not possibly have happened in Europe. There if you arrived in a country with nothing and did well and paid off your debts in a short time, newspaper and magazine writers did not come to your door to ask for interviews. Most certainly not.

Given this earlier experience, he was able to take it in stride when, a few years later, the National Association of Manufacturers honored him at their annual convention at the Waldorf-Astoria. The convention had a theme, which was that America was still the land of opportunity for all. There he had sat on the dais flanked by Henry Ford and Charles E. Wilson, head of General Motors. Then, in one of the more memorable moments of the convention, the assembled NAM members were shown a pageant of Jolson's life, dramatically enacted onstage in one of the Waldorf's ballrooms. While a well-known radio announcer narrated, an actor and an actress made their appearance on the stage, attired in the costume of a middle-class Jewish family in prewar Poland. This was part one of the pageant, his life story having, for the occasion, been divided into four parts. For the occasion, too—and this detail impressed him—the actress had traveled out to his home to study his wife's appearance, the better to represent her onstage. He was a man who admired a complete effort, and would notice such a thing.

In due time, as was natural, people stopped regarding him as a refugee who had made good. To all appearances, he was a wealthy and successful man like any other, though he still enjoyed special honors from time to time. For example, there was the one Italy had given him in gratitude for the foreign currency that the new sewing machine had brought into that country. The President of Italy had given him the Stella Della Repubblica Italiana and bestowed on him the rank of *Commendatore*.

"A *Commendatore*," he would say, rolling the word around on his tongue with relish, with respect, with the air of one who knew exactly how much to enjoy such a thing. In fact, in his sixties he had the look of a man one might address by such a title: he had the unhasty, deliberate walk of someone used to reviewing troops; he was tall and had kept his figure; he wore well-tailored European suits and, in the winter, belted-in-the-back checkered overcoats that clung nicely to his shoulders. Above all, he had a crop of gray-white hair, still thick, and this he wore combed back and to the side in straight, no-nonsense lines, which gave his head what could only be called a tailored look.

Commendatore he might be; he was always quick to say, however, that none of the rewards which had come his way in later years could ever give him as much pleasure as the first, achieved when things had been hard, when he was just getting on his feet again. The first apartment in America, the first dollar earned, the first sense of feeling established again even in a small way. This was something he thought about often in regard to his children, who had been born in America to wealth and to everything they wanted: that they would never know these satisfactions. It was a regrettable truth, but he did not mind contemplating it.

The children would not know what it was to be shorn of every possession but brains and will—that with these things alone one had passed every test, recovered so much, achieved so much. Because they had never had to wait for things they wanted, they would not know what it was to come into possession of them at last.

On this subject, his voice grew velvety. Once, he stretched his arms forward as though to encompass the four walls of the room, and four walls were exactly what he had in mind at the time—the four walls of the apartment on Fox Street in the Bronx, the possession of which had given him a taste of victory his children could never know.

The apartment he lived in now was on upper Fifth Avenue, with a view overlooking Central Park Lake. This one, with its sculptured high ceilings and thick walls, had an aged sort of elegance that gave him the greatest pleasure; but he had taken pleasure in the other residences he had owned, too. He had enjoyed them fully because they were, each one of them, right for a certain stage of his life. Over the years he had owned several fine houses, the last of them on Sands Point, Long Island. Then, when the children had gone off to school and married, he decided that the Long Island period was over. He did not like connection with things that had outlasted their function; furthermore, he felt the need, periodically, to make a change, to be flexible, to adapt to new circumstances— in sum, to practice his skill.

Once, he outlined to a friend all the reasons why it was unlikely that the Jews would ever have to run from America. American democratic tradition was long, its institutions stable; it lacked the entrenched anti-Semitism that had existed in Europe. It was not likely that it would happen here; it was not impossible, either. And though there was no real probability that one would have to become a refugee from America, he could, for argument's sake, list the countries where it would be safest to run. Aside from Israel, there was England. But Sweden was probably safer than England, since Sweden had a more stable economy. By the end of an hour's time he had outlined the flight from America in detail, and in terms that had grown less theoretical by the minute. He did this not for argument's sake but because, like any survivor, he had thought about the problem of where to run, so that the details were quite clear in his mind, quite matter-of-fact and practical.

The move from Long Island to the Manhattan apartment suited him. During the winter season, his wife settled in their Florida residence, where he joined her on weekends. Weekdays, he dined with friends or, more often, he would go dutifully home to eat the dinners his housekeeper cooked for him: she had showed more than once that she was hurt when he called her up from the office to announce that he was dining out that night. He had a great and instinctive sympathy for the efforts of others—for ambition, for work done with a will, work in which the self had been invested—and this sympathy would not let him disappoint his housekeeper, who took pride in the meals she cooked. She was Polish, as were the housekeepers of a good number of well-to-do survivors from Poland. Because they had a common native language—as well, sometimes, as a common lack of facility with English—this was a convenient arrangement both for the housekeepers and their employers, but particularly for the former, many of whom spoke no English at all. Sometimes the housekeepers had emigrated to America, where they could earn good wages, planning only to work several years before returning to Poland, and had therefore no pressing need to learn English.

There were times when the Polish housekeepers brought a faint touch of the past back to their employers, as was so during a large party one survivor gave for his friends. A housekeeper had been lent him for the occasion, a kind of loan that took place often in his circle of friends, who were great partygoers and partygivers. At one point during the festivities, when all the guests were seated eating, the housekeeper's regular employer had an amused sourish smile for the other guests. From the side of his mouth he related to them, in Yiddish, that the housekeeper had confided in him earlier in the evening that she thought some of the people at the party were Jews. He had informed her that not only some but all of the people at

the party were Jews, and that not only they but he and
his wife were Jews, too, which fact had astonished her.
She had no idea that he and his wife were Jews, she had
replied; she could not tell they were Jews, despite the fact
that she had lived and worked in their house for many
months. The other guests laughed when they heard this
story, but the irony of it was not lost on them; most of
them had memories of the Poles who had gone about the
streets of their occupied towns and cities pointing out to
the Germans which of the people passing was a Jew. The
Poles could pick out a Jew anytime, survivors said again
and again. "The Poles, you see, had a nose for Jews."
"The Poles had some kind of radar, some sixth sense,
about Jews." "You could fool the Germans but not the
Poles," they said in introducing the bitter stories about
Polish citizens rushing forth to identify Jews for the SS.
So the Poles were now losing their famous ability to tell
when they were in the presence of Jews, one man at the
party murmured after hearing what the housekeeper had
said. Well, that was only to be expected in a country where
there were no Jews left.

When the subject of the Poles came up, Jolson, who took
pride in not generalizing about people, would tell about a
Polish anti-Semite who had refused to turn him in to the
Germans: the Pole had been a member of the underground, and though he had hated the Jews bitterly, he
would not give away the Jew's hiding place because he
hated the Germans more. Jolson would tell also about
meeting certain decent Germans among the Wehrmacht
soldiers. One of the Germans had been a teacher in a
music conservatory before the war, and while the other
soldiers were busy plundering Jewish goods and businesses
at will, this one had insisted on paying for everything he
took. Then, knowing that his unit would leave Warsaw
in the morning, the German soldier had come marching
to Jolson in the middle of the night to return something
he had borrowed. He had come across other decent
Germans, too, he would say when he told these stories,
and there had been Poles he knew who had helped Jews,

and not betrayed them. He was not going to condemn whole peoples, which was not only irrational but unhealthy and not constructive; this last was the most serious sort of condemnation in his eyes, for when he named something as not constructive, it was as other men might name a prime force for evil in the world. What was constructive was just. The Eichmann trial, for example, had been constructive; and it had been constructive not only for the world as an education but also for him personally. During the war, when he lay curled up in the four-by-three-foot hiding places for months at a time, he had occupied his mind by imagining how the destruction of National Socialism would come about. The final perfect end to that process of destruction had, in his eyes, taken place in 1961, in an Israeli courtroom. "Now I have seen them destroyed in Jerusalem," he observed afterward. The form this ending took had given him the deepest satisfaction; he saw no reason to deny it, nor would he deny anything that gratified him. He was not a man to take gratification from anything he did not approve of in the first place.

In 1972, when he was in his early sixties, and gravely ill, he devised a project that was of great importance to him. For years he had been aware of certain feelings in himself, feelings of obligation, known also to his fellow survivors: the obligation to show that there was meaning in their survival, to do something in their lives that befit people who had been where they had been. Their judgments of one another could be more severe in this matter than in any other: this one did not do enough for Israel, or that one was too busy making money or running around to remember where he came from. They required proofs of themselves and of one another that though they lived normal lives now, normality had not made them disloyal to the past; that material comforts had not made them oblivious, time not made them, like everyone else, indifferent.

He was not different from them in this. Lying in the hospital, thinking about his obligations, he had asked himself certain questions: how should he come to his mother and sisters and his nieces and nephews and the millions of dead? Tell them what: that in his life as a survivor he had sold more sewing machines than anybody?

There and then, he had decided on the project: a monument to the dead, to be established in Israel. As soon as he began to recover from his illness, he set about making arrangements with the Israeli government. Possibly those arrangements had something to do with the speed of his recovery; at any rate, he proceeded determinedly, and whether it was his recovered health or the activity he was engaged in, it seemed to him that he had never felt as well in his life as he did in this period.

As planned, the project was to be an enormous sculpture by Rappaport, to be built on two dunams of land granted by the Israeli government. It was to represent the three faces of Jewish life in the twentieth century: the roundups and the death camps, the Warsaw ghetto uprising, the return to Israel. The depiction of the uprising was particularly important. When visitors came to Israel and asked the usual questions about resistance, and why the Jews had not fought back, there would be the enormous monument to the Warsaw ghetto uprising. The monument would inform those visitors that when sovereign France took no more than eight days to fall and all the countries of Europe fell in only a little more time than that, the Jewish fighters of the Warsaw ghetto had held out for almost two months. The thought of that function alone made the monument seem to him to be worth every penny it would cost.

It would cost him roughly $250,000, a considerable sum, but not too much, all things considered. In addition to everything else it meant to him, the monument project met every standard of merit he held dear: it was educational, it was productive, it would endure. It was to be set in a small garden where visitors could sit and contemplate what they saw in peace and quiet, conditions he always looked for when he wished to think something through. In the winter of 1975, casting for the first section of the monument was begun, a piece of news he received with enormous satisfaction.

II

Emil Wolf had attained nothing like the prosperity that enabled a man to build monuments, which is not to say that he would have built one if he could. In fact, when a group of survivors came to him with plans for a memorial to the dead to be built in their city, he was not enthusiastic.

"Memorials!" he reported furiously to his wife at home that night; now they were building memorials. Probably they would even stick the memorial in a parking lot someplace, just so they could say that they had built one. Not that he had anything against memorials as such; the truth was that he disapproved not of the memorials but of the survivors, and therefore also of most of their enterprises and their activities. They wanted a contribution for their projects, he would always give it to them: here, take the money. But he wished to be left out of their plans and off their committees, he reported to his wife, who was not hearing this from him for the first time. Her husband had for a long time cast a critical eye on his fellow survivors; she knew it quite well, and respected his views, though it was not in her to be so vehement as he was about this or any subject.

Over the years Emil Wolf had come to one conclusion about his survivor friends and acquaintances, and that was that they were a disappointment, a word he used often when he talked about them. Nor was this a mild word in his mouth, for it was uttered more in anger than in sorrow, as were a great many others he spoke. His disappointment in the survivors, as he said, had to do with what they had become—not that he included everyone in this judgment, which would have been unjust, and he was not a person to tolerate lack of justice in himself. He had learned to live by the dictates of a stern inner authority that governed him and told him right from wrong in no uncertain terms, one much stricter than that which seemed to govern the behavior of a great many other people he knew, which was why, perhaps, he seemed to be in the position of judging them so often.

He doubted that his fellow survivors had any idea why he refused to join their organizations, or that they even noticed it. He was, nevertheless, one of them—of "our people," as he called them, as all survivors referred to themselves collectively. The ways our people had disappointed him were quite clear in his mind. He might not be so on top of the world as some of them had become after the liberation; in fact, his was a quite ordinary station in life. He sold insurance; he was comfortably well off, no more, but this he could say at least: that he had tried to keep faith with the past. In all honesty, he did not think he had become, as so many of them had, forgetful of who they were, unthinking, entirely self-interested. For what else but self-interest permitted people to get rich? How, he had been heard to ask, was it possible in this world to go out and make a fortune, as some of these people had done after the war, unless you were devoted to gain? He felt obliged to explain at these times that there was nothing wrong in being wealthy and successful: he was the first to say it. His objection was that many of the survivors had found it in themselves actually to concentrate on these goals; and they had so concentrated, else how could they have achieved these goals so quickly? So soon after everything they had gone through, to become tycoons and empire-builders—materialists, in short. He had expected better from our people—this was the source of his disappointment. After all they had seen and suffered, he had expected that there would come forward from among them a better sort of person, less selfish than the ordinary, perhaps; one more sensitive to humankind, one with spiritual goals that were a little higher than those of most people—otherwise, for what had they survived? Instead, as far as he could see, our people had turned out to be like anyone else—worse, in some cases.

On occasion, when he waxed critical about the materialists and the tycoons, he ventured to suggest there might be some element of jealousy in this criticism of his. But it was soon clear that the suggestion was for form's sake, a disdainful bone thrown to the psychologists, whom he loathed. A moment later, he would dismiss the suggestion, though he himself had made it, and at such times one could catch a glimmer of self-hatred on his face, the look of a man who has caught himself in a politic moment, degrading the beliefs he holds dear.

He knew perfectly well how deep his feelings ran, and that jealousy had no part in his disappointment with our people. And while no dark aspect of human nature, including his own, could ever surprise him, he knew he could not be envious of people whose values were so different from his own.

As a case in point, there was the Adenauer tallis. When he spoke of the Adenauer tallis—which he expected no one to understand without explanation—his usually sober expression brightened, a brightening that only approval brought to his face. He relished humor of the sort the phrase represented; it was sheer malice but, more important, the malice had a moral point very like his own brand. Then he would explain: when Adenauer had first arranged for the West German government to pay reparations to the survivors, the wives all suddenly blossomed out in furs.

Mink stoles—that was what the Adenaur tallis was. His wife never used their reparations money to buy a mink stole, you could be certain of that. She was not the type to show off; as to buying mink stoles with reparations money, he did not even want to dwell on the meaning of that.

He had met her in the tuberculosis hospital in Denver, where he had gone in such dispair in 1949. Still, for all his despair, his case turned out not to be a very advanced one, and he was discharged in two years. The first few weeks at the hospital he had sat around depressed, eating and getting fat. In all, it was a drastic change from the life he had thrown himself into with such a will in Memphis: the long hours at the shoe store, the hasty suppers at his aunt's house, the late-night dates afterward with his fiancée—the fiancée who had broken the engagement as soon as she learned he was ill. For his part, he hardly gave her a thought again once he entered the hospital, for this was an entirely new situation, a grave one, and there were ways he had become accustomed to in dealing with such things. A person had to summon all his wits, and to focus entirely on the present. One had to learn the rules and search for the signals that told how things were done in the new situation, to find out what the dangers were, whom to trust, what resources to count on. In a new situation there was no place for yesterday's problems. It was only when he was much older that he took to brooding. And he did take to it: he had the brooder's memory, the passion for details, the tireless capacity for rage. But that was in the future, when life was easier.

In the hospital, for the first time since his arrival in America, he had found himself in the company of other survivors, and one of them was the girl he eventually married. They suited each other well: he was a talker and she was a listener, a sweet-faced quiet girl, just as his former fiancée had been. The difference was that now he had picked someone with a background like his own, and he never regretted it. She was—in later years, it was the first thing he always said when describing her, a token of the highest praise from him—unselfish. A very fine person, he would invariably add, laying a stress on the word "fine," which summed up all the qualities he cherished in people: refinement, honesty, sensitivity. Furthermore, she was the one survivor whose character he approved of wholeheartedly.

Their wedding ceremony was a sad one. At the end of two years, when both had been discharged from the hospital, they took the train to New York where the girl had relatives. There, in a small barren chapel on Tenth Street and Second Avenue in Manhattan, in the presence of some aunts and uncles, they were married. The ceremony had, of course, begun with the *El Mole Rachamim*, for his mother, father, and brother: "Lord, full of mercy," the prayer asks, naming those who are mourned, "grant them peace."

Years after, he could not go to a wedding, however fancy and gay—and he went to many—without thinking of his own, which had begun with the prayer for the dead. Furthermore, because he was by then a man who

had learned to cherish the private symbol in an existence
—a career—that was not rich in avenues for self-expres-
sion, he refused ever to wear a tuxedo to any of the innumerable formal dinners, weddings, or bar-mitzvah
receptions he went to. There were two reasons for the
business of the tuxedo. First, long ago, he decided that if
he had not had a tuxedo to wear for that wedding of his in
New York, he was not going to wear one for anybody
else's wedding either. More important, not wearing a
tuxedo gave him the opportunity to set a goal for himself:
he would wear one for the first time when his daughter
got married, if and when she married under the proper
circumstances; which is to say, to the proper sort of
person. He felt there was a better chance of having such
a wedding take place if he kept the goal pure and strictly
avoided wearing any tuxedo beforehand. It was a super-
stition, to be sure; he was quite capable of laughing at
himself for it, which he did sometimes, though briefly and
without embarrassment. He had, he pointed out, once kept
himself alive with all sorts of mental tricks that people
could call superstitions, with goals and symbols that might
seem no less trivial than not wearing tuxedos. Therefore,
four hundred men might be in the same room at some fancy
social event, and he the only one among them in an informal suit; he did not mind it in the least.

He supposed that some people, especially other survivors, thought there was a coldness in him, that this
coldness made him separate himself from them. In fact,
the man his wife and children knew was far from cold:
they knew a tender-hearted person—a sentimentalist, even
—a lover of music (he spent long hours Saturday, dream-
ing and listening to his quartets) and books and, above
all, of intelligence. How grateful he was for intelligence!
How happily he would seek out any new acquaintance
who could hold an intelligent conversation, who knew
books, music, or politics! To be sure, he had not come
across a great many, but those he had he remembered, a
huge delighted smile lighting his face suddenly in recollec-
tion of some clever mind, whether of a person he had

known in the camps thirty years earlier or someone he
had met the year before.

He forgot no one who had ever crossed his path; particularly he forgot no one to whom he had ever had to
turn for help. Especially the social workers: the last time
he had run afoul of them was at the tuberculosis hospital
in Denver. The hospital officials had been ready to discharge him as cured, but he protested that there was something else the matter with him which had nothing to do
with lungs. His hands trembled, and he had other disturbing symptoms, he told them at the hospital. But soon
one of the psychiatric social workers had diagnosed his
illness for him: he was an institutional bum, she told him;
he was afraid of going out into the world by now—that
was his trouble. Naturally she knew nothing; none of them
did. A few days before his discharge was to take place,
a doctor at the hospital examined him, saw his trembling
fingers, gave him tests, and diagnosed a severe thyroid
ailment, which kept him there several months more. But
it was not the doctor or the ailment that he remembered
bitterly all the years after: it was the social workers, the
psychiatrists, the mere mention of whom would throw
him into the finest flowerings of rage. Not only the social
workers in the hospital: he had had dealings with the
social-worker types as long ago as the displaced persons
camps, and then, afterward, in his first years in America.
They had provided him with shelter, allowances, jobs, and
even a hospital when he needed it; also plenty of psychiatric attention, which he did not require. Very virtuous,
they had felt, in giving him pocket money and hotel rooms
and a job pushing a broom. He always said that somehow
God had taken mercy on them and given him these fat
jobs, where they had nothing to do but sit there behind
the fat desks lording it over people who had no choice but
to take it. Because in any normal circumstances—if, for
instance, they ever had to compete with other people in
a merit system—they would end up on the rubbish heap
very fast. His own insurance company now sold group benefits to social workers and psychologists for mental-health
care, he pointed out once. The proportion of them that

needed mental care! And he had the records to prove it.

"We're going to go broke from them—that's how sick they are," Emil Wolf announced. And it was no surprise to him. They had sat behind the fat desks, and he, a refugee, age twenty-six, had had to take it because they were the authorities in charge of him. When, several times, social workers had asked him what he thought he would like to do for a living, he told them the truth: he would like to be a professional man, a lawyer. He could see from the noncommittal response, their murmurs about going to work and earning a living, that they didn't approve of this answer. It was too ambitious; they didn't like clients who gave themselves airs. They never said this in so many words, naturally, but their manner spoke for them. When you were a refugee they had brought out of Europe, the manner said, you took what you could get; you pushed a broom during the day and they would tell you where to go to night school to learn English. You should be grateful and practical. Who were you, their attitude said, to have ambitions to be a professional man and go to school to be a lawyer when you were *their* client? That, at any rate, was how he remembered them.

"Social scum," he corrected anybody who referred, in his presence, to social workers. He would say it to any one of them to his face, he promised, staring with burning eyes at the door of his office. No social worker ever materialized there to give him the chance to carry his promise through. One felt, nevertheless, that he would have been as good as his word, especially in a time when he got to talking about the past. He was not, now, a youth of twenty-six, but a man in his early fifties, and possessed of a mature assurance that only seemed to empower his rage.

Once, his daughter brought a girl friend home. By way of making conversation, he had asked the girl what she was studying at college. Social work, she told him; and he replied at once, with the unstoppable, bitter zest this subject always raised in him, "Ah! You're going to be a social parasite, you mean." A minute afterward, he wanted to take the words back, for, much to his surprise, the girl had actually burst into tears. Not very successfully, because he was halfhearted about it, he then tried to explain to her that he had not quite meant what he said. But of course he had meant what he said; he had enjoyed saying it; furthermore, he really wanted the girl to know what he thought of the profession she was getting herself into.

He had, despite his wishes, never got to any professional school himself, a fact he had somewhat accommodated himself to by now—but only somewhat. Just after their wedding, he and his wife went to Dallas, where he had a job waiting. Through friends at the hospital, he had met an insurance broker who took an interest in refugees, and this man had offered him a job with his firm in Dallas. The prospect made him miserable; it was one thing to get used to the idea of not being a professional man, and quite another to think of selling insurance for a living. All he knew about the work was that as a child, in Berlin, he had always heard his mother refer to the insurance salesman who came to their house every few months as "the pest." "Here come the pest," she would say, with a sigh, when the little man with the briefcase appeared at their door, or she might report to the other members of the household that the pest had been there that day.

He would prefer any other job that could be arranged, he told the broker; but the man had only gazed at him, puffed calmly on his cigar, and told him it would be all right, he would do okay in insurance if he put his mind to it. The broker paid him a hundred and forty dollars a month, not a princely sum, especially taking into account the fact that he had already been making eighty-five a week back in the shoe store in Memphis. Still, he felt that the man had taken him under his wing, and—especially since there were no better job prospects available—he stuck it out. His wife went to work as a saleslady in one of Dallas's large department stores, and he busied himself learning the work of an insurance company clerk. In short order, he had learned not only his own work but the work of his immediate superior, the clerk supervisor. This was according to plan, so that he could get the clerk supervisor's job for himself, which was precisely what he succeeded in doing, after a few months, merely by walking into the boss's office and showing him that he was qualified to do the other man's work.

Many years later, he would describe this act of his as typical survivor behavior, though at the time he had only considered it the obvious thing to do to get ahead. But then with the passage of time, as he got further away from the past and into the post-war life, he had, like a good many survivors, absorbed the image of the sort of person a survivor was. One had heard so much: that they were ruthless or opportunistic; that they lied if they thought a lie would get them what they wanted. Had they not had to learn these tricks to survive? And of course, they could not give them up, the tricks had become a part of them, the story went; and on no one did the story have a greater hold than on certain of the survivors themselves: "I'm not like some people; I don't expect that the whole world owes me a living because of what I went through." "I didn't want anything for nothing, that people should say, 'Look at him, he doesn't care to do anything for himself, like the rest of them.' The world doesn't owe me anything." "Don't believe too much what people tell you," survivor A says, referring to survivor B. "It's better to take what some people say with a grain of salt," B says. "What they had before the war, that they were this and that, that this and that happened to them—who knows what they say?" "It happens that some people like to make up stories," C says diplomatically, referring to A and B.

After only a short time in the clerical department, Emil Wolf began to go out on the road selling, briefcase in hand. Did people say, "Here comes the pest" when they saw him coming? Fortunately, he had no time to dwell on such questions, or to think about how little he cared for the work. He was usually exhausted by the end of the day, particularly since he had no car and had to travel his salesman's route by bus for the first few years. But he got on, steadily, and his commissions showed it. In time, he was in a position to ask for a partnership; he would either get a partnership or start looking elsewhere, he had told the broker. The result was that he was given what he wanted, which did not surprise him: he was practiced in the art of making himself indispensable. In addition, he had earned a partnership many times over. It was not necessarily true, he proved, that a person had to be interested in his work to be very good at it; he was exceedingly good at insurance work, and he had no interest whatever in it. To be good required only the will to survive: practically speaking, to earn as much money and get as much authority as possible in a given circumstance. By the time he got the partnership, there were children, a son and daughter, and about one thing he was certain (he used to tell it to his wife, his partner, and anyone else who cared to know): he might have ended up in insurance, but his son never would; he didn't care if they handed him the whole company as a gift.

"Let it end with me," he said once grimly, pointing to his name on the firm's door. Not that he continued to hate the work forever. It took him twenty-three years or so, and finally he acknowledged that it was possible to look at insurance as interesting work—but only, the expression on his face seemed to add, if one looked very hard.

He was balding now, with a fleshy squared-off face: a quiet ordinary middle-age face it would have been but for the eyes, black solids that combined with huge black-rimmed glasses to produce a good deal of interesting glitter. He observed that insurance was useful work; then, wanly, he pointed out that in any work one could behave according to one's ideals. He made decisions on claims in industrial accidents, and in making them he tried to do the fair thing for a worker; he didn't try to talk people into all kinds of insurance that they didn't need. Though, naturally, had he been a professional man, a doctor or a lawyer, he could have done a great deal more for society than it was given him to do now.

"I would have been a good lawyer," he said once mildly. He was in one of his contemplative moods, his great judgmental eyes half closed behind the glasses, his hands folded behind his head. Had it been made possible, he murmured, he had had the mind and will to be a very good one; but it had not been made possible, for there was no way to go to school.

Then, in one of the sharp turns of mood that were frequent with him, he leaned forward. *"Mekimi miofor dol,"* he quoted, in his malevolent low voice. "He raises the lowly from the dust."

The words were from the Psalms and they were not intended as a charge against the Almighty, but against those earthly powers, the social workers, the agencies, the rescue organizations. Like a fool, he had actually expected them to say to him, "We will help you become what you want to be, what you would have been if Hitler and the whole catastrophe had not happened."

A man's life was his ambition. Now he had ambitions only for his children. He was especially hopeful for his son, who was twenty and planned to be a doctor. But the daughter was the source of worry now, a worry so dark that neither he nor his wife could discuss it very often, even when they were alone. The closest and the best of friends, they had shared every problem all the years of their married life; but on this subject, they seemed to tiptoe around each other, avoiding mention of it, each not wanting to disturb the other—feeling, perhaps, that if they talked about it too much, the fear would become reality.

There was a great closeness between him and the children. He had taken a strong hand in their education, particularly their political and ethical education. He had, in addition, brought them up to know they were Jews, not only giving them the traditional schooling but also, when the children were in their late teens, deliberately taking them on a trip to Germany, specifically to Dachau, the camp from which the Americans had liberated him. It was not the first time he had gone back to Germany; in 1970, the year before, he and a number of other German-born Jews had accepted the invitation of West Berlin officials for all former Berliner Jews to return for a visit as guests of the city. At first he scoffed at the idea of going; he was, after all, the person who spat in the water when the boat left the Bremerhaven harbor in 1946, and swore never to lay eyes on Germany again. But then, somehow, he could not resist the chance to go back; Berlin was the place where they had last all been together—his

mother and father, his brother, and himself—a place of
family memories. At the last minute he decided to go, and
at the last minute, too, he became violently sick, attacked
by bouts of nausea and dizziness so severe, the day before
his departure, that he thought of going to a hospital. Instead, the family doctor had come, listened to the story
about the next day's journey back to Berlin, and told his
patient to get on the plane and go.

"What if I get sick there?" he asked the doctor.

"They've got good hospitals in Berlin," the doctor advised him. He was terrified, the doctor had further informed him; that's why he was sick, and it was best to
face up to the fear. It helped, possibly, that the doctor was
not a psychologist, because for once he accepted a psychological judgment with no difficulty, and went on with
the trip.

There were two sorts of people on the plane. The first—
and this was by far the larger group—were happy. Talk-
ative and high-spirited, their faces shining with the prospect
of seeing Berlin again, this group was composed of elderly
Jews who had got out of Germany in the middle or late
thirties. The other group, the one to which he belonged,
was silent and withdrawn, German Jews who had not got
out in the thirties. They were much younger than the first
group, they were few, and there was no happiness in their
excitement.

When the Pan Am plane arrived at the Berlin airport,
he informed his wife that he was not getting off, that there
would be newsmen and photographers, that he would
have to speak to some of them and they to him, and in
German, which was impossible for him. All the while his
wife assembled their belongings, he listed the reasons why
the whole business of his coming here was unthinkable
and an aberration, and then, finally, when there were no
passengers but himself left on the plane, he got off.

A formal welcoming committee waited for the passengers, along with a swarm of German newsmen and photographers. In addition, above the noise and the wind at
the airport, one heard the clear blare of music. Gasping
slightly, because this sight more than any other caught

him like a blow, he saw, stationed off to one side of the welcoming committee, a smartly uniformed German band. They played with a gay brassiness, mostly old Berliner airs, and all the time they played he could not keep from muttering meaningless, nervous, and repetitious asides such as "Don't tell me" and "Do you see that?" to his wife, a Polish Jew who was taking it all in stride. All told, however, the trip went much better than he had dared hope. When, for instance, some person from the press or the reception committee spoke to him, he simply stated that he preferred to speak English. The truth of his problem here was of course stronger than any matter of preference: his German became halting and primitive whenever he tried to converse with non-Jewish Germans, however fluent it might be when he talked to German Jews.

As soon as they had checked into their hotel, he wanted to take his wife to the old apartment where he had lived as a boy, during which trip, his wife later informed him, he had actually hop-scotched down the street. He had to take his wife's word for this, for afterward he had no memory of doing any such thing. But more emotional for him than a visit to the old street on which he had lived as a boy (the apartment itself had disappeared), or anything else he did during the trip, was the meeting they went to in the Berlin Jewish Community Center. The visitors, some Berlin Jews, the Lord Mayor, and various West German officials all assembled in the Center on November 9th, the anniversary of *Kristallnacht*. There were speeches, some of which he thought sounded quite sincere, particularly one given by the Lord Mayor, who spoke of the past with deep emotion. But what he felt they would all hear in their ears forever, what obliterated the memory of any other utterance that night, was the voice of the Berlin cantor: the *El Mole Rachamim* that rose from the hall up to the sky, and tore their hearts out.

The second visit to Germany, on which the children accompanied them, was naturally a much calmer one, in which he occupied himself solely with showing the children around—or educating them, to be more precise. He took a photograph of his daughter—she who was the source of his worry—standing in Dachau, her face twisted with horror and pity. He was later to look at this photograph quite often.

But his teaching had not been only about the Jews and their history—far from it. He wanted his children to know that all humanity was his concern, and that it should be theirs. They saw, in addition, how he had responded to the Vietnam War, a subject that gnawed away at him for a long time. Here he was, said the stern inner authority that governed him, a survivor, supposedly a person with a special obligation not to remain silent when blood was shed, and he would *not* raise his voice against his country's conduct of the war? Of course, the Vietnam War was not the holocaust; he knew it. He was aware, too, that he was playing a kind of mental trick on himself in his response to the war, for he had discovered that the moment he could perceive himself or others around him as citizens who had, by their silence, acquiesced in their government's evil deeds, he began to find it a little more bearable to think about the Germans. Thinking about the Germans—or the Poles or the whole rest of the world, for that matter—was in fact unbearable for him; it was a relief to look away from them, to find acquiescence to evil in himself, however aware he was each time he did this that he was playing a mental trick on himself.

Still, the blood flowed in Vietnam, the houses burned, the people burned; that was no mental trick, but fact. Whatever else he could not do, at least he did not have to be guilty of silence, he told himself. Finally, one night he had confronted the rabbi of his synagogue at a meeting of the congregation and demanded to know when he was going to go on record and speak out against the war; and whatever may have been in the hearts of his fellow survivors, he did not notice that any of them rushed to join him in this public statement, either, he reported afterward. Nor did his question make friends for him in the congregation, most of whose members were bitter anti-Communists, and suspicious of anybody who criticized the war—at any rate, in the early stage of it, the mid-sixties.

He had not wanted to be unthinking and narrow, even on an issue that might be close to his heart. When, for example, the president of his synagogue had referred, in a speech, to the Arab-Israeli wars of 1948 and 1967— Israel's triumphs—as "glorious wars" had he not rebuked the man?

"Glorious wars?" he had asked the president sternly, in private; and the president had conceded that the choice of words was not the best. "Glorious wars, indeed," he had muttered at home. Just wars, yes, but a war must never be called glorious. The children had heard such pronouncements from him before, for theirs was a talk-prone family, their house a place of endless debate, almost always on serious political issues of the day. It was natural that his children had grown up to be politically aware and idealistic. He observed, and it did not surprise him, that they were different in a number of respects from the children of other survivors he knew. For one thing, they were not blindly nationalistic about the Jewish state or about America, either, like so many of those other children. They disliked nationalism, any nationalism, which fact he did not at all mind—approved in some ways, actually. As to wars, there was nothing to speak of so far as wars were concerned: in his children's opinion, and they went him one better in this, there was no such thing as a *just* war either. Now this idea of theirs disturbed him; it would disturb any survivor. Still, he was able to see how they had come to their conclusions, for the children had grown up in the Vietnam era, and their opinions on war and nationalism seemed unassailable.

Nevertheless, when October of 1973 came around, he saw with satisfaction how moved the children were when they thought Israel was in grave danger. His daughter had even insisted on making a donation of her own to the emergency fund for Israel. The October War had had its effect upon them all; he himself no longer talked about Israel giving back some of the occupied territories; but it was the children who showed those effects most dramatically. They had seen the stab in the back on Yom

Kippur, Israel's isolation, her betrayal by once staunch friends who, when their oil supply was threatened, suddenly discovered in themselves the source of a high moral fervor about the injustices of Zionism. Possibly, he reasoned at the time, he would be able to make his daughter see in these events the potential for other betrayals; for this was, in part, what his worry over her was all about.

In her early twenties now, his daughter had for a few years been going out with a man who was not a Jew. There was the possibility, at least, that they would marry, and this prospect had become her father's greatest fear.

"I will never give in to it," he announced flatly. He might just as well be dead as live to see the day. Oh, yes, he hastened to assure one, he would prefer to be dead. Nor was this simply some melodramatic talk, a Jewish parent's traditional carrying on. He was not *any* Jewish parent; he was a survivor, with reasons others did not have for their carrying on, reasons that he had explained in full to his daughter. Once you were branded a Jew, you were always a Jew, he told her: you could expect loyalty from no one but another Jew.

"Didn't I see it?" he demanded. His uncle's wife had been a Gentile; he remembered how, not long after the Nazis came to power, she divorced her husband and watched him go off to the concentration camp. There were other reasons for his attitudes than the ones he gave his daughter, reasons he could not locate, much less articulate, so upset did he become when he tried to name them—he who expressed himself with such ease, who never feared to vent his anger, who was so dauntless in his criticism of rabbis, other survivors, and himself, when necessary.

The idealistic attitudes which he had communicated to his children when he taught them that all mankind was their concern, which permitted him to tell himself that all men, himself included, might have acted as the Nazis did, and had aided him in negotiating some peace with the world, failed now to provide him any measure of comfort. For the truth was that now, in the prospect of his daughter's marriage to a Gentile, he had to confront what he had never been able to bear contemplating: the full force of his hate for the Gentile, a rage too turbulent heretofore not to have been silenced and put away, too dangerous for one who wished, still, to live in the world: particularly one who had discovered the healing power of idealism, and had concluded, as he had, that a survivor's life should be consecrated to the benefit of mankind.

He had no intention himself of letting unhappiness overwhelm him on this subject of his daughter, however, for he knew the importance of optimism. Then, too, there was the pleasing prospect of his son's professional career. In fact, he found a good deal that pleased him in the life he had carved out for himself, including the long early-morning talks with his wife (more and more he was grateful for her these days, it seemed to him), the Saturdays lying around listening to his quartets, the times at the end of a day, even, when he sat eying the names on the door of the insurance firm, seeing his own there one minute and gone the next.

III

In Kansas, Flekier, with a wife and two children, had settled into a fairly peaceful existence. He had, in his words, done everything you were supposed to do, a claim of no small significance to any man making it, least of all him. His one great worry, the suspicion that had kept him tossing and turning in his bed nights after his arrival in the United States, was that he might never learn to get along in a normal society. He mulled over the trouble he had been in in Germany after the liberation, the result mostly of his innumerable fights with local Germans. An older man, a cousin serving with the U.S. Army of Occupation who visited him in jail after one of these scrapes, warned him that unless he watched himself he would get into trouble wherever he went, and Flekier took the warning to heart.

For all his worry, in the course of time, he acquired a wife, fathered two children, earned a good living, and owned his house; and in all his years in America he got into no trouble whatever, though the last may have had more to do with lack of occasion than anything else, for time's passage had not made him more peaceable.

"He's terrible," Flekier's wife said proudly about her husband. One time, in 1973 or thereabouts, when they had driven their two children to Hebrew classes, a member of the American Renaissance Party had appeared in front of the synagogue wearing a placard and giving out pamphlets that denounced Jews as Communists and nigger-lovers. Her husband had gone straight up to him and introduced himself as a Jew; after some words, Flekier broke the placard over the man's head and ripped up all his pamphlets. Then the man had run to look for a policeman, so that he could press charges against her husband, not knowing that all the time there had been a policeman nearby who had seen the whole incident and then quickly disappeared into a store so he wouldn't have to involve himself. She didn't know why the policeman had done that; it might be the fact that her husband was anything but a stranger in the community, and the American Renaissance Party man was. In this community, the stranger was never on an equal footing with the known person. The only thing that worried her, she said, was that the man and some of his friends could come back to the synagogue sometime and hurt the children.

"You saw the sign," Flekier told her.

"I saw."

"Then I have to hit him, don't I? That's all." She was not prone to argue. A native Israeli, she had met Flekier when he visited the Jewish state shortly after his return from service in the Korean War. There followed years of courtship by mail, until, in 1959, she married him and with grim good humor transplanted herself to Kansas, which could not have been less like Tel Aviv than if it had been the moon. For all that, she had come to feel quite at home in the Kansas City suburb where they lived; only once or twice had she had encounters of her own there, additional reminders—as though she needed any— that this was not Tel Aviv. There was the greengrocer who was always very nice to her, always showing her which vegetables and fruit were best. One day the grocer confided he liked to wait on her because she was so nice—not like the Jews who came into the store.

"So I asked him what he meant," she reported. " 'What do the Jews do to you?' I asked him."

Flekier, listening, glowered.

"Then he said to me, 'Oh, you know. The way they come in here and squeeze the fruit.' "

"You should have said to him," Flekier began, and discarded the retort as unsatisfactory.

"I did say to him. Of course I said to him. The way the Jews squeeze the fruit, you hear? All right, I said to this fruitman, whatever he is, I said, 'I have news for you, I am a Jew.' 'Oh, no,' he said to me, 'you're not a Jew!' 'But I *am* a Jew,' I said. 'Oh, no,' he tells me, 'you're not a Jew, you're nice.' "

"Pick yourself up and walk out, that's all," Flekier interposed.

" 'Well, I am a Jew, you can believe me,' I told him. 'I am an Israeli.' 'Oh,' he said, 'you're okay. You're not like the Jews from over here; you're from Israel.' Why I was standing there all this time arguing with him if I'm a Jew or not, I don't know. 'Oh, no,' I said to him. 'We are all the same Jews.' Now every time he sees me, he feels terrible and he hangs his head down. Probably he didn't mean anything bad too much."

Flekier looked forbearing. For, aside from the incident outside the synagogue and several occasions in the army, he had encountered little anti-Semitism in his years in America. There had to be plenty of people in Kansas who didn't like Jews, he allowed, but if there were any in his immediate vicinity—except, of course, for the greengrocer —they certainly kept their feelings to themselves.

All told, he had done well in Kansas, he felt, even if, working as a sales representative for several furniture companies, he had not become so prosperous as other survivor friends who came to America with him. In fact, Flekier took a certain pride in the success of those friends, especially one. His friend Walter had gone through the concentration camps just as Flekier had, and then, after his arrival in America, had gone on to become an enormously successful jewelry salesman. It had not taken Walter long; he was now practically number one in the country in jewelry sales. Flekier had great admiration for someone who could do that: make up his mind to achieve and reach the top, and then, after all the tragic things that had happened to him, go out and do it. And he himself, Flekier said, a touch shyly but nevertheless certain of his facts, he had not come out so poorly, either, had he? "Considering what you started with, which was nothing. You see that you have a wife and children and that you can provide for them."

His friend Walter, however, had not only made up his mind to be an achiever, he had been obsessed by the idea; as soon as Walter got his first job selling jewelry, he also went out and bought a secondhand car.

"Did you ever hear of a person who decides just to get in a car and drive, that he was never behind a wheel in his life?" Flekier inquired. "He was so hot to get started on his route the first day he didn't care, he just went. Took him only a few hours, he smashed the car to pieces."

It was that burning ambition of his that had made Walter such a success, Flekier figured: that, and the fact that he had come to a country like America. How many of the survivors would have found in another country the chance they had found in America to recover? To do what it was in you to do? To become a part of it?

Still, for all that he had these feelings, it amazed him sometimes to see how American Jews sat back so confident that nothing could happen to them here. You would not find a survivor anywhere else who felt confident that way, Flekier predicted. His own conviction was that what had happened to the Jews of Europe could easily happen to Jews again anywhere, anytime, given the right circumstances. Only a trigger was necessary to touch off a holocaust: inflation, perhaps, or political necessity—an attempt to divert the masses from their economic troubles by offering them the Jewish scapegoat. Confidence was wrong; confidence had trapped and killed Jews in Europe.

"You better believe it. You better," Flekier said heatedly. He was far from being a talker, much less an impassioned one, except on this subject, about which he felt absolute certainty. Let better and wiser heads discuss great issues and he would willingly be the listener, but this was something he knew about: what could happen to the Jews at any time, anywhere. His "You better believe it," furthermore, was not a warning so much as a vow: that, as a survivor and a Jew, he would never suffer himself to be deluded, not by his experiences of any country, not by however many signs and proofs there were—as existed in America, for example—that the government was not likely to abandon its democratic principles and begin rounding up Jews.

"Things are always changing," Flekier pointed out. "You hope it doesn't change. You don't want it to change. You have to watch. Keep watching."

Wait, watch, and remember. He was always remembering, whether he wanted to or not. The worst memory was always the same one: his mother running after him when the Germans had thrown him on the truck.

"She was a smart woman," Flekier said. "She was calling to me, 'I'm never gonna see you again.' I didn't pay too much attention, see. I was a dumb kid of thirteen. She's running after me and the Germans are standing there with rifles. I know they're gonna club her any minute. I wanted the truck to move away. I thought, Well, what are the Germans gonna do with kids? They'll make me work a few months and let me come back. But she knew, my mother; she kept saying, 'It's the last time I'll see you.' I still see her running, running after that truck. And that's it. I keep seeing that. She knew it was for the last time. That's what hurts. I never gave her credit, see, for knowing. Something like that."

Flekier tried, though he had scant religious training, to live as much of a Jewish life as possible, going to synagogue and keeping kosher, because, especially in a place like Kansas, it was too easy to forget who you were, where you had been and why. "You have to hold on. Never forget who you are and what happened because of it," Flekier said, echoing an assertion made often by survivors collectively as well as individually.

Every April, survivors come from all over New York to the great annual commemoration of the Warsaw ghetto uprising, the revolt and the destruction of the ghetto having over the years become the focal symbols of all holocaust commemorations. Year after year, particularly in the last decade, the Temple Emanu-El audience seems to grow larger; nor is this the only such memorial observance being held in the city of New York. All over America, the April memorial assemblies have grown more numerous, and the crowds attending them larger.

Temple Emanu-El's side streets are blocked to traffic and closed to passers-by from Fifth to Madison. Everyone sent a ticket has been warned to come early and everyone does: lines begin forming outside the temple at 10 A.M. for a ceremony scheduled to begin at 1:30, but still there are always far too many people to be accommodated in the auditorium, enormous as it is. The tickets mean nothing, assure no one of a seat. In the end, the too many will form a large overflow crowd and stand outside in the raw April wind for hours. The *El Mole Rachamim* comes out to the throng by loudspeakers; they hear the *Ani Maamim* sung, the ancient declaration of faith orthodox Jews sang as they went to their end in Auschwitz and Treblinka, but they do not see, as those inside can, the accompanying procession of New York schoolchildren. The youngest ones in the lead can be no more than five. Shining and solemn, holding candles larger than themselves and in their smallness and fragility inescapably representing others, small and fragile like them, thrown into the blackness of the gas chambers, the children cannot know that every eye under which they pass sees in them the unbearable.

There are in the assemblage sprinklings of older children as well. These are the sons and daughters of the survivors now in their late teens and twenties: children, their parents always noted, who had grown up never knowing grandparents, aunts, or uncles. Some, only finding out for the first time at school or from the child next door that such relations existed, had come home and asked their parents, "What is a grandfather?" "Who is an aunt?" "Where is mine?" But the children grew up; some sit here, greeting people now, very much at home among their parents' friends and no stranger to these occasions. Stella's son is here, as well as Stella herself. She and a large cluster of her friends sit in a corner of the auditorium whispering in Polish and giving one another last-minute instructions. At a signal they are up, pale in their black dresses and head shawls and ready to begin the candlelighting ceremony some of them have taken part in for a number of years now. Tapers in hand, they march in a formation grown quite complicated by the time each of the several dozen women crosses the stage to her appointed place and lights a candle. Black figures swirling in every direction, bending, dipping, lighting, their darkening presence has left the stage ablaze.

Following this ceremony, there are prayers and speeches. Of the speakers, one stands out, a tall, elegant figure of a man who strides toward the lectern with a brisk air, but who, having arrived, leans forward suddenly, all briskness gone. In a fiercely emotional whisper, he greets the audience in Yiddish: "My dear comrades of the ghetto." The greeting is a brief one; in a moment he has done with this whispered Yiddish, token of allegiance and intimacy. He straightens up and begins his English speech, which transforms him instantly: crisp and British, he might now, but for his subject matter, have been speaking from the floor of Parliament. This is Jacob Bar Mor, of the Israeli Mission to the U.N., and he, too, is a survivor. The message he brings today is that Jews must never believe the holocaust danger is past: "We will never again permit ourselves to be deluded." Flekier's very thoughts, if not his accents; there are no differences so great between survivors but that they cannot find a common ground on this, the refusal of delusions.

The closing hymn begins, The Jewish partisan song and exhortation against despair: *Zog nit keynmol az du geyst dem letsen veg*. Outside, in streets grown colder with the passing hours, the overflow crowd still waits. In the darkened temple the survivors surge, spent, toward the exits, toward friends, toward the streets, toward life.